# Spiritual
# Landscape

JAMES L. RESSEGUIE

# Spiritual Landscape

## IMAGES OF THE SPIRITUAL LIFE IN THE GOSPEL OF LUKE

HENDRICKSON PUBLISHERS

Hendrickson Publishers, Inc.
P. O. Box 3473
Peabody, Massachusetts 01961-3473

ISBN 1-56563-827-1

*Printed in the United States of America*

*First Printing — January* 2004

Scripture quotations, unless otherwise noted, are from the New Revised Standard Version of the Bible, copyright © 1989 by the Division of Christian Education of the National Council of the Churches of Christ in the U.S.A. All rights reserved. Used by permission.

Italics in Scripture quotations are the author's emphasis.

**Library of Congress Cataloging-in-Publication Data**

Resseguie, James L.
    Spiritual landscape : images of the spiritual life in the Gospel of Luke / James L. Resseguie.
        p. cm.
    Includes bibliographical references.
    ISBN 1-56563-827-1 (alk. paper)
    1. Bible. N.T. Luke—Criticism, interpretation, etc.
    2. Spirituality—Biblical teaching. I. Title.
    BS2595.52.R47 2004
    226.4'06—dc22
                                                        2003016459

*For Dianne, Timothy, Carin, and Jay*

# Contents

Preface    ix

Introduction    1
    Spirituality    2
    Methodology    5
    Hills Like White Elephants    7

1. Topography: The Landscape of Spiritual Growth    9
    Jordan    10
    Desert    12
    Lake    17
    Mountain    20
    Conclusion    26

2. Journeys: The Itinerary of Spiritual Formation    29
    Emmaus    30
    Journey to Jerusalem    34
    Conclusion    43

3. Families and Households: Models of Spiritual Development    45
    Slaves    46
    Children    53
    Widows    55
    Family Ties    60
    Conclusion    67

4. Meals: Spirituality of Hospitality    69
    Table Etiquette    70
    Feast    78
    Fast    82

Anxiety                                                                    84
Conclusion                                                                 85

5. *Clothing: A Map of the Spiritual Life*                                 89
   Passages                                                  90
   Anxiety                                                   94
   Temple Veil and Cloak of Darkness                         98
   Conclusion                                                99

6. *Consumption: The Spiritual Life and Possessions*                      101
   Peril of Plenty                                          101
   Dispossession                                            108
   Conclusion                                               113

*Conclusion*                                                              115

*Notes*                                                                   121

*Bibliography*                                                            163

*Modern Author Index*                                                     185

*Subject Index*                                                           191

# Preface

The thesis of this book is that Luke uses the physical, social, and economic landscapes of the Gospel to develop and elaborate the contours of the spiritual life. Luke challenges us to think critically about the spiritual life and its implications for everyday living. The physical terrains of the Jordan, desert, sea, and mountain are places of spiritual awakenings. They represent threshold experiences, the terrain where our resolve is tested and our spiritual struggles resolved. Journeys elaborate and develop the itinerary of spiritual formation: the journey outward clarifies the journey inward. The social landscapes of the family and household model spiritual development. The vulnerable and marginalized of first-century society—slaves, widows, and children—exemplify positive characteristics of a self-giving spiritual life. By contrast, members of the dominant culture of the first century with their self-absorbed lifestyle serve best as counterexamples for the Christian spiritual life. The social landscape of meals is an eloquent testimony to our spiritual values. Whom we do or do not eat with expresses our spiritual values. Economic landscape also mirrors spiritual landscape. What we do or fail to do with our possessions is a reflection of our spiritual values and commitments.

I owe an enormous debt to those that have made this book possible. I am especially thankful for several grants from the National Endowment for the Humanities that encouraged me to look at new ways of interpreting biblical texts. Kenneth R. R. Gros Louis's and James Ackerman's seminar on the Bible as Literature at Indiana University taught me to pay close attention to the nuances of the text. To this day their "close readings" of Scripture greatly influence my reading of the New Testament. I am also thankful for Herbert Lindenberger of Stanford University who deepened my understanding of seminal texts in literary theory and challenged me to explore reader-response criticism in his seminar. Giles Gunn's seminar on religion and literature at the University of Florida helped me to see the relevance of Russian Formalism for "making strange" the New Testament. Calum Carmichael's and David Daube's seminar on biblical law at the University of California at Berkeley looked at biblical legal texts in fresh and new ways. I will never look at legal texts in quite the same way. James Phelan's seminar on rhetorical theory at Ohio State University was a welcome addition to my development as a literary critic. He encouraged me to reconsider point of view as an important rhetorical device in the Gospels.

I am especially grateful for a Fulbright fellowship to teach literary theory at the University of Iceland, and to Professor Jon Sveinbjornsson of the Faculty of Theology at the University who served as a most gracious host and made my stay in this wonderful country of ice and fire delightful. The students in the Divinity School at the University were most receptive to my initial forays into literary theory. Little did I know then that three books would develop as a result of their enthusiastic and valuable comments.

I am also thankful for the opportunity to share my initial insights on spirituality in Luke with the adult Bible class of the Norcrest Presbyterian Church in Findlay, Ohio. They helped me to rethink parts of this book with their valuable insights into the desert, mountain, lake, and journey as spiritual terrain. My students at Winebrenner Theological Seminary, through their keen insights and enthusiastic comments, contributed richly to my spiritual reading of the Gospel of Luke. Without the encouragement to incorporate spiritual formation into my biblical classes, this book would not have been possible. I thank the dean for this felicitous suggestion.

I owe a debt to those whose reading of this manuscript strengthened the thesis of the book and saved me from a number of grammatical and stylistic infelicities. In particular, I am indebted to Robert Cecire, John Dasher, and Jeannine Grimm for their enthusiasm and encouragement. I thank my editor, James D. Ernest, who saw the value in this work and offered a home for it at Hendrickson Publishers.

Most important, I thank Dianne for her love and affection. It is one thing to write about the spiritual life, it is another thing to live the spiritual life. Dianne's generosity of spirit and abounding enthusiasm teaches me daily about the latter. I dedicate this book to her and our children, Timothy, Carin, and Jay.

# Introduction

This is a book about landscapes—all types of landscapes: physical, social, and economic. Lukan landscapes develop and elaborate the contours of the spiritual life: its inchoate stages, its tests of integrity and experiences of grace, its moments of glory and agonies of failure, its times of epiphany and periods of distraction.

Physical landscapes include the desert, lake, mountain, and river. They are places of spiritual awakenings, tests of faith, and encounters with bleak interior emptiness. They are threshold experiences in the spiritual life. Social landscapes include families, households, meals, and clothing. Luke does not separate social intercourse from spiritual formation. Images of the family and household serve as surprising models of the spiritual landscape in the kingdom of God. Slavery is an improbable metaphor for Christian leadership; widows are models of strength and abandoned self-giving; children, among the least and at the margins of society, are emblematic of the greatest in the kingdom.

Meals are profound expressions of our spirituality. Whom we do or do not eat with expresses our spiritual values as well as our social values.

Even what we wear has spiritual significance. Clothing marks key transitions in the spiritual life. After his return home, the prodigal son receives the best robe, a ring, and sandals for his feet, representing his passage from death to life (cf. Luke 15:24), from spiritual and social lostness to rebirth. On the Mount of Transfiguration Jesus' clothing testifies to his transcendence; like the prodigal son's, his outward garments reflect his inner character. The demoniac of chapter 8, on the other hand, appears stark naked and departs fully clothed, marking his passage from social and spiritual death to new life. Anxiety concerning what we wear may be a sign of an inadequate, fragile faith, whereas parading around in elaborate and expensive garments, as the scribes do, reflects a meretricious spiritual life.

Economic landscape is the terrain of the rich and poor, of the urban elite and the rural outcasts, of the structures of dominance and oppression. Economic landscape also mirrors spiritual landscape. What we do or fail to do with our possessions is a reflection of our spiritual values and commitments. Zacchaeus gave half of his possessions to the poor and returned fourfold the amount he defrauded his clients. The rich ruler, on the other hand, refused to sell all his possessions and give the money to the poor. One economic decision liberates, the other enslaves.

Why study landscapes to understand the spiritual life? "It is much easier to reflect upon an image than upon an idea," writes Alister McGrath, and, therefore, "biblical images have exercised a controlling influence over Christian spirituality."[1] Images allow us to visualize the ups and downs, the guarded pretensions and resolute commitments, the difficulties and joys, the surprise twists and turns of the spiritual life. Stories and images make the spiritual life come alive. When Jesus eats with Simon the Pharisee, a woman enters and washes his feet with her tears, dries them with her hair, and kisses and anoints them (Luke 7:36–50). What better way to visualize the crippling consequences of a parsimonious and formulaic spirituality than with the story of Simon's discomfort? Or what better way to envision the unfettered spiritual life, freed from the constraints of sin, than with the eloquence of the woman's lavish testimony? A story communicates far more than an idea, and Luke tells his story with startling images. We understand the contours of the spiritual life more clearly because of Luke's consummate storytelling.

## Spirituality

What is Christian spirituality?[2] For Luke spirituality is expressed most clearly in the ordinary world: eating with outcasts and the abject marginalized, giving away possessions to those who have little or none, following Jesus on the difficult road of discipleship, and resisting the lure of hyperconsumerism and immoderate consumption. Spirituality is part and parcel of everyday life: what we wear, with whom we eat, how we spend our money, and what we do with our time. Luke shows us the pretensions of a rule-ridden spirituality and the refreshing sincerity of a self-sacrificing spirituality. He shows us the consequences of spiritual constipation: too much concern with outward show and too little concern with succoring the afflicted. He surprises us with unlikely models of the spiritual life. The marginalized and vulnerable—slaves, children, and widows—are images of strength and greatness in the kingdom, while the self-regarding rich and powerful are exemplars of spiritual decrepitude.

The spiritual life has three defining characteristics in Luke.[3] First, spirituality is portrayed as a journey—an exodus[4] (cf. 9:31) to the new promised land, the kingdom of God. God is our traveling companion, and the journey is an awakening to God's working ways in this world. The Emmaus journey, for example, is an elegant and sublime commentary on God's clarifying presence in our lives. The two disciples are disconsolate and uncomprehending of God's inscrutable ways; but at the moment of their greatest need, Jesus joins them as a fellow pilgrim. His clarifying word burns within their hearts. His clarifying act opens their eyes. They are awakened to God's working ways in this world. How also are we to make sense of God's ways in this world unless God incognito, Jesus, becomes our traveling companion who opens our eyes? How are we to understand Scripture unless the One about whom Scripture bears witness provides the clarifying word? How are we to turn around—as the two on the Emmaus road do (cf. 24:33)—unless God's clarifying actions change our intractable ways?

The journey is not only an awakening to God's surprising ways in this world; it is a pilgrimage to spiritual formation. The journey to Jerusalem (9:51–19:44) outlines its itinerary. Following Jesus requires leaving behind the securities of this life and the pressing obligations that seem so important for survival in this world. Following Jesus wherever he goes means abandoning the encumbrances and distractions of this life. The Lukan landscape, however, is dotted with those who try to take along the accoutrements of success. The rich ruler, for instance, decides that material wealth is more important than spiritual well-being and thus travels another route, a hedonistic exodus that wanders aimlessly through life (18:18–25); others—Zacchaeus, to name one—are happy to part with their wealth because spiritual well-being is more important than material wealth. Social and status boundaries are abolished on this journey. Tax collectors and sinners, the marginalized and the poor, the lame and the crippled join the exodus, while others who are burdened by wealth or power pass it by.

A second defining feature of Lukan spirituality is that material, everyday decisions are inseparable from spiritual decisions. "Faith and wealth belong to the same arena of life. Luke allows for no segregation of life into spiritual and secular, church and world."[5] What we do with our material resources demonstrates our spiritual life. In a passage unique to Luke, self-serving behaviors are abandoned at the Jordan, and God's new agenda is adopted (3:10–14). The multitude comes to John to be baptized, and they ask, "What then should we do?" John tells them to leave behind their self-regarding ways, and adopt a new mode of social interaction for a new era: selfless, self-sacrificing giving. "Whoever has two coats must share with anyone who has none; and whoever has food must do likewise" (3:11). Tax collectors are to abandon the common practice of misappropriation, and soldiers are no longer to extort money. Generalized reciprocity, the new norm of social interaction based on altruism, gifting, and self-giving, replaces negative reciprocity, an old form of social intercourse that seeks to get something for nothing.[6] Material and spiritual decisions are inseparable, two sides of the same coin. In the parable of the Rich Man and Lazarus, for example, the rich man feasts sumptuously daily, while allowing the mendicant at his gate to starve. His material actions comment upon his spiritual indigence.

A third defining feature of the Lukan spiritual landscape is the struggle to know and fulfill God's will. It is well known that the third evangelist develops and elaborates the theme of prayer.[7] On seven occasions, Luke's Gospel alone records that Jesus is at prayer: during his baptism (3:21), before his first clash with the Pharisees and the teachers of the law (5:16), before the selection of the Twelve (6:12), prior to questions about his identity and Peter's declaration of his messiahship (9:18), at the Transfiguration (9:29), before teaching the Lord's Prayer (11:1), and on the cross (23:46).[8] Luke alone has two parables dealing with prayer: the friend that comes at midnight

(11:5–8), and the widow who pleads her case before the unrighteous judge (18:1–8). Luke is the only evangelist who records intercession for Peter: Jesus prays that during Satan's sifting, Peter's faith may not fail (22:32). And Luke alone provides Jesus' injunction for the disciples to pray on the Mount of Olives (22:40; cf. Mark 14:38; Matt 26:41).

The mountain, suspended between earth and sky, is the place of divine-human struggle where we can know God's will and bring our determined, sometimes belligerent, will into conformity with God's will. It is on this stark, serene landscape that the din of the everyday is silenced, we realize the limitations of human resources, our self-will is tamed, and God's will is clarified. It is not only where we speak to God, but also where we *listen* for God's clarifying word. On the Mount of Olives, for example, Jesus struggles to know and fulfill God's will; like an athlete readying himself for the contest of his life, he prays an earnest, submissive prayer.

> A  Father, if *you* are willing,
> > B  remove this cup from *me*;
> > B'  yet, not *my* will
> A'  but *yours* be done. (22:42)

The second-person singular (*you* and *yours*) surrounds and contains the first person (*me* and *my*), and in this way, the will of the self rests entirely within the Father's will. This is the model of Christian prayer. For Luke, the spiritual life involves both the taming of self-will and the clarifying of God's will for our lives.

## Methodology

The method used to analyze landscapes or settings in this work is literary criticism or narrative criticism. Narrative criticism pays special attention to the formal features of a narrative such as rhetoric, point of view, setting, character, plot, tone, atmosphere, style, and so forth.[9] This work examines especially the physical, social, and economic landscapes of the Gospel and the ways they contribute to our understanding of the Christian spiritual life. Settings can highlight the religious, mental, moral, social, and emotional landscapes of the characters.[10] They may also contribute to the mood or atmosphere of the Gospel.[11] A journey, for example, not only describes an outward journey to a particular place; it may also develop an inward journey to emotional or spiritual space. The primary settings of Luke's Gospel—called landscapes in this work—are physical (e.g., Jordan, desert, lake, mountain, journeys), social (families, households, table fellowship, clothing), and economic (possessions, wealth, almsgiving).[12] Physical landscape and the spiritual life is the subject of chapters 1 and 2; social landscape and spirituality are developed and elaborated on in chapters 3, 4, and 5; and economic landscape and the spiritual life is the subject of chapter 6.

What makes the physical, economic, and social landscapes of Luke's Gospel spiritually significant? First, the setting is recognizable in our everyday world as figurative landscape. A turbulent storm is an ideal landscape to represent inner turmoil, while the calming of the sea appropriately represents the calming of inner distress. Similarly, ascending a mountain is a natural setting to develop the theme of drawing closer to God, while a journey ideally portrays an inward emotional or spiritual journey. Landscapes that figure prominently in the spiritual life of the Israelites are important spiritual landscapes in Luke as well. The Jordan, for instance, is a boundary between the threat of the desert and the hope of the promised land; it represents a threshold experience, where we assess where we have come from and where we are going. The desert, on the other hand, is a place of divine testing and succor, and the sea is uncontrollable space that only God tames (cf. Ps 107:23–32). It is an ideal landscape for spiritual awakenings. A setting may also be spiritually important because of repetition and emphasis.

Second, a setting may attain spiritual significance because of characters' speech and actions. The mountain is a place to struggle to know and understand God's will not only because it is the earth reaching toward the heaven, but also because Jesus goes up the mountain to pray. His action and speech supplement physical space; the mountain thus becomes spiritual landscape. The setting of a meal suggests fellowship and acceptance of others. But table fellowship alone does not represent a spiritual setting *unless* the discourse of the characters or the narrator's discourse or the actions of the characters in some way highlight the spiritual or social significance of meals. When Jesus excoriates the religious leaders for seeking the best seats at a meal or for failing to invite the lame, crippled, poor, and blind as guests, he comments upon their social and spiritual values. Similarly, Jesus' fellowship with tax collectors and sinners is a commentary on his social and spiritual values. Some landscapes, however, are spiritually significant because they represent the opposite of common expectations. Slaves, for example, are low on the hierarchic scale of status and do not naturally exemplify greatness. But in the Gospels they are models of greatness in the kingdom.

A brief analysis of a short story by Ernest Hemingway illustrates the method used in this book. In *Hills Like White Elephants*, Hemingway uses physical landscape as an enlightening aperçu of the characters' inner landscape.

## Hills Like White Elephants

The story takes place at a railroad junction somewhere between Barcelona and Madrid. A man and a girl, sitting at a table outside a train depot and waiting for the express train from Barcelona, order drinks, comment on the striking landscape, and discuss an "awfully simple operation." On one side of the depot is a very hot valley with "long and white" hills that look like white elephants, while on the other side is a river with fields of grain and trees along the banks of the Ebro. A shadow of a cloud moves across the field of grain. The girl and the man order Anis del Toro—a licorice-tasting, somewhat bitter-flavored drink like absinthe. Plastered with labels from many hotels, their luggage leans against the station wall.

Outward landscape suggests the contours of the characters' inner landscape. Dry, sterile hills that resemble white elephants suggest an etiolated, rocky relationship. White elephants, an object of little or no value, are a clever description for a barren relationship. The fecund landscape on the other side of the train depot may be a description of what their relationship could be. And bags decorated with labels from all the places they stayed suggest an aimless, empty relationship. Physical landscape, however, only suggests the contours of their relationship. Landscape must be supplemented with the characters' dialogue to elevate the physical setting to a description of the characters' emotional landscape.

When the girl says that the drinks taste like licorice, the man agrees and says that everything tastes that way. He means that everything in that part of Spain tastes the same. But the girl enlarges upon his comment: everything they have waited so long for tastes like absinthe. The bitterness of the drinks thus becomes emblematic of the way their relationship has developed: her hopes and expectations have turned bitter. On the other hand, when the girl looks to the other side of the train depot and sees the lush, fertile landscape, her remarks are a commentary on what the relationship could be. They could have all this but every day they make it more impossible, she says. Their views on the "awfully simple operation," an abortion, are amplified by the landscape. For the man, the white elephant is the fetus in her womb—a hindrance to their relationship, for he wants only her. For her, the white elephant is their barren relationship, which her wry comments on the landscape and bitter drinks amplify. The multiple labels on their luggage suggest an aimless lifestyle. All they ever do, she says, is look at things and try new drinks. The train junction symbolizes the dilemma they face. Where will they go? Will they change directions, go different ways, or continue to live their lives in the same way? Their choice is highlighted by the striking landscape: dry, brown hills on one side and fields of grain on the other.

The method used in this book is to examine physical, social, and economic landscapes along with the action and discourse of characters to develop and elaborate Luke's understanding of the spiritual life. The mutual dialogue between the variegated landscapes of the Gospel and the actions and speech of the characters clarifies Lukan spirituality.

# Chapter

## 🍂 1

# Topography:
# The Landscape of Spiritual Growth

External terrain is a map of inner terrain. The Jordan, desert, lake, and mountain are not only places plotted on a physical map; they are also spiritual landmarks—threshold experiences, epiphanies, trials, awakenings, and so forth. The Jordan, for instance, is a threshold experience, liminal space where we assess where we have come from and where we are going. The desert is foreboding, feral landscape that threatens the pleasant fertility of inhabitable land; it is the habitat of noxious, terrifying creatures and the wasteland of devil and demons. In this "fierce,"[1] rugged, untamed landscape our resolve is tested and our loyalties made known. Will we rely upon God in the desert or on the fretful self?

The lake or sea is uncontrollable space. The movie *The Perfect Storm* (2000), based on a real-life story that occurred off the coast of Gloucester, Massachusetts, in 1991, is a reminder that the unpredictable, relentless sea is uncontrollable space. In the movie, the captain of a fishing boat gathers his crew to go out for a big haul on short notice, while three brutal storms converge off the coast to create the storm of the century, the perfect storm. The protagonist and his crew are unable to make it back to coast in time and are lost in the tumultuous storm. Whether in the twenty-first century or the first century, the raging sea cannot be calmed by human efforts. Only God tames the sea. The sea is uncontrollable terrain where we awaken to life's uncertainties and our own frail egos. As spiritual landscape, the sea or lake is where we become aware of our need for God to tame the unpredictable in our lives.

The mountain is a different kind of spiritual landscape. As the earth reaching heavenward, it represents humankind's striving to draw closer to God and to know God's will. The mountain is a place of spiritual strengthening where our recalcitrant wills are brought into conformity with God's will. It is on the mountain that we gain a new vantage point, a different perspective on life. In the movie *Dead Poets Society* (1989), John Keating, played by Robin Williams, is a charismatic English teacher in a private prep school in New England who instills within his students the need to think outside the box and to "seize the day" (*carpe diem*). In one scene, the students march in single file to his desk and stand on top of it to gain a different perspective. By going higher physically, the students also go higher intellectually, spiritually, and emotionally; they envision new possibilities—or at least that is John Keating's hope—that eluded them in their staid, conformist environment. In Luke, the mountain is that higher ground where we not only gain a new perspective on life but also are provided with the necessary resources to "seize the day." Everything looks different from the mountain, and the impossible no longer seems impossible.

## Jordan

The Jordan River is a boundary that separates the threat of wilderness from new life in the promised land. It represents a break with past, aimless ways and the beginning of a new phase in our lives.[2] It is at the Jordan that the question "What then should we do?" (3:10, 12, 14) is asked. In the movie *The Year of Living Dangerously* (1983), the same question is posed by Billy Kwan, a Chinese Australian who lives in Jakarta, Indonesia, in the '60s under the oppressive rule of Sukarno. "What then must we do?" is the question Tolstoy asked (who is quoted in the movie). In one scene, Billy tells a foreign correspondent, Guy Hamilton, that Tolstoy sold all he had to alleviate the pain and suffering of those around him. And when Billy is faced with the stifling poverty of Jakarta under Sukarno, he, too, asks the same question. Billy tries to alleviate suffering and the squalid poverty of others. He helps a young prostitute and her child, but the child eventually dies from drinking polluted water. He even takes the bold step of placing a banner over the balcony of a hotel to challenge Sukarno to feed his people. But Billy is hurled to his death for his act of defiance. Like Billy's Indonesia, which stood at the threshold of rebellion (Sukarno was overthrown in 1965), the Jordan is the threshold experience where we ask the question "What then should we do?"

The Israelites crossed the Jordan, leaving behind their desert wandering for a new life in a new land; similarly, the new Israel[3] crosses the Jordan once more in 3:7–17—a crossing that takes the form of baptism of repentance for the forgiveness of sins. The crowd's baptism in the Jordan signals their departure from recalcitrant, self-serving ways to complete surrender to God's new aims.[4] Their threshold experience is described in 3:10–14: those who have two coats share with those who have none, those with food share with the hungry, tax collectors stop overcharging, and soldiers no longer extort money from others. "Negative reciprocity," which desires something for nothing is left behind for "generalized reciprocity," which is characterized by altruistic, self-sacrificing transactions.

Jesus also has a threshold experience at the Jordan.[5]

> Now when all the people were baptized, and when Jesus also had been baptized and was praying, the heaven was opened, and the Holy Spirit descended upon him in bodily form like a dove. And a voice came from heaven, "You are my Son, the Beloved; with you I am well pleased." (3:21–22)

The opening of heaven testifies to the uniqueness of this event and provides God's point of view on Jesus' threshold experience. In Revelation, for instance, the opening of heaven provides access to God's perspective, revealing the mystery of heaven to those on earth (cf. Rev 4:1; 19:11).[6] In Luke's baptismal account, the mystery revealed is that Jesus is endowed with the Holy Spirit and proclaimed Son of God; he is the new earthly representative anointed for divine service (cf. Luke 4:18–19).[7] But before he leads the new Israel into the new promised land, the kingdom of God, he is tested as to *his* resolve in the desert. The threshold experience is followed by a desert testing, which confirms and validates the Jordan crossing—a common pattern, indeed a necessary sequence, in the spiritual life.

# Desert

Desert is austere, feral, forbidding landscape.[8] It is the habitat of wild, terrifying animals and demonic beings.[9] The desert represents the world at the edges, untamed, uninhabitable land that threatens the pleasant fertility of inhabited spaces and human existence.[10] The desert tests our resolve. Untamed space is where we come face-to-face with our own limitations; the terror without reveals the terror within. Yet the desert is also where God's grace, divine succor, turns the stark emptiness of wilderness into an empyrean of spiritual and physical nourishment.[11] In the desert we "quickly come to the end of what [we] have depended upon to give continuity and meaning to [our] life."[12] The desert takes us to the edges of our lives: we realize what we have and do not have; what is important and what is irrelevant; what is needful and what is empty. Our own bleak emptiness is clarified in the nakedness of untamed space. It is at the edges that we learn to set our priorities straight and to rely upon unexpected, all-sufficient grace. The fidelity of the Israelites was tested in the desert, but they also received divine, unsayable grace there. In Luke the desert is a place of testing our resolve and realizing our limitations. It is also a place of unexpected succor.

## Luke 1:80; 3:2, 4

The initial reference to the desert recalls the desert wandering of the Israelites. In the desert John prepares a new Israel for a new exodus (1:80).[13] His is the voice of the one crying out in the wilderness,

> Prepare the way of the Lord,
>> make his paths straight. (3:4b)

The "way of the Lord" is the way Jesus travels as he gathers followers on the "way" to the new promised land, the kingdom of God—a way that is described in 3:5, where radical upheavals in the physical landscape symbolically represent unexpected transformations in the socioeconomic, political, and spiritual landscape.[14]

Every valley shall be filled,
> and every mountain and hill
>> shall be made low,
> and the crooked shall be made straight,
>> and the rough ways made smooth. (3:5)

In this new exodus, everything is turned upside down: the lofty made low ("mountain and hill . . . made low"), and the low made high ("every valley filled in"); the hungry filled, and the rich impoverished (cf. 1:52–3; 14:11; 18:14).

## Luke 4:1–13

Jesus' unblinking faithfulness to God is put to the test in the desert where two radically different points of view clash. Life's choices are clearest in the vast starkness of desert wasteland. One point of view, which is the devil's strong suit, is material, concrete; it exults in the securities of this life and the allure of this world.[15] The material point of view is a spiritual putsch on the loyalties of the human heart; it revels in superficiality, in the concreteness of this world, and in the frailty of the fretful ego. The other point of view rejects life's beguiling temptations and finds its security in uncompromising loyalty to God.[16] The one is self-serving and specious; the other recognizes God as the author and sustainer of life. The one leads to certain death; the other, to eternal life.

The devil's self-serving point of view feeds ferociously upon an irresolute ego. His self-referential posture is apparent in the tribute to himself.

To you
> I will give their glory and all this authority;
> for it has been given over to *me*,
> and I give it to anyone I please.
> If you, then, will worship *me*,
it will be all yours. (4:6–7)[17]

Although the passive voice ("it has been given over to me") acknowledges in a roundabout way that God delegates the authority to the devil, he buries this information within a paean to himself. First-person verbs[18] and pronouns[19] exult in the self. In 4:6, for example, the devil begins with "I will give" and closes with "I give." Like a persistent salesperson who is closing an important sale, his speech accentuates what *he* can do for *Jesus*: "to you" and "to me" are placed in the emphatic position. "*To you* I will give their glory and all this authority; for *to me* it has been given" (4:6, author's translation). His self-regarding posture elevates the material point of view to new heights: the "self" becomes the object of worship.

By contrast, Jesus' speech is utterly devoid of first-person verbs and pronouns. Whereas the devil is full of himself, so to speak, Jesus is "full of the Holy Spirit" (4:1). He repeatedly refers to God, not to the self. With a string of quotations from Scripture, Jesus, unlike the devil, shifts attention from himself to God. In 4:8, he borrows from Deut 6:13: "Worship the Lord your God and serve only him," and in 4:12, he quotes from Deut 6:16: "Do not put the Lord your God to the test." In the single instance where the self might surface, no "I" is found; only a generic reference: "One[20] does not live by bread alone" (4:4).

The material point of view also determines the devil's exegesis of Scripture. In the third temptation, he interprets Ps 91:11–12 (LXX, Ps 90:11–12) in a literal, concrete way to tempt Jesus to adopt a self-regarding posture.

> "He will command his angels
> > concerning *you*,
> > to protect *you*,"

and

> "On their hands they will bear
> > *you* up,
> so that *you* will not dash
> > *your* foot against a stone." (4:10, 11)

Here the devil employs a tactic similar to his overfull usage of first-person pronouns in the second temptation, although this time using second-person pronouns. He tempts Jesus to rely on God's promises for *his own* benefit and to use Scripture in a crass and materialistic way to test God's faithfulness. "Concerning *you*," "to protect *you*," "they will bear *you* up," and "*you* will not dash *your* foot." [21] Jesus, however, rejects the emptiness and fatuity of the devil's offer and refuses to "put the Lord your God to the test" (4:12).

Jesus' desert temptation is not only the necessary way to spiritual development; it is also the desired way. The material is seductive. Its bewitching attractiveness is without question. Yet its stark emptiness is too real to doubt. The nakedness of the devil's material way of thinking is reflected in the vast, raw barrenness of the desert. He offers merely an ephemeral existence, bankrupt of lasting significance: kingdoms of this world, the glory and authority of this world, *this* world, this *world*. Like the unreceptive wilderness terrain, his solace is empty. On the other hand, the desert test strengthens confidence in God who provides in desolate times and parched places. This confidence allows us to turn our backs once and for all on a vacuous, material point of view. In this act of turning, we learn to rely upon the uncommon fullness of God's grace.

## Luke 9:10–17

In the desert ("deserted place," 9:12) the disciples are tested and face their own bleak emptiness. They also learn to rely upon God's uncommon grace. Their test is straightforward yet daunting: Jesus commands them to give the five thousand something to eat (9:13).[22] But the disciples, prone more to rely on the self than on God, fail their test; they offer a human solution to a problem that can only be resolved preternaturally.[23]

> We have no more than five loaves and two fish—*unless* we are to go and buy food for *all* these people. (9:13)

The "unless" and the "all" underscore the difficulty of the task. "Unless"[24] expects a negative answer: "Of course, you do not expect us to buy food for all these people." They are right, of course: Jesus does not expect them to purchase food. And "all these people"—five thousand or more—reveals the utter impossibility of human solutions. Because they view bread as a mere commodity[25] that can be bought and sold, the disciples flounder in their spiritual test. The material poverty of five loaves and two fish is like the disciples' spiritual poverty: the limited resources are all too apparent. Bread on this exodus, like the manna in the desert, is *not* a commodity; it is a miraculous gift from God.

This desert experience prepares the disciples for the relinquishment of their self-sufficiency. When they rely on their own frail egos, they fail; when they rely on Jesus, they succeed. At Jesus' direction the disciples gather the crowd into groups of fifty, creating order out of chaos, shaping community out of entropic brokenness. Jesus then shows the way the vast emptiness can be filled: *he prays*.

> And taking the five loaves and the two fish,
> he looked up to heaven,
> and blessed,
> and broke them. (9:16)

After saying the blessing and dividing the food, he keeps on giving[26] an unlimited supply of manna for this exodus. Poverty of resources is miraculously turned into excess:

> And all ate and were filled. What was left over was gathered up, twelve baskets of broken pieces. (9:17)

The narrator's annotation summarizes the benefit of traveling with Jesus: God's extravagance far exceeds our meager resources. We end up with much more than what we started with. As Israel approached the promised land, they were promised that they would eat their fill (Deut 8:10)—a promise fulfilled in the feeding of the five thousand. All[27] ate and were satisfied.[28] The *twelve*[29] baskets of leftovers—one for each of the twelve disciples, the representatives of the new Israel—is a surfeit of food, an extravagance of grace, which feeds all on this exodus to the new promised land.[30] Jesus thus turns the untamed, broken, deserted places of life into a land of abundance. Unexpected grace. The desert is where we come face-to-face with our immense poverty, and where we realize our bleak emptiness. Yet it is in the stark nakedness of vast, terrifying space that we learn to rely on God's uncommon grace.

# Lake

As uncontrollable space, the lake tests the limits of human endeavor and reveals the infinite power of God.[31] Since God alone tames the uncontrollable (cf. Ps 65:7; 89:9; 106:9; 107:23–32),[32] the unpredictable lake is an ideal landscape for spiritual awakenings. The disciples awaken to the bankruptcy of the self and the need to rely on Jesus.

## Luke 5:1–11

Peter's call is a spiritual awakening that includes an awed sense of unworthiness in the presence of the numinous and a radical break with the past. Luke uses the technically correct designation—"Lake" of Gennesaret—instead of Mark's "Sea" of Galilee. But like Mark's sea, which is rich with overtones of raging chaos and divine calm,[33] Luke's lake is a spiritually rich symbol. Of the Synoptic Gospels, only Luke associates the miraculous catch of fish with the call of Peter *on a lake*.[34]

The lake narrative begins in stark and dismal poverty. The disciples have brought their boats ashore and are "washing their nets" but have caught nothing after an entire night of fishing (5:2, 5). Simon expresses their failure: "Master, we have worked all night long but have caught nothing" (5:5). Yet in this dreadful failure Peter's awakening begins, as Jesus tames the recalcitrant lake and makes it yield its bounty. Without Jesus the disciples are fishermen with no fish; with him their failure is turned to success.

As Jesus gets into Simon's boat and teaches the crowds, the peripety begins (5:3). He joins symbolically with the disciples in the common activity of fishing; but Jesus' fishing is uncommon.[35] He directs Simon to put out a little way from the shore and then commands him to put his nets into the stubborn lake one more time. When Jesus becomes captain of *this* boat, the niggardly lake is transformed into a place of overwhelming excess. With its unwieldy weight, the immense catch threatens not only to break the nets but to capsize the boats: newfound success where there was only bleak failure.

A spiritual awakening begins with the discovery of our brokenness and poverty; our own stark emptiness is clarified in the presence of the numinous. "Simon Peter" recognizes his unworthiness and re-coils in the presence of the Other: "Go away from me, Lord, for I am a sinful man!" (5:8). Luke's usual pattern is to call Peter "Simon" (5:3, 4, 5, 10), but at this seminal moment he expands his name—"Simon Peter"—as if to call attention to Peter's awakening.[36] An expanded name corresponds to an expanded vision. Peter's expanded under-standing is also represented in the titles he uses for Jesus. No longer does he call him "master" but "Lord,"[37] which is not a polite address to a superior, but a recognition that he is in the presence of the Other.[38] Peter's self-designation "sinner" underscores the distance between Jesus and himself. A sinner can be many things in Luke,[39] but in this passage a sinner is one whose immense poverty and bleak nakedness are uncovered in an encounter with God's unexpected, undeserved gift of abundance.

The concluding scene is a reminder that the success Jesus brings is not material success. The surfeit of fish is a metaphor for a more important catch: "Do not be afraid;[40] from now on you will be catching people" (5:10). The "from now on"[41] marks a decisive separa-tion from the past.[42] In response to Jesus' call and commission, the disciples "left everything and followed him" (5:11). A spiritual awak-ening to our brokenness includes not only an awed sense of unwor-thiness in the presence of the numinous but also a decisive break with the past.

## Luke 8:22–25 (cf. Mark 4:35–41; Matt 8:23–27)

In a second lake narrative the disciples awaken to their fragile faith. The tempest on the lake is not simply a squall without; it also represents a spiritual tempest within the troubled disciples.[43] The storm within is a fragile faith that assumes that Jesus has left his fol-lowers to perish. It is an inner turmoil troubled by the riptide of failed confidence. The disciples lack confidence in Jesus' ability to tame the unpredictable in life.[44]

The narrative contrasts are made with simple elegance. A calm forms an inclusion around the distressed lake and the troubled dis-ciples. At the beginning, Jesus falls sound asleep in the boat—a calm the disciples obviously lack. At the end, Jesus calms the troubled sea. In between are the roiling sea and the rueful disquiet

of the disciples; troubled waters and troubled disciples are sur-
rounded by divine calm.

> And while they were sailing *he fell asleep*. (8:23)
> And he woke up and rebuked[45] the wind and the raging waves; they
>      ceased, *and there was a calm*. (8:24)

Also forming an inclusion around the disciples' fretful anxiety is
Jesus' awaking from sleep. A common theme in the Old Testament is
the awakening of God (cf. Ps 35:23; 44:23–24; 59:4). Like God, Jesus
awakens to those who cry for help. He arises while they sink.

> They went to him and *woke him up*, shouting,
>      "Master, Master, we are perishing!"
>           And *he woke up*. (8:24)

A "whirlwind or hurricane"[46] of wind sweeps down from the Galilean hills and stirs the resting lake, and the disciples' boat begins to
sink. The disquiet of the lake is recorded from the disciples' perspective: they were being swamped.[47] This is ambiguous: are they
swamped by the raging storm, or are they swamped by their own spiritual poverty, their broken faith? Luke's personalizing of the danger
(*they* were being swamped) allows for both, and the narrator's annotation ("they were in danger"), also in a continuous past tense, underscores their anxious uncertainty and impending destruction. Further,
the disciples' speech amplifies their tempestuous state. The double
title "Master, Master,"[48] which is a frantic cry to the captain of *this*
boat, conveys unsettling urgency,[49] while terror and disbelief overcome their fragile faith: "We are perishing." On the surface their
prayer seems to apply only to the immediate physical danger; yet it
aptly summarizes the depth of their spiritual poverty, identified by
Jesus' question: "Where is your faith?" Jesus conquers the external
threat of the raging sea; now he turns to the more difficult task of
calming the internal threat of failing faith.

To what are the disciples awakened? Their reaction to Jesus' mir-
acle and their puzzled query suggest that they are learning to rely on
Jesus in troubled times.

> They were afraid and amazed, and said to one another, "Who then is
> this, that he commands even the winds and the water, and they obey
> him?" (8:25)

Their fearful[50] and amazed response is altogether appropriate in the
presence of the numinous.[51] But, more important, their question reflects the conviction that God alone controls the raging sea (cf. Ps
107:23–30). Their awakening is "the beginning of the sense of awareness"[52] that security in the midst of danger requires unencumbered
trust in Jesus. This is faith (cf. 8:25, "Where is *your* faith?"). "Being
swamped" and "perishing" need not end in destruction; instead it can
lead to the sanguine discovery that Jesus controls the vast uncertainties of our lives.[53] No danger is too great to overcome, no tempest
too formidable to calm. Like God, who is "our refuge and strength . . .
in trouble" (Ps 46:1), Jesus calms the troubles within and without.

## Mountain

"The image of ascending a mountain [is] a natural choice to il-
lustrate or undergird a central theme of Christian spirituality: drawing closer to God in the Christian life."[54] As the earth reaching
toward the heavens, the mountain,[55] suspended between earth and
sky, is a natural place for God and humankind to meet. [56] It is where
the eternal and transcendent break into this world with clarity. The
mountain is where God's ways are made known to humankind: a
place of prayer and of revelation. As an image of the spiritual life, the
mountain represents our desire to draw closer to God, to know God's
will, and to confirm God's plans for our lives.[57] But the mountain also
represents our willingness to give up control and to allow God to
speak to us in surprising ways. On the mountain God determines the
agenda, not we; on this rugged terrain our self-will is tamed. And it is
on this stark, mysterious, eerie landscape that the din of the everyday
is silenced, and God's clarifying word is heard.

In Luke God speaks on the mountain (9:35). It is a place of refuge in times of trouble (21:21) and a retreat from a busy day (21:37).
Three times Luke records that Jesus went up the mountain to pray:
6:12; 9:28; 22:39, 41.

## Luke 6:12

The only place in the New Testament where Jesus spends the entire night[58] in prayer is before the selection of the Twelve, which underscores the seminal importance of this event.[59] A twofold reference to Jesus' reason for ascending the mountain adds to its solemnity and emphasizes that the selection of the Twelve from a larger group of followers is divinely sanctioned.

> Now during those days he went out to the mountain *to pray*;
> and he spent the night *in prayer* to God.[60]

## Luke 9:28–36

On the Mount of Transfiguration, God's will is made known and confirmed. This brooding, mysterious, cloud-covered place of terror and tranquility accents the importance of *listening* for God's clarifying word.

Twice prayer is mentioned as the purpose for going up the mountain.

> Now about eight days after these sayings Jesus took with him Peter
> and John and James, and went up on the mountain *to pray*. (9:28)
> *And while he was praying*, the appearance of his face changed, and his
> clothes became dazzling white. (9:29)

David Crump divides the Transfiguration narrative into two parts. The first part records what the disciples *see* (9:28–34); the second part develops what they *hear* (9:35–36).[61] The *hearing* interprets the *seeing*; God's clarifying word interprets the meaning of Jesus' altered appearance. The act of seeing is insufficient because it leaves the event clouded in mystery and at the level of appearances. Its mysteriousness leaves it open to misunderstanding, as Peter's suggestion to build three booths demonstrates. Without hearing God's word, the event of seeing is left naked.

This seeing/hearing pattern is prominent elsewhere in the New Testament, especially in the book of Revelation.[62] In Rev 5, for example, John *sees* a lamb but *hears* about a lion. The Lion of the tribe of

Judah is a stock messianic expectation; but this familiar expectation is "made strange,"[63] defamiliarized by the appearance of a slain lamb. The hearing interprets what is seen; what is seen reinterprets what is heard. In chapter 12, John *sees* a heavenly battle between Michael and Satan, but the meaning of the struggle remains a mystery until he *hears* a voice interpret the vision of 12:7–9. And in 13:11, John *sees* a beast with two horns like a lamb, but he *hears* the voice of the dragon. In this last instance, appearances are deceptive, open to misinterpretation; it is the hearing that reveals the inner reality and unmasks the true nature of the beast.

The seeing/hearing pattern occurs elsewhere in Luke. In 3:21–22, the heavens open, and the Holy Spirit descends upon Jesus in bodily form like a dove. The descent of the Holy Spirit is *seen*, but the heavenly voice is needed to clarify the significance of the baptism: "You are my Son, the Beloved, with you I am well pleased" (3:22). Even if Jesus is the only one who sees and hears what happens, the reader is given a report of the seeing and hearing.

At the transfiguration the clarifying action ("seeing") is completed by the clarifying word ("hearing"). In the nine verses of the transfiguration narrative, seeing or references to sight are mentioned no less than five times.

> The *appearance*[64] of Jesus' face and clothing is visible to the disciples. (9:29)
> Moses and Elijah are introduced with the words "and *look*." (9:30)[65]
> Moses and Elijah *appear*[66] in glory. (9:31)
> Peter, James, and John *see*[67] the glory of Moses and Elijah. (9:32)
> The disciples keep silent and tell no one of the things they *had seen*. (9:36)[68]

The act of seeing brackets the transfiguration (9:29, 36), highlighting the importance of visual revelation. Yet until the clarifying word of 9:35 comes to the disciples, their dullness clouds their understanding of the new revelation. Peter wants to construct three dwellings, one each for Jesus, Elijah, and Moses, but the narrator's aside confirms his incondite exuberance: "not knowing what he was saying." Visual revelation is naked without the clarifying word.

In part two of the transfiguration narrative (9:35–36), the emphasis shifts from seeing to hearing. From the cloud, which is God's mysterious, exquisite clothing,[69] comes the clarifying word.

> "This is my Son, my Chosen; listen to him!"[70] When the voice had spoken, Jesus was found alone. (9:35b–36a)

Jesus alone is God's spokesperson, and the disciples are to give undivided attention to his voice ("listen to him!"). They are to follow his authoritative voice as he leads a new Israel on a new exodus[71] to a new promised land, the kingdom of God. The parallels between the exodus of the Old Testament and the transfiguration reinforce this theme. In the exodus three men accompanied Moses on a mountain (Exod 24:1; cf. Luke 9:28), an impenetrable cloud covered the mountain as God spoke (Exod 24:15–18; cf. Luke 9:34), and Moses' countenance shone as he descended the mountain (Exod 34:29; cf. Luke 9:29). An allusion to the prophet like Moses predicted in Deut 18:15 ("listen to him," 9:35)[72] further accents the connection between Israel's exodus from bondage and a new exodus from bondage.[73]

The cloud-covered, serene mountain is where Jesus receives God's unmistakable answer to his prayer.[74] The changed appearance, dazzling clothes, two Old Testament figures, mysterious cloud, and clarifying voice all provide divine commentary on Jesus' identity. This may not have been the answer Jesus was expecting; nevertheless, it was *God's* answer to *his* prayer. In prayer we receive God's clarifying word for us, even if it is not the expected response. Prayer is also a time to confirm where we are going in life. Jesus' journey to Jerusalem is divinely confirmed and sanctioned during the transfiguration. His *exodos*, which was discussed with two heaven-sent representatives in 9:31, leads to Jerusalem, the place of death and resurrection. It was thus through prayer that Jesus confirmed God's will for his life, and it is on the mountain that we confirm God's will for our lives. The transfiguration also highlights the importance of prayer as a time to *listen* for God's clarifying word. Again, what the disciples heard may not be what they were expecting; yet it was unmistakably God's singular word for them: "Listen to him [i.e., Jesus]!"

### Luke 22:39–45

Jesus' prayer on the Mount of Olives is an earnest and agonizing struggle to know and to follow God's will. Like an athlete who endures rigorous training to attain physical fitness, Jesus shows the way to spiritual fitness through intense, relentless prayer. "As was his custom" he went to the Mount of Olives, "and the disciples followed him." (22:39). The disciples follow Jesus up the mountain literally, but Luke certainly intends the figurative sense: they are to follow his example in intense, resolute prayer.[75] Five times, prayer is mentioned in the eight verses:

> "Pray that you may not come into the time of trial." (22:40b)
> Then he withdrew from them about a stone's throw, knelt down, and prayed. (22:41)[76]
> In his anguish, he prayed more earnestly. (22:44)
> When he got up from prayer. (22:45)
> "Why are you sleeping? Get up and pray that you may not come into the time of trial." (22:46)

The structure of Jesus' prayer is a model for Christian prayer.[77] Jesus' request to remove the cup is bracketed by a reference to God's will: the second-person singular surrounds the first person. In this simple and elegant way, the will of the self rests totally within the will of the Father.

> A   Father, if *you* are willing,
>      B   remove this cup from *me*;
>      B'  yet, not *my* will
> A'  but *yours* be done. (22:42)

The disputed text in 22:43–44 intensifies Jesus' agonizing struggle.[78] After an angel appears to strengthen him, he prays "very fervently."[79] The metaphor of an athlete training for a strenuous sporting event captures the spiritual struggle: "his sweat became like great drops of blood falling down on the ground" (22:44). The intensity of his struggle parallels the strenuousness of the task; it requires all his energy not only because the task is enormous, but also because the opposition is great.[80] Three times, Luke records Jesus at prayer: in 22:41, as he kneels to pray; in 22:44, as he prays with earnestness; and in 22:45, as he gets up from prayer. The final reference marks the completion of the struggle and his unblinking resolve to follow God's will.[81] Crump symbolically interprets the phrase, which reads literally: Jesus "stood up from prayer."[82] On the one hand, Jesus arises from prayer and returns to the disciples. This is the concrete understanding of the phrase. On the other, he is able to *withstand* his trial *because* of prayer. This is the figurative understanding of the phrase.

If Jesus is faithful to the divine will, discerned and accepted through strenuous prayer, the disciples fail because they do not pray. The need to sleep is stronger than the command to pray. Jesus' twofold command to pray forms an inclusion, which magnifies Jesus' struggle and success on the one hand and the disciples' resistance and failure on the other.

> Pray that you may not come into the time of trial. (22:40)
> Get up and pray that you may not come into the time of trial. (22:46)

Two metaphors capture the different outcomes: 1) Jesus sweats profusely as he wrestles with the divine will and accepts his destiny. 2) The disciples fall fast asleep. The twofold reference to the disciples at sleep (22:45, 46) emphasizes their defeat: nodding off is equivalent to spiritual somnolence. They are unable to resist temptation because they have not sought the divine strength available through prayer.[83] Although Luke offers a reason for falling asleep, "because of grief"[84] (22:45), Brian Beck notes that no explanation is given in the text for grief. Beck, therefore, prefers to render "grief" as "stress." Unlike Jesus who was able to overcome angst with angelic help, the disciples were totally exhausted—physically, mentally, and spiritually—in their struggle.[85] "In . . . anguish"[86] (22:44) Jesus struggles like an athlete preparing for the contest of his life, while the disciples nod off "because of stress." The way to overcome temptation is modeled by Jesus: "through persistent, intense, submissive prayer . . . not through sleeping!"[87]

Jesus at prayer on the Mount of Olives is a paradigm for spiritual fitness. He shows how to deal with life's incessant stresses.

Strenuous prayer overcomes both mental and spiritual exhaustion. Although Jesus' prayer does not remove the passion, his prayer provides the added strength to deal with the battle.[88] Similarly, Christians are strengthened to face the peril of temptation through prayer. Jesus' final words to the disciples apply today: "Rise and pray that you may not enter into temptation" (RSV). As Jesus "rises up" from prayer, strengthened to do battle, so also the disciples are to "rise up" and pray. Prayer is an all-important, powerful weapon, especially "when . . . human resources are so obviously limited."[89]

## Conclusion

Spiritual landscape mirrors physical landscape. The spiritual life begins at the Jordan where our past, recalcitrant ways are abandoned. Through baptism we submit to God's new aims and begin the journey to the new promised land. Left behind are self-centered ways of dealing with others. The one with two coats gives to the one who has none; those with food share with those who are hungry; the tax collector no longer overcharges; the soldier abandons extortion. Altruism replaces the desire to get something for nothing. Generalized reciprocity becomes the norm, while negative reciprocity recedes into the distant background.

The threshold experience is tested by a desert experience. The fierce, harsh landscape of the desert prepares us to relinquish our self-sufficiency. When we rely on our own frail ego, we fail; when we rely on Jesus, we succeed. In the desert we confront the vast emptiness within: there our resolve is tested; there life's choices are starkly defined. Will we rely on the allure of the material, the concrete, or will we rely totally on God's grace? Will we depend on the fretful self and our own brokenness in the harshness of feral space, or will we rely on unexpected, divine succor? In the desert we learn to rely on God.

As uncontrollable space, the lake is an ideal landscape for spiritual awakenings. Human frailty is more evident when the need to rely on God is more certain. Only God quells the storms on lake and sea. It is on the lake—i.e., in the midst of life's uncertainties—that we awaken to Jesus' comforting presence. Peter recognizes his unworthiness when he comes face-to-face with the numinous, and the disciples are awakened to their fragile faith on the lake. Faith in

Jesus is confidence that he controls the uncontrollable and tames the unpredictable.

The mountain represents humankind's desire to draw closer to God. It is a place of divine-human struggle: to know and to obey God's will. The stark, brooding terrain is not only a place to speak to God but also a place of solace where we can listen for God's clarifying word. The answer may not be the anticipated response; yet it is God's singular, clarifying word for us. It is on this rugged terrain suspended between earth and sky that we confront the limits of our human resources. Despite our rugged individualism that wants to do it all, the mountain is a strong reminder that we cannot. It is on the mountain that Jesus prays for the cup to pass from him, yet he realizes that the only meaningful way is God's will. And it is on the mountain that Jesus is strengthened for the battle he faces. It is also where we struggle to know and obey God's will, and where we are strengthened, especially when our resources are so obviously limited.

One of the most important images of the spiritual life is the journey. A journey involves a destination or goal and a route traveled. Jesus' destination is Jerusalem where he suffers and dies; the disciples' destination is the new promised land. The next chapter develops and elaborates the itinerary of the route traveled, an itinerary of spiritual formation.

# Chapter

## 🌿 2

# Journeys:
# The Itinerary of Spiritual Formation

J ourneys in Luke—the journey to Emmaus (24:13–35) and the journey to Jerusalem (9:51–19:44)—outline the itinerary of spiritual formation. The Emmaus journey is a journey to understanding, a spiritual awakening to God's mysterious ways in this world.[1] On this journey the disciples learn to realign their expectations with God's expectations and to view death and resurrection—brokenness in its most profound sense—as God's new way of acting in this world. The journey to Jerusalem develops and elaborates a spirituality of brokenness. The disciples learn to relinquish control over the securities of this life that seem so important for daily existence. They leave behind family ties, possessions, and the accoutrements of success and experience to follow Jesus.

In the journey to Jerusalem, Jesus' exodus (cf. 9:31) to death and resurrection makes possible a new exodus to a new promised land, the kingdom of God. On the way, the spiritual landscape of the kingdom and the itinerary of spiritual formation are clarified.[2] Jesus, however, does not travel the journey alone. Others join the exodus, a new Israel traveling the same difficult way[3] of brokenness. Other gospel writers, of course, develop the figurative as well as literal sense of following (e.g., Mark 2:14; 10:21; Matt 8:18–22),[4] but Luke greatly expands the journey and the itinerary of spiritual formation. Luke's journey to Jerusalem is nearly seven times longer than Mark's and nearly six times longer than Matthew's. Four hundred and twenty-three verses in the United Bible Societies' text are devoted to Jesus' pilgrimage to Jerusalem in Luke 9:51–19:44, while Matthew has seventy-five verses, and Mark, only sixty-two.

## Emmaus (Luke 24:13–35)

The Emmaus narrative is a spiritual journey in which the two disciples awaken to a new way of seeing the world. God's surprising ways transform their mundane vision. Jesus appears incognito, an unexpected stranger in their downtrodden circumstances, and becomes their traveling companion (24:15). Yet deep incomprehension prevents them from recognizing the stranger-companion in their midst (24:16). He begins the conversation (24:17a)—as God always does—and allows them to tell their story with its hopes, expectations, and disappointments. Cleopas and his friend, however, are disconsolate (24:17b) because they do not understand God's mysterious ways in this world. The impediments to spiritual formation—disappointment, dullness, foolishness, mirthless trudging, and slowness of heart—are abandoned on this journey, and the disciples' eyes are opened to God's working ways in this world.

The Emmaus narrative begins with the disciples' traveling the wrong way: *away from* the place of new revelation *to* an insignificant village, Emmaus, approximately seven miles[5] away (24:13). Yet the wrong way turns out to be serendipitous when the stranger becomes their companion. They tell their story to him "on the way," as if this journey—and life's journey in general—is somehow incomplete without a complete understanding of *that* day's puzzling events. Journeying is not simply traveling from point A to point B, as is often the case today. It is also a time of deep, spiritual reflection; a time to look inward while traveling outward. The importance of reflection while journeying is reinforced with the commingling of words for journeying and reflection. They *"were going to a village"*[6] and *"talking*[7] with each other about all these things that had happened"* (24:13, 14). *"Jesus himself"*[8] *goes along with them*[9] (24:15) and asks: "What are you *discussing* with each other *while you walk along*[10]?" (24:17).

Striking reversals enrich and complicate the story's artistry. It is the "first day of the week" (24:1), the "third day" (24:21), i.e., resurrection day, which is *the day* of reversals. A chiasm—itself an artistic reversal of structural patterns (ABBA)—represents the reverse pattern of this spiritual awakening. Unseeing eyes begin to see.

A    But *their eyes*
    B    *were kept*[11] from recognizing him. (24:16)
    B'   Then *they were opened*,[12]
A'   *the eyes*, and they recognized him. (24:31, author's translation)

At the clarifying moment as the stranger becomes host—the moment of recognition, as Geoffrey Nuttall calls it[13]—their eyes, which were closed to Jesus' presence, are opened. Who or what *holds* their eyes? Does God hold their eyes and open them at an opportune time?[14] Or is Satan the subject of the passive voice ("were kept" and "were opened"), restraining the disciples' eyes?[15] Or is lack of understanding the blinding influence?[16] If God is the subject of the passive voice, his action is certainly not "whimsical": "God holds human eyes in the sense that God's ways necessarily appear meaningless to humans who understand events in terms of their own purpose and ways of achieving them."[17] Until Easter is seen from God's point of view, God's ways remain imperceptive. An everyday, familiar point of view, which is filled with shattered hopes, is abandoned on this journey, and God's point of view, which turns the impossible into the possible, is adopted. Thus the Emmaus story is a story of two points of view: that of the disciples—which is also ours—and that of God. When the disciples see the bewildering story from God's perspective, their direction is altered, and their itinerary is changed. They turn back to the city of reversals (24:33), the place of death and resurrection, and proclaim the good news, bearing fruits worthy of repentance (cf. 3:8).

## Disciples' Point of View

Three descriptive phrases frame the disciples' story and express their bewilderment.

They stood still, *looking sad.* (24:17)[18]
"Oh, how *foolish*[19] you are,
    and how *slow of heart*[20] to believe all that the prophets have
      declared!" (24:25)

Gloom and fatuity characterize the disciples' itinerary. Although they relate the events of that day with remarkable *completeness*, they *completely* misunderstand what happened.[21] The events are publicly available; yet their understanding is clouded by intractable dull-wittedness, for they can only imagine God acting according to their expectations.

Irony heightens the gap between the disciples' expectations and God's actions: the disciples are caught at a lower level of understanding, unaware of a higher level.[22] They exegete at the surface and thus miss the deeper meaning. As they discuss "with each other about all these things that had happened," the very person[23] about whom they are talking joins them (24:14, 15). The one who can open their eyes becomes their traveling companion. But the Jesus of their discussion—the Jesus of their expectations—is not the Jesus that joins them on this journey. Like Mary Magdalene who sees a gardener but not Jesus (cf. John 20:15), they expect another Jesus—one who liberates Israel from oppressive political powers (cf. 24:21). Yet this is not the Jesus who appears before them on this journey.

Cleopas stumbles over his own words, or, as Nuttall puts it, "We watch the two friends tripping as they charge *him* with unbelievable ignorance—'didn't you *know* . . . ?'"[24]

> Are you the only stranger in Jerusalem who does not know the things that have taken place[25] there in these days? (24:18).

The named disciple overstates his case with an emphatic "*you alone,*"[26] as if everyone else clearly understands what has happened in Jerusalem. He intensifies the irony by calling Jesus a "stranger."[27] Indeed, he is a stranger to them until their eyes are opened. "The things that have taken place" confirms the public knowledge of Jesus' crucifixion and death, but this "open" event is "closed" to their understanding. A clarifying word and clarifying action are needed to open their eyes.

In their second speech, the emphatic "we"[28] and the past-continuous tense ("we were hoping"; NRSV: "we had hoped") underscore "their pathetic disappointment."[29]

> The things about Jesus of Nazareth, who was a prophet mighty in deed and word before God and all the people, and how our chief priests and

leaders handed him over to be condemned to death and crucified him. *But we had hoped that he was the one to redeem Israel.* Yes, and besides all this, it is now the third day since these things took place. (24:19–21)

They understand redemption[30] as the liberation of Israel from the oppressive rule of the Romans,[31] and, although Jesus is a messianic deliverer, he does not fulfill this familiar expectation. Hence the itinerary of this spiritual journey requires a radical readjustment of human expectations with God's mysterious plans. The disjunction between God's ways and the disciples' expectations is what makes their story *our story.* How are we to make sense of our own unfulfilled, shattered expectations unless the Jesus about whom the story is told comes alongside us and opens our eyes?

### God's Point of View

With the breach between human understanding and God's ways magnified, Jesus offers a reproach and a clarifying word.

Oh, how foolish you are, and how slow of heart to believe all that the prophets have declared! Was it not necessary[32] that the Messiah should suffer these things and then enter into his glory? (24:25–6)

The phrase "was it not necessary" summarizes divine surprise: what appears as unmistakable failure turns out to be God's surprising plan of salvation.[33] Although God's saving purpose seems to have failed, the cross is the unexpected reversal that assures salvation. The disciples' doleful dull-wittedness is remedied by the one to whom "all the scriptures" testify. Without Jesus' clarifying word, Easter remains recondite, and the disciples continue their journey in gloom and fatuity. But with the opening of Scriptures their hearts burn (24:32).

The moment of recognition finally occurs in the breaking of bread.

When he was at the table with them, he took bread, blessed and broke it, and gave it to them. *Then their eyes were opened, and they recognized him.* (24:30–31)

The clarifying word is completed by a clarifying act: the host who opens Scripture becomes the host "in the breaking of bread" (24:35b). The clarifying moment is the realization that Jesus is now present in a new way[34] with the disciples as they journey to the new promised land. The breaking of bread also brings to consciousness their own "brokenness" and "the false hopes they brought into their relationship to Jesus in the first place."[35] Thus the itinerary of spiritual formation begins with a startling awakening to the false expectations that we bring on this journey and to the new way God works in this world.

## Journey to Jerusalem (9:51–19:44)

The journey to Jerusalem, during which Jesus leads a new Israel to the new promised land, the kingdom of God, develops the itinerary of brokenness: the attachments and accoutrements of this life wane in importance to the decision to follow Jesus.

In 1919 Karl Ludwig Schmidt concluded that although Jesus journeys to Jerusalem, he never really makes any progress.[36] It is not a "route [that can] be reconstructed on the map."[37] In 9:51 Jesus leaves Galilee and arrives at the village of Mary and Martha (10:38); yet he is still travelling somewhere between Samaria and Galilee in 17:11, and the goal of the journey, Jerusalem, is not reached until 19:45.[38] The travel notices (*Reisenotizen*) of the "central section"[39] are vague.[40] The topographical notations are colorless,[41] and chronological references are languorous.[42] "No event, no conversation, no speech is precisely located."[43] Luke 13:22 illustrates the listless character of the travel notices:

> Jesus went through one town and village after another, teaching as he made his way to Jerusalem.

Thus Luke's journey is not simply a pilgrimage from Galilee to Jerusalem; it serves another purpose. Four suggestions as to the purpose of this journey are noteworthy: (1) the journey is modeled on an Old Testament literary model; (2) the journey serves a theological or christological purpose; (3) the journey serves a practical function of instruction for the early church; (4) the journey is a spiritual journey that prepares a new Israel for a new exodus to a new promised land.

## Literary Model [44]

C. F. Evans suggests that Luke shapes his material to form a Christian Deuteronomy.[45] Jesus is the prophet like Moses of Deut 18:15, and the events in the central section correspond to stories in Deuteronomy. More recently, David Moessner outlines broad thematic correspondences between Deuteronomy and Luke's central section.[46]

> As the Prophet like Moses of Deuteronomy, Jesus must journey to die in Jerusalem, not simply because God so willed it but because God so willed that the Exodus redemption led by Moses be consummated in the Exodus of the Prophet who, like him [i.e., Moses], must die to effect new deliverance for the people.[47]

Moessner's parallels between Deuteronomy and Luke's central section, however, are less obvious than parallels found in Isaiah.[48] Mark Strauss, for instance, shows that the more important exodus parallels are found in Isa 40–55, not Deuteronomy.[49] Nevertheless, Moessner is correct to point out that Jesus is a prophet like Moses who gathers a new people for a new promised land. "Like its counterpart [Deuteronomy], the central section depicts a prophet gathering and leading the covenant people to redemption by teaching them the will of God and faithful obedience to that will."[50] The itinerary of the journey is thus spiritual formation: "teaching them the will of God and faithful obedience to that will."

## Theological/Christological

For Hans Conzelmann, the central section is a symbolic journey that expresses Jesus' consciousness that he must suffer.[51] What distinguishes the journey to Jerusalem from the Galilean phase of the Gospel (4:14–9:50) is that Jesus travels in "a different manner." "The fact that the goal is fixed, and that there is no real change of place for the major part of the period of the journey shows that the latter is primarily symbolical, and is meant to express the changed emphasis in Jesus' ministry."[52] This "changed emphasis" is his awareness of a divine mission to suffer and die in Jerusalem, which is summarized in 13:33: "Yet today, tomorrow, and the next day I must be on my way, because it is impossible for a prophet to be killed outside of Jerusalem."

Although Conzelmann ignores a vast amount of the material in the central section to draw this conclusion, his observation that the journey is symbolic remains indisputable.

## Practical

Several writers underscore a practical purpose for the journey to Jerusalem. Walter Grundmann, for example, argues that Jesus, God incognito, discloses his messiahship through suffering and instructs the disciples on discipleship.[53] He is a "teacher in the face of death."[54] Peter von der Osten-Sacken agrees. "Luke understands the journey of Jesus to suffering, resurrection, and ascension . . . as a time in which Jesus instructs the community for its own life in the period between his ascension and parousia."[55] Similarly, Johannes Schneider argues that the central section serves "to show the community and above all the leaders of the community how they are to live and act according to the will of Jesus."[56] Finally, Bo Reicke argues that Luke arranges the material of the travel narrative in alternating blocks of material to instruct the disciples on the one hand and to carry on a discussion with adversaries on the other.[57]

## A Spiritual Journey

We agree with Conzelmann that the journey to Jerusalem is *symbolic*. Only with great difficulty can the journey be sketched on a geographical map; rather it must be plotted on a spiritual map.[58] It is a spiritual exodus in which Jesus resolutely determines to travel the hard road to suffering and death. On the journey he gathers together a new Israel for a new promised land, the kingdom of God.[59] Yet the journey is not an arbitrary scaffold to underscore Jesus' awareness that he must suffer, as Conzelmann argues, and it is not simply a framework to provide instruction for the disciples, as Reicke suggests. Rather the journey motif itself is important. *Journeying with a resolute purpose is a fundamental characteristic of the spiritual life*. Or, as David Gill argues, "Jesus' journey is . . . a type of the Christian life, but, more than that, as a journey toward suffering it gives a rationale for the difficult things in the living of the Christian life, the things that are the biggest stumbling blocks and causes of misunderstanding for the community here and now."[60] Jesus determines to travel to Jerusalem to suffer and die because this is God's saving will. The journey also provides an itinerary of spiritual formation for the disciples, which includes: (1) the hard road of suffering and death that Jesus travels, (2) the way of brokenness that the disciples travel, and (3) the self-indulgent path that the disciples are to avoid.

### The hard road (Luke 9:51; 13:33; 18:31–34)

For Luke, the spiritual life is characterized by journeying with a resolute purpose, as Jesus models in his unwavering resolve to go to Jerusalem. Luke 9:51 is "one of the most remarkable and characteristic sentences Luke composed,"[61] and it establishes an atmosphere[62] of resolute determination.

> When the days drew near for [Jesus] . . . to be taken up, he set his face to go to Jerusalem.

Clearly, this is no ordinary journey. Jesus "sets his face"[63] to go to Jerusalem, an expression found frequently in Ezekiel[64] as well as in Jeremiah,[65] which implies "fixedness of purpose."[66] His resolve to go to Jerusalem "to be taken up"[67] can narrowly refer to his death, or it can refer to the whole chain of events leading up to and including the ascension. In either case Jesus' decision to go to Jerusalem is not one of reckless abandonment; his is a resolve rooted in divine purpose.[68] His determination to travel the hard road to suffering and death in Jerusalem is a fulfillment of the *exodos* discussed with Moses and Elijah on the mountain (9:31) and summarized in 13:33.

> Yet today, tomorrow, and the next day I must be on my way, because it is impossible for a prophet to be killed outside of Jerusalem.

As Conzelmann notes, the end of the journey at Jerusalem is not only important to achieve the goal of suffering and death, but the journey itself is "something of a divine appointment, which may not be brought to an end too soon, because it has a function of its own."[69] Some Pharisees urge Jesus to "go and travel from here," for Herod wants to kill him (13:31). But Jesus has another reason for traveling, and it is not to escape Herod's predatory plot; rather he travels because it is of divine necessity ("I must[70] be on my way"). The itinerary of this journey is "a well-mapped plan of salvation."[71] It is a way that Jesus goes "today, tomorrow, and the next day," which accents Jesus' determination to go to Jerusalem without the usual (or unusual) daily interruptions that overshadow most journeys.

This same determination to travel the hard road is underscored in Jesus' pronouncement at the conclusion of his journey to Jerusalem.

> See, we are going up to Jerusalem, and everything that is written about the Son of Man by the prophets will be accomplished. For he will be handed over to the Gentiles; and he will be mocked and insulted and spat upon. After they have flogged him, they will kill him, and on the third day he will rise again. (18:31–34)

Only Luke has the motif of Scripture and its fulfillment in this third passion prediction (cf. Mark 10:33; Matt 20:18): "everything that is written about the Son of Man by the prophets will be accomplished." Jesus voluntarily takes the difficult path ("we are going up") in fulfillment of a mandate ("will be accomplished").[72] The hard road is the way the disciples are to travel also.

### The way of brokenness (Luke 9:57–62; 14:25–35; 18:29b–30)

In 9:57–62, three sayings of Jesus outline the itinerary of spiritual formation and the requirements to join this exodus. Only Luke records the sayings on discipleship while Jesus and others were travelling "on the way"; cf. Matt 8:18.[73] The third discipleship saying emphasizes singleness of purpose. "No one who puts a hand to the plow and looks back is fit for the kingdom of God" (9:62).[74] Just as Jesus "sets his face" to go to Jerusalem in 9:51, potential disciples are to "put their hands to the plow" without a hesitating glance behind. The resolute determination that characterizes Jesus' journey is to characterize the disciples' spiritual journey also.

The rigorous demands of this journey are set forth in the first saying. A would-be disciple wants to follow Jesus wherever he goes (9:57); but unbridled eagerness is not sufficient for this journey:

> Foxes *have* holes
> and
> birds of the air *have* nests;
> but
> the Son of Man[75] *has* nowhere to lay his head.
>     (9:58; author's translation)

The rhythmic pattern amplifies the disparity between the haves and have-nots.[76] The security that even foxes and birds enjoy is a security unknown to those who follow Jesus on this journey. Some commentators assume that Jesus' "homelessness" is a sign of the rejection he faces as he journeys,[77] for as recently as 9:52–56 the Samaritans rejected him. But, more likely, Jesus and his followers are homeless because the exodus to the new promised land has little time for the stockpiling of possessions, climbing the ladder of personal success, performing filial duties, and so forth. The journey is characterized by brokenness: the encumbrances and accoutrements of this life are broken to follow Jesus.

The second discipleship saying intensifies the stringent requirements to join this pilgrimage. Jesus' invitation to a potential disciple to follow him is met with eagerness yet hesitation. The would-be disciple asks permission to "first" fulfill a sacred filial duty (cf. Tob 4:3; 6:15): "Lord,[78] first let me go and bury my father" (9:59). Jesus' response when faced with this seemingly unavoidable duty, however, is nothing less than "provocative and shocking."[79] "Let the dead bury their own dead; but as for you, go, and proclaim the kingdom of God" (9:60). Despite attempts to soften these words,[80] they remain harsh.[81] Not even a solemn act of filial piety takes priority over following Jesus and proclaiming the kingdom of God.[82] "One can hardly think of a better excuse for postponing the demands of discipleship, but even this excuse is rejected."[83] Spiritual formation requires setting priorities befitting the kingdom of God: the responsibilities and obligations of this life are not more important than following Jesus.

The third saying on discipleship (9:62) allows for no delay. The request to say farewell to one's family is similar to a farmer who glances back while attempting to plow a straight furrow: the distraction makes the goal impossible to achieve.[84] The grammar underscores the farmer's ambivalence. He takes hold of the plough in a decisive act of commitment, but continually looks behind to the sheer detriment of the goal.[85] The resolute determination that characterizes Jesus' commitment to go to Jerusalem in 9:51 must also determine the disciples' journeying. Neither the usual securities of this life nor the delays and distractions of the everyday have any part in this journey.

In Luke 14:25–35, a second series of sayings outlines the itinerary of brokenness.[86] Large crowds[87] "were traveling"[88] with Jesus (14:25). The crowds are not committed disciples, but potential followers who may either follow Jesus or go their own ways. Once again, the concept of "leaving behind" is prominent in this second series of sayings. Just as the farmer of Luke 9:62 cannot achieve the goal of a properly furrowed field while looking behind, so a disciple cannot follow Jesus on this exodus and look back. In 14:33, the verb for "renounce" or "give up" also means to "say farewell (to)" or "take leave (of)."[89]

> So, therefore, none of you can become my disciple if you do not give up[90] all your possessions. (14:33)

Luke uses a present tense to indicate that this is not a one-time action but a continual action that characterizes spiritual formation.[91] Just as the journey is a continual, ongoing process, the abandonment of the securities of this life is more than a one-time action; it is an orientation to life that characterizes a spirituality of brokenness.

The abandonment of the securities of this world is also the point of the parables of the tower builder and the king contemplating a campaign (14:28–32). The usual understanding of these parables is that one must count the cost before setting out to follow Jesus. "The disciple should be sure that he is able to pay the cost, lest his life should resemble a task half-completed and worthy of scorn."[92] Yet Thomas Schmidt notes that counting the cost of discipleship is not the action required of the tower builder and the king. In fact, the opposite action is demanded,[93] for 14:33 requires the abandonment of all resources to follow Jesus. Schmidt's observation hinges on the repetition of the phrase "is not able."[94]

> Whoever comes to me and does not hate father and mother . . . *is not able to be my disciple.* (14:26)[95]
>
> Whoever does not carry the cross and follow me *is not able to be my disciple.* (14:27)[96]
>
> Or what king, going out to wage war against another king, will not sit down first and consider *whether he is able*[97] with ten thousand to oppose the one who comes against him with twenty thousand? (14:31)

> So therefore, none of you *is able to become my disciple*[98] if you do not
> give up all your possessions. (14:33)

The stress of this section is not upon committing one's meager and inadequate resources to accomplish the task; this only results in painful mockery and certain surrender. Rather one must abandon all resources and securities to follow Jesus. The parables underscore the impossibility of relying on one's own inadequate resources. Not only are our resources unequal to the task, they provide a false sense of security. Spiritual development begins when we realize the inadequacy of our resources and abandon our tenacious grip on life's securities.

The metaphor that summarizes the itinerary of this exodus is the cross. "Whoever does not carry the cross and follow me cannot be my disciple (14:27)." In contemporary western culture, the cross is romanticized with unembarrassed insouciance. It is worn as a trinket around the neck or as a piece of fine jewelry that identifies one as a Christian;[99] but this concept is completely alien to 14:27. "To carry the cross" is an "attitude of self-denial which regards . . . life in this world as *already finished*."[100] The cross is an instrument of a painful and violent death, an extreme form of execution that deprives the person of any form of dignity; it was a public reminder that Israel was subjugated by a foreign power.[101] Hebrews 12:2 calls the crucifixion a sign of extreme "shame." Those who bear the cross—and Luke uses a present tense to stress the continuous process[102]—relinquish control over all attachments and securities of this life to follow Jesus. They live as persons on death row with no worldly attachments, no possessions to stockpile, no angst-ridden desire to climb the ladder of personal success, no ties to ordinary obligations of this life, no incessant distractions.[103] They are completely free to identify with Jesus and to follow him.

### The self-indulgent path

The itinerary of the religious leaders—notably the Pharisees and scribes—serves as a negative foil. Some of the Pharisees, for example, represent values and activities that hinder travel to the new promised land.[104] They substitute rules and guarded pretensions for the difficult path that Jesus and the disciples travel.[105] In 11:37–54, Jesus outlines the way some of the Pharisees (and

scribes) travel.[106] Their outward spirituality is a front for inward rapacity and wickedness (11:39). Their self-directed quest for honor
and recognition shapes their social intercourse (11:43). Their punc-
tiliousness in tithing neglects the weightier issues of justice and
love of God (11:42; cf. also 5:33). Their appearance of virtue conceals inner corruption (11:44). In 12:1, Jesus identifies the yeast or
leaven of the Pharisees as hypocrisy. Yeast is a powerful transforming agent that works surreptitiously to alter flour and water so that
it becomes dough.[107] Though concealed at first, it invades flour and
water and changes their nature (cf. 12:2–3). Self-serving forms of
spirituality invade and corrupt like the leavening agent for bread.
The Pharisees' leaven is "hypocrisy": they create "a public impression that is at odds with [their] real purposes or motivations."[108]
Luke does not elaborate on their hypocrisy, but 11:37–52 hints at a
spiritual life imbued with pretense and outward show, while the exodus Jesus follows—and calls his disciples to follow—is incompatible with play-acting.[109] Yet the disciples are not immune from a
spiritual life of outward show, and that is why Jesus directs this
warning not to the Pharisees but to the disciples (12:1).

Another negative trait of some Pharisees that the disciples are
warned against is the desire for self-promotion.[110] In Luke 14 Jesus
is invited to a meal by a leader of the Pharisees and notices how the
guests jockey for positions of honor.[111] This blatant self-promotion
turns out to be a source of embarrassment and shame when the person who has chosen the seat of honor is given the lowest seat.
Rather, Jesus advocates a self-deprecating stance in regard to others (14:11). Although self-promotion may be highly valued in a society that is driven by one-upmanship, in the eyes of God it is an
"abomination" (16:15).[112] Luke criticizes self-promotion in the parable of the Pharisee and the Tax Collector: "He also told this parable
to some who trusted in themselves that they were righteous and
regarded others with contempt" (18:9). It is perhaps within this
context that the characterization of the Pharisees as "lovers of
money"[113] should also be understood (16:14). The religious leaders'
unctuous spirituality is focused on the things of this world and not
on God. Wealth and status or self-glory are closely related. Halvor
Moxnes shows that the desire for status, honor, and praise from
others goes hand in hand with a desire for wealth in the ancient

world.[114] More important, the Pharisees' self-serving spirituality contrasts with the self-sacrificing, generous spirit (e.g., almsgiving) that Jesus directs the disciples to follow. The Pharisees' emphasis on ritual purity reduces the stranger, outcast, and needy to "the other,"[115] whereas the exodus Jesus envisions welcomes the stranger and the outcast as "kin" (cf. 18:9–14).

## Conclusion

The itinerary of spiritual formation begins with God who initiates the journey and becomes our traveling companion. Like the two on the Emmaus road, we cannot grasp God's inscrutable ways in this world: God's ways are not our ways; our expectations are not God's expectations. This fundamental disjunction requires that Jesus, God incognito, be our traveling companion. Left to our own devices, we would travel a different route, a hedonistic exodus that wanders aimlessly throughout life. But God's clarifying word and clarifying act convince us to do otherwise.

The journey to Jerusalem outlines the itinerary of spiritual formation: the brokenness that enables the disciple to travel the hard road. The route is simple yet demanding. We need only to follow where Jesus leads. The requirements to travel this road are laid out at the beginning (9:57–62). The securities of this life are left behind. The obligations that seem important—indeed essential to normal strategies of survival in this world—wane in comparison to following Jesus. Spiritual fitness requires that followers not be distracted by what lies behind; rather with single-minded devotion they set their sights on the destination, the kingdom of God. The journey also requires the abandonment of all presumption of self-sufficiency. The resources we bring on this journey—money, accomplishments, self-importance—are not only inadequate; they get in the way. The cross symbolizes the nature of this journey. There are no possessions to stockpile and no ladder of personal success to climb.

The journey to Jerusalem also outlines some of the dangers to spiritual formation: self-promotion may weigh heavier than self-denial, outward forms of spirituality may mask inward corruption, status and self-glory may become more important than sincerity of heart. The spiritual life is characterized by inward transformation as well as outward change. A spiritual life that separates outward forms of spirituality from the renewal of the inner life is not part of the itinerary of this journey. Luke, however, does not simply provide negative models of the spiritual life; he offers positive models for spiritual development, such as slaves, children, and widows. The positive models for spiritual growth and development are discussed in the next chapter.

# Chapter

## 3

# Families and Households: Models of Spiritual Development

Luke uses the social landscape of the natural family and household—slaves, children, and widows—as models of spiritual development. Alister McGrath argues that human beings need to "picture" or "visualize" spiritual matters before they apply them.[1] Slaves, children, and widows are improbable models that enable us to visualize the new landscape of the kingdom of God, while familiar models of spirituality such as the religious elite are frequently exemplars of the old landscape. The religious leadership are too influenced by self-serving forms of spirituality to be useful as positive examples of the spiritual life. They are more concerned with the accrual of status and honor and the formation of power bases than they are with serving God and others. Jesus makes their spirituality seem strange by offering alternative "pictures" of the spiritual life. Slavery, for instance, is an unlikely metaphor for leadership; yet this is precisely the image Jesus uses to describe his own leadership style. Slave-related metaphors develop the contours of a spiritual life of integrity. Children are among the least and at the margins of society, yet they are emblematic of the greatest in the kingdom. Widows are stereotypical models of vulnerability and weakness, yet in Luke they exemplify courage and strength, a self-giving spirituality.

## Slaves

Slave-related metaphors develop and elaborate a spirituality of integrity. It is important to note that first-century slavery differed from New World slavery of the seventeenth to nineteenth centuries. In his article in the *Anchor Bible Dictionary*, S. Scott Bartchy highlights several differences between Old and New World slavery.[2] Slavery was a temporary status in the ancient world: the majority of slaves could anticipate being liberated by the age of thirty. Racial factors played no role in the institution of slavery. Slaves carried out highly responsible social functions. They were encouraged to seek education, which, in turn, enhanced their value as slaves. No laws prohibited the assembly of slaves. They could own property, including other slaves, and their cultural and religious traditions were the same as those of the freeborn.

The Old Testament imagery of "slaves of God" and Paul's reference to manumission of Christians by Christ (1 Cor 7:22) are important for understanding the imagery of slave-related metaphors. The spiritual life of the Christian or Jew is defined in terms of liberation from slavery. In Lev 25:55, the Israelites are described as "slaves [of God]" after their liberation from slavery in Egypt,[3] and in 1 Cor 7:23, Paul tells the Corinthians that they are bought for a price, and, therefore, must not become slaves of human masters.

Slave-related imagery models a form of leadership that is immune to status or honor. In 22:24–27, slave imagery is used to deflate the disciples' incondite exuberance concerning the greatest among them and to describe Jesus' own style of leadership. By modeling a new concept of leadership and benefaction based on status reversal, he makes strange the disciples' understanding of discipleship.

> But he said to them,
>> "The kings of the Gentiles lord it over them;
>>> and those in authority over them are called benefactors.
>> But not so with you;
>>> rather the greatest among you must become like the youngest,
>>> and the leader like one who serves.
>> For who is greater, the one who is at the table or the one who serves?
>>> Is it not the one at the table?
>>> But I am among you as one who serves." (22:25–27)

The disciples assume that greatness is equivalent to lording (or ruling) over others,[4] and Jesus acknowledges that this is so in contemporary society: Gentile kings lord over others and those in authority are called "benefactors."[5] Similar to a Gentile king, a benefactor "lords over others," i.e., he places his clients in an inferior position of obligation by his generosity.[6] The patron expects a reciprocal response of honor or some other form of indebtedness from his clients. Slave-related imagery, by contrast, overturns the familiar concepts of benefaction. The table servant is obligated to perform a duty to the benefit of others, but, unlike kings and benefactors, he cannot wield power and authority to gain indebtedness from those he serves with his form of "benefaction."[7] At issue, thus, are two forms of benefaction: a commonplace form of benefaction that places others in obligation to the self, and a different form of benefaction that serves others without expectation of personal gain.[8] The disciples operate under the first assumption; Jesus' modus operandi is the second. The two points of view are outlined as follows:[9]

| Position A | Position B |
|---|---|
| kings and benefactors | Gentile subjects (22:25b–c) |
| the greatest | the youngest (22:26c) |
| the diner | the table servant (22:27a) |
| the diner | Jesus, the table servant (22:27b–c) |

The rhetorical strategies of the text reinforce position B by undermining position A. In 22:25, a chiasm places at center a common and desirable form of leadership in the ancient world—"ruling" or "lording" over others.

A   Gentile kings
   B   lord it over them
   B'   those in authority over them
A'   are called[10] benefactors

Gentile kings and other rulers lead by lording over others; they maintain a position of honor and leadership by serving as benefactors. Even someone who uses his power to benefit others creates a power base and a following that is at best a form of power wielding. This norm, however, is overturned with the negative injunction: "But not so with you" (22:26). Christian leadership and benefaction cannot follow the norm established by Gentile kings and leaders;[11] rather ruling must be completely transformed, which the parallelism reinforces.

> A   the *greatest* among you
>> B   must become like the *youngest*,[12]
> A'  and the *leader*
>> B'  like *one who serves*.

Unlike kings and benefactors who are concerned with accrual of status and honor, the disciples are to adopt the role of those at the lowest rungs of society: the young and the table servants.[13] But Jesus' rhetorical question sets a trap for the disciples: "For who is greater, the one who is at the table or the one who serves? Is it not the one at the table?" (22:27a,b). The intended response is clear: "Certainly it is the one at table, is it not?"[14] With the disciples leaning in the wrong direction, Jesus now turns the expected answer on its head: "But I am among you as one who serves" (22:27c). The rhetorical trap overturns the conventional assumption of greatness and "a new pattern of human relationships" is instituted.[15] Great leadership is not found in "lording over others" or in acts of beneficence that ultimately benefit the self more than others. It is found in the lowly status of a slave whose acts of benefaction are reserved *solely for the benefit of others and not for the self.*[16] The metaphors of "the youngest" (i.e., children) and "servant" indicate that leadership is nearly egalitarian.[17] Kings and benefactors lead by wielding power, whereas those who are like children and slaves can only lead by serving. Christian leadership uses acts of benefaction not to secure a power base for the self, or as an opportunity to elevate the self above others, but as an opportunity to serve others without expectation of return.[18]

Other slave-related images highlight the spiritual value of indifference and attentiveness. Attentiveness (*agrypnia*) is knowing what to pay attention to; indifference or detachment (*apatheia*) is knowing what *not* to pay attention to.[19] In 12:35–38, the parable of the doorkeeper or watching servants accents the importance of distinguishing what needs attention from what needs to be ignored. As is often the case in parables of departure and return, the slave's true colors emerge when the master is absent. That is when issues of integrity come to the forefront. In the parable's introduction, a clothing metaphor illustrates spiritual attentiveness (12:35). Like the Israelites who were prepared for a hasty exodus with their "loins girded" (Exod 12:11), the disciples are to "to gird themselves."[20] They are to draw up their long ankle-length robes with a belt so that their feet are unhindered for "work, for travel, for battle, etc."[21] Those with drawn robes are spiritually alert, while those with loosened garments are indifferent when they should be attentive.[22] The second-person pronoun in the emphatic position accentuates the differing states of readiness: "you[23] be dressed for action." The disciples are to be spiritually attentive *in contrast to* those who are ill prepared for the arrival of the master.[24]

In the parable a master attends a wedding banquet that goes late into the night, even until dawn, and, consequently, the slaves whose task is to open the door cannot know the hour of the master's return.[25] A. J. Mattill describes the scenario: "The faithful servant sits up all night, if necessary, fights off fatigue, and is ready to run with his garments tucked up at his waist ("loins girded about"), with lighted lamp at hand to greet the master at the gate, so that one may recognize him and he may find the entrance ("lights burning"), when he returns."[26] If the master finds the slaves alert and prepared to open the door, *he* takes the unusual step of fastening his garments with a belt and serving them.

The alert slave, undistracted by sleep or other activities that divert attention from serving the master, is a model of laudable spiritual indifference and wakefulness. Spiritual fatigue occurs when the Christian is overcome by endless tasks, a busy schedule, and the drive for upward mobility.[27] The discipline of inattention—that is, apathy to matters of unimportance or detachment from matters that *seem* entirely essential—requires that we learn to ignore what is not important and that we know when to apply the discipline of inattention. Attentiveness, on the other hand, requires that we pay attention to what is important and that we know when to apply this discipline. In the parable, the slaves have to fight off fatigue to fulfill their task, and, therefore, they separate what needs their attention from what needs to be ignored, the essential (staying alert for the master) from the unessential (sleep). This discipline requires the reordering of our lives according to God's will, ignoring our desires, abandoning what is unnecessary (even though it may seem necessary), and concentrating on what is important. Particularly in Western societies, the trivial seems important, and sheer busyness passes for sincere dedication. Yet nothing is more important in the spiritual life than learning when to pay attention and when not to pay attention, what to pay attention to and what to ignore.

In 12:43–48, Jesus tells another parable about a master who puts a faithful and prudent manager[28] in charge of his slaves while he is away. Once again, a slave's true colors are revealed in the master's absence. A slave is given great responsibility, which may be used for the benefit of others (e.g., distribution of food to the other slaves) or as an opportunity for license (e.g., abuse, drunkenness). If he is found at work upon the owner's return, he is blessed; but if he beats the other slaves and gets drunk while the master is absent, he will be cut in two.[29] With acerbic irony, the slave's punishment corresponds to his divided loyalty;[30] he is literally given a divided self in exchange for divided loyalty to his master. Like the slave of this parable, the Christian is given great responsibility in Jesus' absence for which he or she will be held accountable. Spiritual integrity does not use responsibility as an occasion for self-aggrandizement but as an opportunity to serve others.

The parable of the unprofitable slave (17:7–10), however, is a reminder that spiritual integrity is not a means to gain honor or special rewards. In contrast to the serving master of 12:35–38, this parable offers the normal social script for slaves in the Greco-Roman world.

> Who among you would say to your slave[31] who has just come in from plowing or tending sheep in the field, "Come here at once and take your place at the table"? Would you not rather say to him, "Prepare supper for me, put on your apron and serve me while I eat and drink; later you may eat and drink"?[32] Do you thank the slave for doing what was commanded? (17:7–9)

After working all day in the fields, a slave cannot expect to return home and be served by his master; rather he is to "gird himself"[33] and prepare the master's meal. By doing the expected, *ça va sans dire*, he does not place the master in debt to himself.[34] The slave expects no

honor or reward for accomplished tasks or designated responsibilities. Similar to Jesus' saying in Luke 22:24–27, this parable catches
the hearer completely off guard. It opens with the hearer/disciple
identifying with the slave owner of the parable—"which one of *you*
will say to *your* slave" (17:7a)—but closes with uncertain identification with the slave.

> So *you* also, when *you* have done all that *you* were ordered to do, say,
> "*We* are worthless[35] slaves; *we* have done only what *we* ought to have
> done!" (17:10)

"The rhetorical genius of the parable"[36] is this shifting perspective
from the master to the slave. At first, we identify with the master, concluding that it is absurd that a slave should expect to be served; but,
to our surprise, the perspective shifts, and we find that we are the
serving slaves.

This winning strategy forces us to recognize that there can be no
seeking of honor for the completion of expected tasks, in contrast
perhaps to the self-congratulatory seriousness of the Pharisees,[37]
who expect approbation from God and others for tasks completed (cf.
14:7–11; 16:15).[38] The parable is a reminder that the tasks of the
Christian follower are not self-determined. That is, the slave of the
parable cannot decide that since he has worked hard in the field all
day, he will take the remainder of the day—or, more likely, night—off.
The master determines the tasks. The completion of discipleship
tasks is not compensated on the basis of *our* merits; they are compensated on a completely different principle—namely, what God has already done in Jesus Christ. *Obedience is based on divine initiative and human
obligation, rather than on human initiative and divine obligation.*[39]

In the parable of the pounds (Luke 19:11–27 = talents in Matt
25:14–30), slave imagery highlights the peril of a self-protective spiritual life. What is freely given to use for the master's benefit cannot be
hoarded for fear of taking risks. A nobleman goes away to a distant
country to receive royal power. In his absence he gives ten slaves ten
pounds[40] to "do business with"[41] until his return. When he returns
home, he summons the slaves to report on their trading activities.
The first made ten additional pounds with the one, an increase of one
thousand percent, and as his reward, he is given rule over ten cities;

the second multiplied the one pound to five, an increase of five hundred percent, and as his reward, he is put in charge of five cities. But a third slave hid his pound in a handkerchief and returned the pound to the king because he was fearful of his harshness: "You take what you did not deposit, and reap what you did not sow" (19:21). The king judges the slave by his own words and orders his pound to be given to the slave with ten pounds.

> I will judge you by your own words, you wicked slave! You knew, did you, that I was a harsh man, taking what I did not deposit and reaping what I did not sow? Why then did you not put my money into the bank? Then when I returned, I could have collected it with interest. . . . Take the pound from him and give it to the one who has ten pounds. (19:22–24)

As in the parable of the talents, the focus in the Lukan parable is on the third slave. William Herzog argues that the third slave is not a tragic figure, but is actually the hero of the parable [of the talents] because he steps forward and exposes the exploitive practices of the wealthy elite.

> By digging a hole and burying the aristocrat's talent in the ground, he has taken it out of circulation. It cannot be used to dispossess more peasants from their lands through its dispersion in the form of usurious loans. By his actions, the third retainer dissociates himself from the system he has so cleverly exploited to attain his position of power and influence. . . . He describes the master for what he is and acknowledges his fear of his power. The whistle-blower is no fool. He realizes that he will pay a price, but he has decided to accept the cost rather than continue to pursue his exploitive path.[42]

Perhaps in the real world the slave would be a hero, but in the narrative world of the parable he is simply tragic. His actions are punished and he is labeled a "wicked slave."[43] Bernard Brandon Scott notes that the slave's image of the master deprives him of a future, "for it freezes the servant in fear."[44] John Nolland concurs: the slave has "a preference for doing nothing rather than running the risk of doing too little."[45] The slave's *hamartia* is not acting on what he believed to be true. If, indeed, the master is an exacting taskmaster who "expects to get blood out of a stone,"[46] why did he not, at the very least, invest the pound in the bank to accrue interest?

The slave's response to the dilemma accents a prominent hazard of the spiritual life. The slave is neither slothful (unlike Matt 25:26) nor dense, and he is an excellent judge of character; but he allows the fear of failure to overcome his good judgment. He is immobilized by the real possibility of a failed venture, and rather than taking the necessary and unavoidable risks to please his master, he is paralyzed by fear.[47] It is not necessary to look for allegorical equivalents of the "pound" or "talent,"[48] for the parable is concerned more generally with an attitude toward life. The faithful slave takes risks and multiplies what is given to him, while the unfaithful slave adopts a *soi-disant* safe course of action and loses all. A gift requires responsibility, and although the slave willingly accepts the gift, he rejects the responsibilities that come with it. Instead he adopts a self-protective behavior that increases his fear of taking risks. He lapses into a victim mentality, which saps him of vitality and undermines the spiritual life. Such is the peril of a self-protective spirituality.

## Children

Scholars today routinely reject the romanticized notion that Jesus commends children's innocence, moral purity, or trusting dependency.[49] The problem with the romantic idealization of children is seen, for instance, in Joseph Fitzmyer's stammering paean to children. The parenthetical remark at the end of the following quote undercuts his argument.

> Jesus is . . . extolling the openness and sheer receptivity of these tiny human beings. Their freshness, their lack of guilt or suspicion, their loving warmth, and their lack of a claim to achievement are what is being held up to adults accosted by the message of the kingdom. The little child . . . becomes the symbol of the ideal entrant into the kingdom. (The modern reader may wonder about the other side of a little child's character, which is only too apparent to any parent or grandparent [cruelty to siblings, lying, shifting blame, etc.]; but once again, to reflect on that aspect of the comparison is to miss the point.)[50]

Like slaves, children are at the margins of society—dependent, vulnerable waifs.[51] The high mortality rate of children increases their vulnerability, and the practice of infanticide and exposure (child abandonment)[52] in the Greco-Roman world underscores their status as castaways. The modern tendency to dote on children is alien to ancient culture. Children's relative lack of importance in the ancient world makes them striking models of the kingdom.

In Luke 18:15–17, some *even* brought infants[53] to Jesus that he might touch them, but the disciples "sternly ordered" them not to bring the children. No reason is given for their rebuke, but the infants' diminutive standing in the culture makes them, so to speak, not worth the time of day. Jesus, however, sees the children otherwise.

> Let the little children come to me, and do not stop them; for it is to such as these that the kingdom of God belongs. Truly I tell you, whoever does not receive the kingdom of God as a little child will never enter it. (18:16–17)

The Lukan scene underscores the marginality, weakness, and vulnerability of the children. Unlike the parallels in Matt 19:13–15 and Mark 10:13–16 where the children may be toddlers, in Luke they are clearly infants. They are babes in arms, "wholly passive"[54] and, in a sense, objects, not persons in their own right. They cannot display attitudes of trust or take initiatives to humble themselves. Yet the kingdom of God belongs to insignificant and inconsequential members of society like these[55]—not to the powerful and the elite.

The children are models for spiritual development. Not only does the kingdom belong to these marginalized representatives of society, but also one must receive the kingdom "as a child."[56] This ambiguous phrase may be interpreted in three ways:[57] 1) One must receive the kingdom "as one receives a little child," 2) a person receives the kingdom "as though one were a little child," or 3) the kingdom is received "as a little child receives it." The last suggestion is impossible in the Lukan context since the infants are completely passive. Joel Green prefers the first interpretation: one receives the kingdom in the same way one receives a little child, i.e., by granting hospitality to a child. This also is unlikely in the cultural script of the day, for no one would be inclined to extend hospitality to a child.

More likely, the kingdom is received as though one were of the same status as a little child. The kingdom comes as a gift to infants[58] and remains hidden from the wise (cf. 10:21).

A child is not self-sufficient or self-determined or independent—those highly prized virtues of our upwardly mobile society—and, therefore, a child is an uncomfortable model of spiritual development for today's world. A child is unencumbered with the accoutrements of success and has no pretension "to greatness and achievement."[59] A child is vulnerable and at the margins of society—virtues dismissed by society but highly prized in the kingdom.

In 9:46–48, a child once more takes center stage. The disciples argue concerning which of them is greatest. Aware of their inner thoughts, Jesus takes a little child and places her in a position of honor by his side. He says:

> Whoever welcomes this child in my name welcomes me,
>> and whoever welcomes me
>> welcomes the one who sent me;
> for the least among all of you is the greatest. (9:48)

The child represents the least, the social inferior, a castaway, and yet this emblem of marginality is a model for spiritual formation. The least is the greatest—an irresolvable paradox until it is realized that the values of the kingdom overturn the most prized values of ancient and modern societies. In fact, they are exact opposites, which is the point Jesus tries to get across to the disciples. To receive a little child is "to accept and esteem even the lowliest of human society."[60] This attitude is not highly valued in a society that regards competence as the sure measure of greatness. Yet if the least are the greatest, then the disciple is freed from the usual strivings for greatness. The need to prove or bolster one's self-worth recedes into the distant background. And the desire for preeminence and one-upmanship is seen to be worthless.

## Widows

Like children, widows are vulnerable and marginalized.[61] But, unlike children, widows are models of uncommon strength and persistence. In first-century society, widows were at a distinct disadvantage if there was no male voice to champion their cause. They were "stereotypically vulnerable"[62] and in need of special legal protection along with orphans and strangers.[63] Although victimized by the rich and powerful (cf. Luke 20:47; Job 24:3), widows model spiritual strength, engaging in acts of radical self-giving that shame both the powerful and the rich.

In Luke 21:1–4, the example of the poor widow is sometimes seen not "as praise for her piety, but rather as a scream against the distortion of religion that makes her a victim of abuse."[64]

> He looked up and saw rich people putting their gifts into the treasury; he also saw a poor widow put in two small copper coins. He said,
>
> A   "Truly I tell you, this poor widow has put in more than
> B   all of them;
> B'  for all of them have contributed out of their abundance,
> A'  but she out of her poverty has put in all she had to live on."

In an important article, Addison Wright argues that Jesus uses the widow's example to condemn the callous religious authorities and the unjust religious system of the day. Jesus laments the tragedy of a religious value system that deprives widows of their livelihood or subsistence. Wright's argument is as follows: Jesus does not praise the woman for her action; he merely contrasts her gift with that of the rich. And since the immediately preceding context (20:47) denounces the scribes for devouring widows' houses, Jesus continues the diatribe against the rich scribes by highlighting the widow's action. She is not only a victim of an unjust religious system, but her gift supports the corrupt religious system. And, finally, the *corban* saying of Mark 7:10–13 makes it unlikely that Jesus would commend a widow whose contribution would further impoverish her.

The problem with Wright's interpretation is that the poor widow is victimized twice: first by the scribes and a second time by this interpretation—for her gift giving is seen as a tragic virtue.[65] She is not merely poor and a widow; she is also a fool. S. John Roth, for example, leaves the widow no dignity. "The audience's sympathy for the poor widow adds pathos to the narrative critique of the wealthy religious leaders. The narrative presents her as a foil to the shallow and devious scribes, but not as a paradigm for discipleship, *for her virtue is tragic."* [66] But is self-sacrificing giving a tragic virtue in the Gospels? Perhaps Roth would also say that Jesus' self-sacrificing giving is a tragic virtue. On the contrary, the widow's contribution represents radical self-abandonment in service to God, not a foolhardy gesture by a poor woman who is duped by an unjust religious system. An apparently weak and poor widow who gives all that she has *does not act out of weakness but out of strength.*[67] And the seemingly strong rich, who give far smaller amounts by comparison, *do not act out of strength but out of weakness or cowardliness.* Like Jesus who gives his whole life, the woman gives "all [her] life."[68]

The contrast between rich and poor and between trifling gifts given out of abundance and substantial gifts given out of poverty represents two types of spirituality.[69] A spirituality of self-giving shames the self-protective giving of the rich. In the surprising logic of the parable, the weak are actually strong. The woman gives abundantly with the clear strength of abandoned self-giving, while self-protective giving is utterly foreign to her. She is an example of spiritual strength.

In Luke 2:36–38, the prophet Anna is another model of stalwart dedication. Anna is the ideal widow: her marriage lasted only seven years whereas her widowhood spanned nearly eighty-four years.[70] Her strength is not found in a male counterpart who has long ceased to be a part of her life, but comes from within, from her complete dedication to God.[71] The only other characteristic Luke highlights is her total dedication to God; the parallelism in 2:37 accents her spiritual life.

> She never left the temple
> > but
> worshipped there
> > with fasting and prayer
> > > night and day.

Anna's physical fast is a visible expression of her spiritual hunger, a plea for God to usher in the promised redemption of Israel.[72] Her dedication to worship "night and day" in the temple is a self-abandoned display of spirituality that makes her perceptive to the extraordinary: God at work in the "lowliest member of human society," a child (2:38–40).[73] Anna and Jesus' disciples—also models of spirituality—frame the Gospel. Luke opens the Gospel with Anna in the temple; he closes with the disciples in the temple (24:53). The Gospel opens with a female model of spirituality, and closes with male models. The disciples "continually" blessed God in the temple; the widow "never left the temple" and "worshipped there with fasting and prayer night and day." Hunger ("fasting") opens; satisfaction ("blessing") closes.

A final model of a spiritually strong person is the helpless widow who pleads her cause to an unjust judge in the parable of Luke 18:1-8.[74] The portrayal of the judge is disheartening, for he "neither feared God nor had respect for people" (18:2)[75]—a characterization the judge accepts in 18:4. "He thus acts contrary to Jewish legal practice according to which the complaints of orphans and widows are to be given precedence."[76] His attitude also exemplifies a corrupt judicial system that exploits rather than protects the disenfranchised.[77] When Jehoshaphat appointed judges in Judah, he set forth a standard of impartiality.

> Consider what you are doing, for you judge not on behalf of human beings but on the Lord's behalf; he is with you in giving judgment. Now, let the fear of the Lord be upon you; take care what you do, for there is no perversion of justice with the Lord our God, or partiality, or taking of bribes. (2 Chron 19:6–7)

And the stranger, orphan, and widow were protected classes to which God shows special favor.

> You shall not wrong or oppress a resident alien, for you were aliens in the land of Egypt. You shall not abuse any widow or orphan. If you do abuse them, when they cry out to me, I will surely heed their cry; my wrath with burn, and I will kill you with the sword, and your wives shall become widows and your children orphans. (Exod 22:21–24)[78]

The widow takes an active role in the parable, refusing to be a victim of hapless circumstances; the judge, on the other hand, is a model of stolid indifference.[79] For a while[80] (18:4) he refuses her request, and then retreats within himself to soliloquize. Unlike the openness of direct speech, interior speech reveals and conceals at the same time. The interior monologue uncovers the judge's inner thoughts and motivations to the reader, while concealing his true motivations from the public. His speech thus hides his less-than-honorable motivations for granting the woman's request: self-protection.

> But later he said *to himself*, "Though I have no fear of God and no re-spect for anyone, yet because this widow keeps bothering me, I will grant her justice, so that she may not wear me out by continually com-ing." (18:4b–5)

Only after it is apparent that "she may . . . wear [him] out" with her continual[81] coming, does he grant her request (18:5). The phrase, however, could be translated, "so that she might not finally come and blacken [his] eye."[82] The woman's unrelenting, astonishing behavior forces the judge to exact justice. The judge's soliloquy is thus a reluc-tant tribute to her wearisome persistence.

In contrast to the judge's almost cowardly behavior, the widow is active and strong. Unlike the judge's speech that is hidden within him, the widow's speech is direct and confrontational. The opposing forms of speech highlight two points of view and express two differ-ent ways of dealing with the same problem. Instead of giving up, she forces the judge to give up. Although the judge is a social superior, she offers no respectful title[83] and refuses to coat her language with treacle. "Grant me justice against my opponent," she demands (18:3). "There is no 'Sir, I request' nor [sic] 'There is no other possibility for me because my husband is dead . . . thus, I have had to turn to you, O King, to obtain justice.' "[84] The imperative, "grant me justice,"[85] an-nounces unmistakably her implacable will, and a past-continuous tense[86] testifies to her refusal to settle for a one-time encounter with the judge. Her request is insistent.

The parable is an argument from lesser to greater.[87] If the wicked judge vindicates the widow, how much more will God vindicate the elect, i.e., the believers?[88] Or, "if an unrighteous judge could not with-stand the supplications of this widow, all the more would God's lack of response be unthinkable."[89] Luke uses a helpless, vulnerable widow as a model of uncommon spiritual strength. She is a paradigm of the powerless and the disenfranchised; the judge, a model of power and privilege. Yet, in the world of the parable, the weak (i.e., the widow) is strong; the strong (i.e., the judge), weak.[90] Her unwavering importunity in the face of insurmountable obstacles (her widowhood and the judge's indifference) characterizes confident Christian prayer. On the surface, the social script requires that the widow admit certain defeat. For she has no hope of altering the imbalance: no male voice to plead her cause,[91] no bribe to placate the indifferent judge, and a legal system that is unjust. But her unflagging persistence and resolute desire for vindication overcome the obstacles of this undesirable social script. She is a model of spiritual strength, especially when difficulties and odds seem insurmountable, and a model of persistence in prayer, especially when prayer is the only recourse and resource in a difficult situation.

## Family Ties

Among the Synoptic Gospels, Luke offers the most radical critique of conventional family ties.[92] Family ties are part of the structures and securities of this life that are broken, set aside, to follow Jesus. The old family structure is no longer the place of identity and social relations for the Christian;[93] instead, a new spiritual family based on the hearing and obeying of the word of God replaces conventional family ties. Brokenness, however, is never an end in itself in which the Gospel writer celebrates; it is always *"for the sake of the kingdom of God "* (18:29; cf. Mark 10:29; Matt 19:29; cf. also Luke 9:60 and parallels, and Luke 9:62).[94]

### Traditional Family Ties

In four passages Luke develops a spirituality of brokenness (12:52–53; 14:26; 18:29–30; 17:26–30). In 12:52–53, two family members are pitted against three and three against two. The numerical imbalance testifies to the "imbalance, instability, tension"[95] that occurs with a spirituality of brokenness. The securities of this world are broken to make way for a new ordering of priorities. To the crowds (cf. 12:54), Jesus asks: "Do you think that I have come to bring peace to the earth? No," he says, "but rather division!" (12:51). Jesus then sketches the divisions that occur within a single household.

> From now on five in one household will be divided; three against two and two against three; they will be divided:

> A    father
>     B    against son
>     B'   and son
> A'   against father,
> A    mother
>     B    against daughter
>     B'   and daughter
> A'   against mother,
> A    mother-in-law
>     B    against her daughter-in law
>     B'   and daughter-in-law
> A'   against mother-in-law. (12:52–53)

In Mic 7:6 and in the parallel passage in Matt 10:35, the hostility is strictly one-directional: the young against the old. In Luke, on the other hand, a chiastic structure amplifies the mutual tension: the younger generation against the older, the older against the younger.[96] The pleasant harmony of the household is disrupted by the decision of discipleship; it unsettles the "balance and restfulness of symmetry"[97] within the traditional family. [98]

In Luke 14:26, the spirituality of brokenness is intensified to include one's spouse and even the self; the traditional fabric of the family is set over against the personal call of discipleship.

> Whoever comes to me *and* does not hate
>     his own father *and* mother
>     *and* wife *and* children
>     *and* brothers *and* sisters
>     *and* furthermore his own life
> cannot be my disciple. (author's translation)

Luke's form of the saying is harsher than the parallel in Matt 10:37. Matthew uses a comparison and the word "or": "loves father or mother more than me is not worthy of me." Luke, on the other hand, intensifies the choice by the usage of parataxis[99] and the word "hate."[100] Each family tie is named and highlighted as a potential obstacle to discipleship. Some commentators consider "hate" to be a Semitic hyperbole that means to "love less than," but it cannot have this meaning here.[101] A comparison with 16:13 shows that "hate" must mean disown or renounce.[102]

> No slave can serve two masters;
>     A   for a slave will either *hate* the one
>         B   and *love* the other,
>         B'  or *be devoted* to the one
>     A'  and *despise* the other.
> You cannot serve God and wealth.

"Hate" is parallel to "despise," and "love" is parallel to "be devoted." Thus "hate" does not mean to love one master more than another; it implies leaving one master behind to serve another. Similarly, in 14:26, "hate" refers "to disowning, renunciation, rejection. . . ."[103] The expansion of the list of family members to include father, mother, wife, children, brothers, sisters, and even one's own life amplifies the brokenness: none of the usual securities of this life can get in the way of following Jesus. In contrast, Matthew has only father or mother, son or daughter.

In Luke 18:29–30, brokenness results in gain, not loss. Unlike the parallels in Matt 19:29 and Mark 10:29–30, Luke includes "wife" along with "brothers or parents or children."

> Truly I tell you,
> there is no one who has left house or wife or brothers or parents or
>     children,
>         for the sake of the kingdom of God,
> who will not get back very much more in this age,
>         and in the age to come eternal life. (18:29–30)

In the new social landscape, the disciple receives "very much more" in this age and in the age to come than what he or she gave up, and although Luke, unlike Mark,[104] does not specify the gain, he assures the follower that the gain[105] far exceeds the loss.

In a final passage on family ties (17:26–30), Luke shows how the ordinary strategies for survival in this world are inadequate for the kingdom. A spirituality of brokenness requires that we view survival strategies in this world differently; the ordinary must be seen in terms of its cessation, in terms of the End. In his book, *The Sense of an Ending*,[106] Frank Kermode illustrates the way a sense of an ending influences how we view the everyday. He uses the *tick tock* of a clock to make his point. The *tick* immediately creates the expectation of the *tock*. This is a particularly astute observation because there is, of course, no such thing as *tick tock*. The sounds are identical, but we create the fiction that they are different sounds: *tick tock* instead of *tick tick* or *tock tock*. The "*tick* is our word for a physical beginning, *tock* our word for an end."[107] A *tock* enables us to perceive a special kind of middle between the *tick* and the *tock*. In other words, the *tock* allows us to "confer organization and form on the temporal structure. The interval between the two sounds, between *tick* and *tock* is now charged with significant duration."[108] Without a sense of an ending (i.e., the *tock*), the mundane occupies our entire field of vision, looming large as life's goal; but with the sense of an ending, the everyday (i.e., the interval between the *tick* and the *tock*) is placed within a proper perspective. At any time, the ordinary, including marrying and offering a daughter in marriage, may come to a sudden, unpropitiously apocalyptic end. It is only when the repetition of daily activities abruptly ceases—or, at least, is viewed as possibly coming to an end—that everyday activities gain a new perspective. The sense of an ending is part of a spirituality of brokenness. The lethargy of the habitual no longer exerts its anesthetizing influence on our everyday activities; the trance is broken, allowing us to set kingdom priorities.

In Luke 17:26–30, a sense of ending breaks the rhythm of the routine.[109] We normally view the everyday as timeless, but in this passage Luke makes us aware of the ephemera of the everyday. Staccato phrasing, repetition, and asyndeton (omission of conjunctions that ordinarily coordinate words or clauses) lull us into the routine of the everyday. The rhythmic pattern then comes to a grinding halt with an abrupt change in tenses and style, mimicking the cataclysmic disruption that occurs on the day of the Son of Man. The oscillation between "days" and "day," like the *tick tock* of a clock, sets ordinary activities in the context of an extraordinary day.

> And as it happened in the *days* of Noah, so it shall be in the *days* of
>     the Son of Man.
> They *were eating, drinking, marrying, being given in marriage,*
>         until the *day* Noah entered into the ark,
>             and the flood came
>             and destroyed all.
> Likewise as it happened in the *days* of Lot:
> They *were eating, drinking, buying, selling, planting, building,*
>         but on the *day* Lot left from Sodom,
>             it rained fire and sulfur from heaven
>             and destroyed all of them.
> —it will be like that on the *day* that the Son of Man is revealed.
>     (17:26–30, author's translation)

Asyndeton expresses the monotony of routine daily activities. Although the NRSV captures the rhythm of the ordinary with the past continuous tense ("were eating and drinking, and marrying and being given in marriage"), it mollifies the rhythmic cadences by using "ands" which are absent in the Greek.[110]

> They *were eating,*
>     *were drinking,*
>         *were marrying,*
>             *were being given in marriage. . . .*
> They *were eating,*
>     *were drinking,*
>         *were buying,*
>             *were selling,*
>                 *were planting,*
>                     *were building. . . .*

This continuum of ceaseless activities is broken, however, with usage of a simple past tense (aorist) and parataxis.

Noah entered . . .
>    *and* the flood came
>    *and* destroyed all.
It rained . . .
>    *and* destroyed them all.

A similar pattern occurs with the oscillation between "days" and "day." "Days" underscores the routine, mundane pattern of ordinary days.

>    *days* of Noah;
>    *days* of the Son of Man;
>    *days* of Lot.

On the other hand, the singular, "day," marks the cessation of the ordinary.

>    *day* when Noah entered the ark;
>    *day* when Lot went out;
>    *day* when Son of Man is revealed.

Eating, drinking, marrying, and being given in marriage are "various kinds of irreproachable normalities in life,"[111] the stuff of ordinary days, which aims at securing the future. There is nothing in the text to suggest that these activities are immoderate or heedless; drunkenness or lechery is not involved. Only the routine of the ordinary, which contributes to complacency, is critiqued. The text makes the reader aware of the limits of the ordinary, which, in turn, transforms the ordinary into something else.[112] Everyday activities, including the formation of families, are natural, good pursuits but cannot be viewed as ends in themselves—only pursuits on the way to the End. In the examples of Noah and Lot, the common factor is that the activities aim at preserving ordinary life. "Food and drink are normally necessary in order to live, while contracting marriage is primarily directed towards procreation and the legitimate future life of the human race. In other words: the usual physical strategy for survival is inadequate as eschatological readiness."[113] Our normal strategies for survival in this world—which include not only marrying and being given in marriage but also conspicuous consumption and building larger barns—are inadequate strategies to secure the future. Something more is needed to break through a spirituality lulled by complacency: the sense of an ending.

## A New Spiritual Family

Two sayings of Jesus (Luke 8:19–21; 11:27–28) develop and elaborate the new, spiritual family. In Luke 8:19–21, the crowd informs Jesus that his mother and his brothers are outside waiting to see him, and in response, Jesus defines a new family: "My mother and my brothers are those who hear the word of God and do it" (8:21). Although Luke establishes a critical distance between Jesus' biological family and the spiritual family, he avoids the hostility to Jesus' biological family that is found in Mark 3:31–35.[114] Luke lacks Mark's rhetorical question, "Who are my mother and my brothers?" (cf. also Matt 12:48). More important, he avoids the gestures of Matthew and Mark that distinguish the spiritual family from the natural family. In Mark 3:34, Jesus' glance at those seated around him singles them out as the new fictive family, and in Matt 12:49, a gesture with the hand identifies the disciples as the new family. In Luke, however, no distinguishing gestures are offered. Thus Luke does not exclude the natural family from the spiritual family;[115] but he does transfer kinship ties from the natural biological categories to a spiritual category. The criterion for being a part of the new family is hearing God's word and doing it. And this new family is directly related to Jesus, for it is "*my* mother and *my* brothers."

This criterion is reinforced in Luke 11:27–8. A woman in the crowd raises her voice and blesses the womb that bore Jesus and the breasts that nursed him. Jesus again defines a family that is not based on traditional kinship ties: "Blessed rather are those who hear the word of God and obey it" (11:28). The woman in the crowd attributes Mary's blessedness to her role as a mother—i.e., her function within the natural family. But Jesus corrects the woman[116] and shifts attention from conventional roles in the natural family to new roles that define the spiritual family. Blessedness lies not in "the fecundity of . . . belly and breasts" [117] but in hearing and obeying the word of

God. If Mary is blessed, it is not because she is Jesus' mother; it is because she has heard the word of God and obeyed it.

Yet a spirituality of brokenness does not necessarily disband the traditional family. The traditional family may still operate alongside the new spiritual family. The saying on divorce in 16:18 recognizes that although a new suprafamily is taking shape, the conventional family continues to function.

> Anyone who divorces his wife and marries another commits adultery, and whoever marries a woman divorced from her husband commits adultery.

While Mark 10:2–12 and Matt 19:3–12 provide more positive instruction concerning marriage and against divorce, Luke offers the most radical critique of marriage. The linking "and" should perhaps be understood in a final sense, in which case the divorce is for the purpose of remarrying another.[118] Thus the prohibition would read: "Anyone who dismisses his wife *in order to* marry another commits adultery." The point of the divorce logion is not to forbid divorce but to prohibit divorce for the purpose of remarriage.[119] "Luke 16.18 is not concerned with those who remarry after divorce, but excludes the possibility of remarriage by those disciples who have left their wives without necessarily divorcing them (cf. Luke 14.26 and 18.29). The same applies to new marriages with abandoned wives."[120]

## Conclusion

Families and households are surprising, sometimes uncomfortable models for spiritual development. The model for Christian leadership, for example, does not draw upon familiar examples of power and prestige. The religious elite, the wealthy, or the prominent leaders in the first-century community—those concerned with accrual of status and honor and the formation of power bases—are inadequate models of Christian leadership. Instead, Luke uses unlikely models such as slaves, children, and widows. Slaves' acts of beneficence are solely for the benefit of others. Greatness is not found in self-promotion but in self-giving.

Children and widows are vulnerable and at the margins of society. Contemporary society values upward mobility: self-sufficiency, self-determination, one-upmanship, status, honor. But the kingdom values downward mobility. Disciples are called to be like children, who are unencumbered with the accoutrements of success and have no pretensions at greatness or achievement. The least and the youngest have no need to bolster self-worth with an endless array of self-promoting activities. Widows are models of spiritual strength and devotion. Their strength is clarified in acts of selfless giving.

Family ties are rendered relative in relation to the fulsome expectations of contemporary discipleship. Luke's spirituality of brokenness views family ties as part of the securities of this world that must be broken to follow Jesus. The family and indeed the self and possessions cannot occupy the place of primary allegiance if one is to follow Jesus. A new spiritual family, however, is taking shape; it is an all-inclusive family formed on the basis of hearing and doing God's word. "My mother and my brothers are those who hear the word of God and do it" (8:21).

Meals bring out the best and the worst aspects of the social and the spiritual life. The landscape of table fellowship is the subject of the next chapter.

# Chapter 4

## Meals:
## Spirituality of Hospitality

Table fellowship is a "timeworn symbol" that designates "a special relationship between the participants at the meal"; it implies the acceptance of others' social values and status.[1] The ones we exclude from the table testify to our social and spiritual values as much as, if not more than, the ones we include. Pharisees and scribes, for instance, grumble because Jesus "welcomes sinners and eats with them" (15:2; cf. also 5:30; 7:34). He includes at table society's excluded: the castaways, the people at the margins, the undesirables, the unseen. On the other hand, Jesus censures the elite for dining with their well-positioned friends—rich neighbors, for example—while excluding society's expendables: the poor, the crippled, the lame, the blind (14:12–13). The social landscape is turned upside down when the excluded are included at table and the included are excluded from table fellowship.

Table fellowship is a metaphor for joyous[2] participation in the kingdom of God. Eating bread together is a happy, privileged event that mirrors the expectations of intimate fellowship in God's reign: "Blessed is anyone who will eat bread in the kingdom of God!" (14:15; cf. also 22:16, 18). Table fellowship may be inclusive, reflecting the open, boundless diversity of the empyreal kingdom, or it may be exclusive, mirroring a self-serving, adamantine spirituality of closed barriers and insurmountable barricades. Hospitality, whether inclusive or exclusive, self-promoting or self-effacing, is an eloquent testimony to our spiritual values.

## Table Etiquette

Table etiquette observes socially accepted patterns of behavior that prescribe where we sit (or recline) at table, with whom we eat, types of food we eat, preparation of food, and so forth. Etiquette establishes acceptable boundaries so that persons know the "proper" way of dining with others. Boundaries separate insiders from outsiders and eliminate polluting influences, such as unclean persons, unclean foods, and so forth. Yet boundaries also contribute to self-serving, unctuous forms of spirituality that increase comfortable smugness while ignoring "the other." By excluding "the other," the purpose of table fellowship is nullified.[3] Meals are a joyous expression of social and spiritual hospitality; but hospitality fails miserably when restrictive regulations and guarded pretensions govern group behavior. In the call of Levi, Jesus shows why those guarded pretensions are wrong.

### Luke 5:27–32

When Jesus calls Levi, the tax collector,[4] he hosts "a great banquet"[5] for Jesus and for other tax collectors. The authorities grumble[6] at this scandalous event that threatens the identity of the group by opening it up to outsiders. They ask Jesus' disciples, "Why do you eat and drink with tax collectors and sinners?" (5:30). Jesus responds that his ministry is to the sick, not to the healthy.

> Those who are well have no need of a physician, but those who are sick; I have come to call not the righteous but sinners to repentance. (5:31–32)

For the religious leaders, "sinners" are those who do not follow rules of purity,[7] or persons who "are outside the boundaries, beyond the margins."[8] For Jesus, "sinners" are defined more simply as "those who are sick" and in need of "repentance." By denying table fellowship with "tax collectors and sinners," Jesus would exclude the very people who need healing and forgiveness. Thus table fellowship, as Jesus envisions it, is not the like-minded sharing a meal with the like-minded ("sinner" with "sinner" or "righteous" with "righteous"), but the crossing of boundaries ("sinner" and "righteous" sharing a meal). A meal is an occasion to receive the other, the stranger, the one at the margins. The refusal to receive the other has crippling consequences for the spiritual life, as the following narrative illustrates.

## Luke 7:36–50

Simon the Pharisee illustrates the consequences of social and spiritual constipation: his preference for human boundaries restricts his view of the way God works in this world.[9]

"A certain one of the Pharisees" invites Jesus to a meal when "a woman in the city, who was a sinner,"[10] a stigmatic, enters Simon's house and lavishes hospitality on Jesus. Although Simon is "the one who invited" Jesus (7:39, cf. 7:36), he treats him as a total stranger, not a welcomed guest. The woman, on the other hand, welcomes him as an honored guest. The woman at the margins takes center stage, while a prominent member of the dominant culture is pushed to the margins. The lofty (e.g., Simon) are brought down, the lowly (e.g., the woman) are raised up.[11] The striking reversal heightens the contrasts between "sinner" and "religious," and outlines the contours of the new spiritual landscape of the kingdom: the prodigal actions of the woman model a new type of spirituality, while Simon's parsimony is a remnant of an old spirituality.

The woman's effusive attention, which contrasts with Simon's egregious passivity, represents a grateful reception of God's visitation in Jesus. Luke highlights her reception with parataxis (a heaping up of "ands") that allows each action to stand as a testimony to her gratefulness.

> She began to wet his feet with her tears,
>> *and* dried them with the hair of her head,
>> *and* she continued kissing[12] his feet
>> *and* anointing[13] them with the ointment.
>> (7:38, author's translation)

Simon's muted reception, by contrast, is underscored with clipped, staccato phrasing that testifies to his frugal hospitality. By placing each glaring omission of hospitality *first* in the clause, Luke accentuates Simon's feckless behavior.

> Water to me for my feet you did not give.
> A kiss to me you did not give.
> With oil my head you did not anoint. (7:44–46, author's translation)

Three antitheses then contrast Simon's passivity with the woman's fulsome reception.

> But *she* wet my *feet* with her tears and with her hair she dried.
> But *she* from the time I entered did not cease to kiss my *feet*.
> But *she* anointed my *feet* with ointment. (7:44–46, author's translation)

The threefold repetition of "but she"[14] along with the repetition of "feet, feet, feet" hammers into Simon's head her excess and his lack. His failure to offer even minimal acts of hospitality, which begin in a humble position with the feet and proceed to a more elevated position,[15] is astounding when placed next to the woman's humble yet teeming exuberance. Although Simon invited Jesus into *his* house,[16] he did not give water for the *feet*, a kiss for the *cheek*, and oil for the *head*, while a stigmatic bathed his *feet*, kissed his *feet*, and anointed his *feet*.

Simon's spiritual constipation—his restricted view of the way God works in this world—actually prevents him from seeing who Jesus is.[17] He concludes that because the intruder is a sinner and because Jesus allows her to touch him, he cannot be a prophet.

> If this man[18] were a prophet, he would have known who and what kind of woman this is who is touching him—that she is a sinner. (7:39)

His formulaic spirituality, which stereotypes both the woman and Jesus, blinds him not only to the true identity of the woman (she is forgiven!) but also to Jesus' true identity. Simon sees the woman *only* as a sinner, not as *a person* in her own right worthy of God's unsayable forgiveness. This restricted perspective prevents him from seeing who Jesus is. Jesus' query highlights Simon's limited vision: "Do you *see* this woman?" (7:44).[19] Until Simon *sees* the woman as a forgiven sinner, he will continue to believe that Jesus cannot be a prophet, and thus he will not *see* Jesus.[20] Perhaps Jesus also wants Simon to *see* this woman as one who models new behaviors: a new, exuberant spirituality that flows over boundaries, like God's overflowing love, because of the unexpected gift of forgiveness.[21]

The clarifying question, "Do you see this woman?" is complemented by the clarifying action: Jesus turns to the woman in 7:44.[22] Although she was behind Jesus,[23] Jesus now turns to her, leaving Simon behind. The act of turning is approval of the woman's actions, while at the same time rebuking Simon's spiritual and social constipation; it is as if he turns his back on Simon. The dramatic turning also brings the woman to center stage and forces Simon and his point of view to recede into the distant background.[24] By this action, Luke illustrates the consequences of a formulaic, hidebound spirituality. By seeking to erect barriers that keep the outsider out, those same barriers block access to Jesus who identifies with the outsider; in excluding the outsider, the insider is outside.

Luke 7:47 explains the reason for the woman's prodigal spirituality.

> Therefore, I tell you, her sins, which were many, have been forgiven; hence[25] she has shown great love.

Because she has been forgiven much, she loves much. In contrast to Simon's frugal spirituality, she is generous because she experienced firsthand the extravagance of a canceled debt. She demonstrates, therefore, the same kind of love that *she* experienced. In the following narrative, Luke develops in more detail the spiritual poverty of a conformist culture.

## Luke 11:37–54

The topic of Jesus' table conversation with the Pharisees in 11:37–54 is a rigid self-certainty that neglects the inward life but delights in outward expressions of spirituality: purity rules, supererogation such as tithing mint and dill, and so forth.[26] What are we to make of the vituperative utterances in this section? Certainly, the rhetoric is not an indictment of all Pharisees. Rather, it must be seen as a literary device to awaken the hearers from the lethargy of the habitual so that the unseen dichotomy between action and thought, outer and inner life, is pressed on the hearer/reader with shocking clarity.[27]

> While he was speaking, a Pharisee invited him to dine with him; so he
> went in and took his place at the table. The Pharisee was amazed to
> see that he did not first wash before dinner. Then the Lord said to him,
> "Now you Pharisees clean the outside of the cup and of the dish, but
> inside you are full of greed and wickedness." (11:37–39)

Social conventions require the ritual washing of hands before a
meal,[28] which Jesus neglects to his host's amazement. This minor
breach of custom, however, sets the atmosphere for an agonistic lec-
ture. Although the Pharisees exhibit a life of deep spirituality on the
outside, they are impure, "full of greed[29] and wickedness" (11:39), on
the inside. Despite their desire for purity, they are impure; despite
their eagerness to be clean, they are unclean (cf. 11:44).[30] How can
this be?

The religious worldview held purity in high regard as a faithful
response to God: the religious leaders sought to honor a holy God by
keeping their world clean and unalloyed.[31] Leviticus 10:10 is a key
text for this *Weltanschauung*: "You are to distinguish between the holy
and the common, and between the clean and the unclean." Yet ritual
rules of purity not only identify clean from unclean and pure from impure, they also create rigid, impenetrable barriers. John Elliott describes the class-stratified landscape of purity rules.

> This organization of society along purity lines called for a careful
> avoidance of contact with all that was judged impure or unholy
> (sinners, lepers, blind, lame, menstruants, corpses, toll collectors,
> Samaritans, Gentiles) and proper respect for holy places (temple,
> synagogue), holy persons (temple personnel), acts of purification
> (hand washing before meals) and holy times (sabbath, festivals). Ac-
> cording to this system of economic and social stratification legiti-
> mated by purity classifications, the rich were ranked above the poor,
> the clergy above the laity, urban dwellers (especially in Jerusalem)
> above the rural peasantry (especially in distant Galilee), men above
> women, married above unmarried, healthy above ill, conformists
> above deviants.[32]

Purity rules create a "map" that designates special times and
special places: with whom we can eat, what can be eaten at meals,

how vessels are cleansed, the manner of washing hands, and so forth.[33] Maps, however, contribute to a stultifying spiritual life, forming a landscape of multiple barriers, complex boundaries, immoveable barricades. By following an outward purity map, the authorities ignore a more important inward spiritual map. They emphasize outward purity, but cultivate an inner life of rapacity and moral corruption, which includes grasping for status (cf. 11:43) as well as plundering by "violent means something that belongs to others."[34] They are guilty of "wickedness,"[35] which, similar to the "evil"[36] eye of 11:34, signals inner darkness (e.g., duplicity and internal corruption).[37] Both rapacity and wickedness are marks of "negative reciprocity," which tries to get something for nothing either by violent or nonviolent means.[38]

Jesus, however, offers a way to cleanse and renew the inner life.

> So give for alms those things that are within;[39] and see, everything will be clean for you. (11:41)

Almsgiving radically alters the spiritual map of the Pharisees and others. If rapacity is excessive grasping, then almsgiving is excessive giving. Almsgiving should not be confused with the sort of charitable giving that parts with "trifling sums from one's abundance."[40] It is "an expression of genuine social solidarity, of embracing those in need as if they were members of one's own kin-group."[41] Almsgiving shatters the barriers between the social elite and the needy; it destroys the boundaries of the purity map. It turns negative reciprocity into generalized reciprocity, excessive grasping into excessive giving, rapacity into altruism. Some of the religious authorities reduce the spiritual life to outward expressions that give the appearance of inward vitality. Jesus, however, allows for no separation between the outward and inward life. Negative reciprocity is abandoned and generalized reciprocity is adopted, giving replaces taking.[42] In this way, the petrified spiritual life is renewed.

In 11:42, Jesus excoriates a spiritual life that substitutes superficial expressions of spirituality for weightier issues. Outward form replaces inward substance. The spiritual discipline of tithing mint and rue and herbs (which Jesus does not forbid) is more important than the weightier spiritual discipline of economic and social justice.

> But woe to you Pharisees! For you tithe mint and rue and herbs of all
> kinds, and neglect justice and the love of God; it is these you ought to
> have practiced, without neglecting the others.

In 11:44, Jesus attacks a spirituality that appears holy on the
outside but is inwardly corrupt. Although this spirituality appears an-
odyne, it actually contaminates the purity of others in the same way
that persons who walk unsuspectingly upon unmarked graves are
rendered ritually impure (cf. Num 19:16). In 11:43, the Pharisees love
to receive recognition in both the religious (synagogue) and economic (marketplace) centers, an aggrandizing behavior centered in
the self, not in God. This spirituality of self-promotion is developed
and elaborated further in the parables of Luke 14.

## Luke 14:1–14

In a symposium-like setting, Jesus goes to the house of a leader
of the Pharisees to eat a meal (14:1), where he limns the spiritual
landscape of the kingdom of God.[43] The first parable (14:7–11) uses
the seating arrangement at a wedding banquet to outline the angst
that characterizes a spirituality of self-promotion.

> When he noticed how the guests chose the places of honor, he told
> them a parable. "When you are invited by someone to a wedding ban-
> quet, do not sit down at the place of honor,[44] in case someone more
> distinguished than you has been invited by your host; and the host
> who invited both of you may come and say to you, 'Give this person
> your place,' and then in disgrace you would start to take the lowest
> place. But when you are invited, go and sit down at the lowest place,
> so that when your host comes, he may say to you, 'Friend, move up
> higher'; then you will be honored in the presence of all who sit at the
> table with you. For all who exalt themselves will be humbled, and
> those who humble themselves will be exalted." (14:7–11)

Self-promotion leads to shame, while self-deprecation leads to
honor. God brings down the lofty and exalts the lowly (14:11).[45] Despite the commonplace desire for recognition and honor, honor is a
gift that cannot be grasped.[46] In the parable, an invited guest seeks
public recognition from others by taking the preeminent position at

the banquet, the "first seat." But when another person with greater status arrives, he is shamed into taking the "lowest place." On the other hand, the person who takes the lowest seat may be pleasantly surprised and asked to go higher. In both scenarios, the host bestows the honor or shame. Persons are powerless in their bid for honor no matter how hard they try, for in the world that Jesus describes, the only safe course of action is to cast aside the desire for approbation from others. The clause, "in case someone more distinguished than you has been invited by your host," reinforces the uncertainty attached to spiritual one-upmanship. How can one be certain that a more eminent person will not arrive later? A spirituality of self-promotion is thus held captive to the gnawing anxiety of uncertainty. By seeking honor from others, one runs the risk of shame and social embarrassment because ambition overestimates the importance of the self.

If everyone seeks the places of least rather than greatest honor, the spiritual landscape is radically altered. Honor and status from others is no longer the motivating factor, and all are on an equal plane. Self-seeking makes little sense because the system of rewards—honor and status from others—is destabilized, and the desire for one-upmanship and upward mobility is rendered impotent. The only one who will bestow honor and status is God, not one's peers.

A second parable (14:12–14) takes issue with the common practice of inviting "friends," "brothers," "relatives" or rich "neighbors" to a luncheon or dinner (14:12). Jesus recommends an uncommon guest list.

> But when you give a banquet, invite the poor, the crippled, the lame, and the blind. And you will be blessed, because they cannot repay you, for you will be repaid at the resurrection of the righteous. (14:13–14)

Four can repay the host with a return invitation, while four cannot. A threefold repetition of the word "repay" contrasts a reward in the present with an unforeseen reward in the future.

> In case they may invite you in return, and you would be *repaid*. (14:12)[47]
> And you will be blessed, because they cannot *repay*[48] you, for you will be *repaid*[49] at the resurrection of the righteous. (14:14)

Whether in an ancient Mediterranean society or today, normal patterns of etiquette favor inviting those who can reciprocate—a balanced form of reciprocity that receives payment in the present. The uncommon guest list that Jesus suggests, however, is based on generalized reciprocity: persons who lack all means or status to repay the host.[50] There is no reward in the present for inviting the marginalized, only a future reward "at the resurrection of the righteous" (14:14). Giving without expectation of return replaces the normal system of rewards, overturning conventional modes of social intercourse. The "other" is treated in the same way one treats friends and relatives, shattering the distinction between insider and outsider. The drive for self-seeking honor from one's peers is undermined, for the system of rewards in the new spiritual landscape comes not from others but from God. A spiritual life characterized by selfless generosity replaces self-seeking ambition for present rewards.

## Feast

Feasts fall into two categories: self-absorbed banquets, and those that anticipate the messianic banquet.[51] Everyone feasts. Some, like the rich man in 16:19–31, feast now; others, like Lazarus, feast at the messianic banquet. Feasting is part of the reverse rhythms of the Gospel: those who are filled now will go hungry; those who hunger now will be filled (6:21).

The cares and concerns of this world, however, are more important for some than participation in the messianic feast.[52] The parable of the great banquet highlights this sad fact (14:15–24). In the parable a householder invites many to a banquet, yet when the time for the celebration arrives, "all alike[53] . . . make excuses" (14:18).

> The first said to him, "I have bought a piece of land, and I must go out and see it; please accept my regrets." Another said, "I have bought five yoke of oxen, and I am going to try them out; please accept my regrets." Another said, "I have just been married, and therefore I cannot come." (14:18–20)[54]

The householder is enraged[55] and commands the slave to "bring in the poor, the crippled, the blind, and the lame" from the "streets and lanes of the town" (14:21). Still there is room, and, therefore, the householder orders the banquet hall filled with outcasts from outside the city gates.[56]

> Go out into the roads and lanes, and compel people to come in,[57] so that my house may be filled. (14:23)

Willi Braun argues that the parable is about the host's conversion from hobnobbing with the wealthy and social elite to eating with the socially marginalized.[58] Eating with the marginalized implies acceptance of their values and rejection of social approval from peers. The householder at first seeks "to define his social self in terms of allegiance to the circle of the urban élite and their aspirations, values, prejudices and paranoias."[59] Despite the host's good intentions to honor his wealthy peers with a banquet, his well-positioned friends and neighbors snub him, denying him the honor he desires. Predictably, the host is angered at the loss of face among his peers. The conventional cultural script for this indignity calls for the use of "avenging strategies" to reclaim his honor, but the host rejects this course of action. Instead he opens a new chapter in his "social biography," offering the socially and morally marginalized people an invitation to attend the banquet.[60] In this way, the householder flouts the social values of the urban elite, and converts from arrogant aristocrat to patron of the disenfranchised.

Several interpreters[61] accept Braun's analysis. Yet his reconstruction of the host's motivations goes beyond the textual evidence. Although the host is "angry" at the no-shows, it is problematic to infer that his anger is due to a loss of face among peers, family, and friends. More likely, he is angry because the invitees decide to forego the party at the last minute to pursue a more pressing obligation. Although shame and honor are crucial to the understanding of the parable in 14:7–11, this parable is silent concerning the householder's loss of honor. There are few clues that the stress falls on the shunned host and his honor.[62] Instead, the parable's emphasis is on the guests, their excuses, and the unexpected guests who take their place.[63]

Luke 14:15 is about the messianic banquet.[64] "Insiders" refuse the invitation to the banquet, while "outsiders" fill the banquet hall.

The "insiders" excuse themselves because the material, everyday obligations of life are more important than the banquet. "These excuses identify the would-be guests as persons whose lives are wrongly embedded in their possessions and family relationships."[65] The invitees are "devoted to the material and physical aspects of life."[66] The first-invited are more concerned about the cares and concerns of this world than their participation at the festive meal.[67] On the other hand, the material aspects of this life do not distract the socially marginalized and destitute from attending the banquet. Since they have "virtually no hope of improvement in their condition,"[68] the invitation to the feast comes as an "unexpected gift."[69] Although they are not among the first invitees to the feast, and even though some do not even belong within the city gates, the householder makes it clear that the party will go on and they will be a part of the festivities.[70] As for the first invitees, they have indicated their preference by their excuses. The parable thus criticizes a self-absorbed lifestyle that is distracted by the material, everyday obligations of life, while those who attend the banquet lack the multiple distractions of this life and are delighted to attend. The next narrative (Luke 22:14–23) develops and elaborates a new mode of feasting that contrasts with the self-referential and self-absorbed posturing of the world's feast.

### Last Supper (Luke 22:14–23)

Luke repeatedly mentions the Passover and Unleavened Bread as the religious setting of the Last Supper.

> Now the festival of Unleavened Bread, which is called the *Passover*, was near. (22:1)
> Then came the day of Unleavened Bread, on which the *Passover lamb* had to be sacrificed. (22:7)
> So Jesus sent Peter and John, saying, "Go and prepare the *Passover meal* for us that we may eat it." (22:8)
> "Where is the guest room, where I may eat the *Passover* with my disciples?" (22:11)
> So they went and found everything, as he had told them; and they prepared the *Passover meal*. (22:13)

He said to them, "I have eagerly desired to eat *this Passover* with you
before I suffer." (22:15)

The Passover is a celebration of God's gracious act of deliverance of
the Israelites from Egypt (Exod 12–13). The Passover here outlines
the way that the new Israel will be delivered to the new promised
land: the pouring out of blood—an imagery of violent death (Gen 9:6;
Ezek 18:10; Isa 59:7)[71]—and a new covenant of inner renewal (cf. Jer
31:31–34).[72]

Jesus' table manners alter the spiritual landscape once and for
all: gift-giving becomes the new mode of social and spiritual intercourse. In Luke 14, the world's feast represents self-absorbed forms
of spirituality: one-upmanship, status seeking, contests of honor, and
meretricious posturing (cf. 14:7–14). The Last Supper, however, is an
act of selfless giving in which Jesus establishes a new contract between himself and the disciples. The Last Supper, with its repeated
emphasis on what Jesus will do for the apostles, the representatives
of the new Israel (22:14; cf. 6:13),[73] stands in striking contrast to
meals (e.g., Luke 14) in which the participants seek to enhance their
own self-worth at the expense of others. In 22:19–20, the first-person
singular underscores the selfless act of gifting ("my body"; "my
blood"); the second-person plural emphasizes that the act of giving is
for the benefit of others ("for you"; "for you").

A   This is *my* body,
   B   which is given for *you*.[74]
A'   This cup is the new covenant in *my* blood.
   B'   which is poured out for *you*. (22:19–20, author's translation)

In place of self-regarding posturing and meretricious one-
upmanship, Jesus shows a new way characterized by self-giving
and self-sacrifice. Yet even the apostles, by their self-referential
posturing, want to turn this meal of unprecedented *self-giving* into a
shameful contest of honor.

A dispute also arose among them as to which one of them was to be
regarded as the greatest. (22:24)

Jesus, however, overturns their blatant status seeking and one-upmanship and shows a different way of relating to others: honor in serving.[75] The instruction to the apostles to "Do this in remembrance of me" should have had "the effect of drawing forth responses reminiscent of Jesus' own table manners—his openness to outsiders, his comportment as a servant, his indifference toward issues of status, honor, and the like—so that these features of his life would come to be embodied in the community of those who call him Lord."[76] But apparently this was lost on the disciples.

## Fast

Fasting in the Old Testament is an expression of loss or an act of religious devotion (Lev 16:29). In 2 Sam 1:12, for instance, David and his men "mourned and wept, and fasted until evening for Saul and for his son Jonathan, and for the army of the Lord and for the house of Israel, because they had fallen by the sword" (cf. also 2 Sam 3:35; 12:16–23). Bruce Malina and Richard Rohrbaugh view fasting as "a form of self-humiliation intended to get the attention of another so that that other will offer assistance to the one fasting."[77] Fasting is a plea for God to give assistance.[78] The widow Anna, for instance, "never left the temple but worshipped there with fasting and prayer night and day" (2:37). Her fast represents a spiritual hunger: a plea for God to fill the nation with good things and bring about "the redemption of Jerusalem" (2:38).[79] This may also explain why John's disciples fast because the Baptist's ministry is a time of anticipation and preparation for the Messiah. Jesus' disciples do not fast because doing so would amount to a denial that God has sent the Messiah.

Fasting communicates refusal to cross boundaries and join with those who consume. It is "a means of withdrawing from society, a way to communicate non-involvement."[80] It is thus a boundary-creating activity, identifying a group as different from others. "The practice of group fasting necessarily entails the rejection of reciprocities with other groups and their members and thus further highlights group boundaries."[81] In the parable of the Pharisee and the Tax Collector, the Pharisee draws attention to his meretricious spirituality by fasting twice a week (18:12)—a pious act of supererogation that intentionally creates boundaries. Jesus, however, is critical of fasting when we should feast and of feasting when we should fast. The next narrative illustrates this.

### Luke 5:33–35

In Luke 5:33–35, fasting represents the wrong form of spirituality at the wrong time. Some[82] object that Jesus' disciples, unlike John the Baptist's, do not "frequently fast and pray"; instead they "eat and drink" (5:33). Jesus' riposte draws upon a wedding analogy.

> You cannot make wedding guests fast while the bridegroom is with them, can you? The days will come when the bridegroom will be taken away from them, and then they will fast in those days. (5:34–5)

The issue is not the appropriateness of fasting and praying as an expression of the spiritual life. The problem is that the religious are encumbered with a hidebound spirituality—a pious conservatism—that is blind to new revelation: they want to fast when the time for celebration has arrived.[83] The time for fasting is in the bridegroom's absence, not in his presence.

Fasting during a period of celebration forms boundaries: it is a refusal to join in the festivities, or perhaps a failure to recognize that the party has begun. The authorities adopt an old form of spirituality that does not fit the new age. Their pious conservatism, a formulaic, boundary-creating spirituality, prevents them from seeing and welcoming new revelation. While fasting is appropriate as a plea for God to usher in the messianic age, in this passage fasting represents a stubborn refusal to acknowledge that God has done so. Yet the problem is deeper than whether one should fast. Jesus recognizes that comfortable, familiar forms of spirituality exert a narcotic effect that blurs perception to new revelation. Even though Jesus brings "new wine," those accustomed to the "old" find the "new" inferior.[84]

> And no one after drinking old wine desires new wine, but says, "The old is good." (5:39)[85]

Using a different metaphor, Jesus emphasizes that old expressions of spirituality cannot simply be carried over; they are incompatible with new. New expressions of spirituality must be found.[86]

> And no one puts new wine into old wineskins; otherwise the new wine will burst the skins and will be spilled, and the skins will be destroyed. But new wine must be put into fresh wineskins. (5:37–8)

By putting new wine into old wineskins, both the wine and the wineskins are lost; new wine must be put into new wineskins.[87] Similarly, the new revelation that Jesus brings cannot take the form of old, formulaic expressions of spirituality. Just as a wedding party does not celebrate by fasting, so the new economy of salvation cannot be held captive to old forms of spirituality.[88] The expressions of the spiritual life must change in appropriate ways as God breaks into our world in new ways. It is right both to feast and fast; but it is never right to feast when we should fast, or to fast when we should feast.


## Anxiety


*Luke* 10:38–42

Martha is emblematic of a spiritual life overburdened by anxiety.[89] When Jesus visits the home[90] of the two sisters, Martha "welcomes"[91] him, but the welcome he gets is not the welcome he wants. Martha is occupied with "many" distractions, and lacks the "single-hearted"[92] response of Mary. "Many" is compared to "one." "Many tasks"[93] (10:40a) and "many things"[94] (10:41) distract Martha. She loses focus of the "one thing" that is needful (10:41).[95]

Martha's story is about herself, not about the "Lord."[96] Her self-referential and self-absorbed posture[97] keeps her from focusing on Jesus. Her speech betrays where her interests lie, and they are not where they should be.

> Lord, do you not care that *my* sister has left *me* to do all the work *by myself*? Tell her then to help *me*. (10:40b)

Even though she recognizes Jesus as "Lord," Martha does not hesitate to accuse him of failing to help *her* achieve *her* goals, and to tell *him* what *he* must say.[98] She assumes that Jesus will side with her in what seems to be a reasonable request; yet she is corrected.

A twofold reference to her distraction brackets her request, and two different verbs for angst ("worry" and "distract," 10:41)[99] underline her anxiety. The doubling of her name[100] and alliteration draw attention to her anxious behavior: *Martha, Martha, merimnas*.[101]

> But Martha was *distracted* [102] by her many tasks. (10:40a)
> But the Lord answered her, "Martha, Martha, you are *worried* and *distracted* by many things." (10:41)

Anxiety is a serious distraction because it slowly erodes the unifying center found in Christ. In the parable of the sower (8:4–8; 11–15), for example, the seed that falls among the thorns represents those who hear the word of God but "are choked by the cares[103] and riches and pleasures of life." Anxiety suffocates the word of God. In Luke 12, Jesus warns the disciples not to "worry"[104] about what they eat or about what they are to wear (12:22)—a warning repeated in 21:34: "Be on guard so that your hearts are not weighed down with dissipation and drunkenness and the worries[105] of this life." Anxiety weighs down the spiritual life. It suffocates. Instead of worrying and being distracted with "many things," Jesus wants Martha to choose, as Mary has, the "one thing," "the better part"[106] (10:42), which is to give undivided attention to their guest.[107] The angst-ridden, divided spiritual life, overburdened with concerns, cannot hear the word of God through the din of the everyday.

Although Martha is perhaps a negative model for Christians today, she is, nevertheless, an endearing model. She is a follower of Jesus; but the cares and concerns of this world distract her from hearing the clarifying word that Jesus speaks. She is harried with the busyness of the everyday, the stuff of ordinary days. This is what makes Martha a poignant model of spirituality: she is exactly like us.

## Conclusion

Whom we do or do not eat with expresses our spiritual values. Eating with others implies acceptance of their social values, while refusal to share a meal is a rejection of the other's values. Boundaries serve to distinguish the acceptable from the unacceptable. The rich do not eat with the poor, the upper echelon of society with the lower echelon, the professional class with blue-collar workers, the indigent with middle-class, and so forth. In Jesus' day, "sinners" did not eat with "righteous," the clean with the unclean, the wealthy with the poor. Boundary-making allows us to know whom we can eat with and whom we should avoid. Yet this is not the way it is in the kingdom.

Jesus reserves his harshest criticism for the religious authorities who want to protect the spiritual life with firm barriers and purity maps. The spiritual map that Jesus outlines is radically different. He accepts prodigal expressions of thankfulness from the stigmatized and marginalized. His modus operandi creates an open, boundary-breaking society in contrast to the boundary-making society of the first century. He rejects balanced reciprocity for generalized reciprocity. Instead of inviting friends and relatives and rich neighbors who can return the favor of a meal invitation, a follower should invite those who cannot repay: the poor, the crippled, the lame, and the blind (14:12–13). The landscape is radically altered in this upheaval of social protocol.

The feast is an important image of the kingdom of God. The kingdom is likened to a great banquet in which guests sit down with the host, Jesus. The feast is an image of abundance. Food and drink satisfy human hunger, and human hunger suggests spiritual hunger. In the feeding of the five thousand a surfeit of food feeds all. Jesus feeds the hungry both physically and spiritually. The feast also marks important transitions in the spiritual life. On his return home, the prodigal son receives a festive banquet to celebrate his figurative resurrection to new life (Luke 15:11–24). Similarly, those who are resurrected to new life in the kingdom receive a banquet to mark their transition from death to life. Yet some are more concerned with the cares and concerns of this world and, therefore, forego the feast (Luke 14:15–24).

Fasting is an important discipline of the spiritual life. It is a plea to God to make things different. Physical hunger is an outward expression of inner, spiritual hunger. Anna, for example, fasted as a plea to God to intervene with the Messiah and set things right (2:36–37). Yet fasting can be the wrong expression of spirituality at the wrong time. It can be a stubborn refusal to take part in the celebration, an act of pious conservatism that forms new boundaries by nonparticipation in the celebration. Should we feast or fast? We feast because the messianic celebration has begun in Christ, yet we fast as a plea to God to set things right in a world gone wrong. It is right both to feast and fast; but it is never right to feast when we should fast, or to fast when we should feast. Fasting is also a reminder to a society that revels in excess that the feast so earnestly desired by humankind is not material but spiritual.

Clothing is a luminous map of the spiritual life. Clothing marks important transitions in our social and spiritual life, and it may also suggest where our loyalties lie. Lavish clothing in Luke, for example, represents a solipsistic spiritual life, while anxiety over clothing signals a restless, inadequate faith. The role of clothing in the social and spiritual life is the subject of chapter 5.

# Chapter
## 5

# Clothing:
# A Map of the Spiritual Life

In Luke, clothing[1] is a map of one's spiritual state or inner character as well as social status.[2] The scribes, for example, are criticized for their love of fine clothing and the recognition that comes with their high office (20:46). Their outward lavishness testifies to a meretricious spiritual life that craves public approbation. Clothing also marks transitions in the social and spiritual life. When the prodigal son returns home, he receives the best robe, sandals, and a ring—a sign of his social and spiritual regeneration (15:22, 24). Similarly, a discarded tunic in a tomb symbolizes the transition from death to life and announces death's certain defeat. Excessive concern with clothing, on the other hand, signals an insufficient, restless faith—a sign of attachment to this world and failure to trust God. The way clothing is worn is also symbolic. Girded garments, for example, represent spiritual readiness or alertness, while ungirded garments represent lack of spiritual preparation, even indolence.

In the ancient world, the quality of the fabric (wool, linen, cotton, or silk), the condition and length of the garment, the color of the dyes, and the type of ornamentation indicated social status. Linen and fine silk were expensive fabrics available only to those of high social status. Unblemished garments were essential for social and religious duties. The color and quality of dyes testified to social status; purple dye was very expensive and available only to the wealthy. A "fulled" garment was thoroughly washed and bleached in a special clay to make it as white as possible. This was a costly process and thus available only to a very few persons of means. On the other hand, unbleached garments—dark brown and gray—were the standard of the poor and hoi polloi. The length of the garment was also an important indicator of social status. The poor and slaves dressed with short tunics and cloaks, while long cloaks and tunics were common among the rich and dignitaries. Footwear and ornamentation also signaled social status. Long fringes, ornate hems, rings and headgear, for instance, were common among the wealthy and those of high status, while slaves not only lacked all ornamentation but also went barefoot.

## Passages

Like special meals, clothing signals important transitions in the spiritual life. Lack of clothing is a sign of spiritual impoverishment or alienation from community, while new clothes represent spiritual rebirth and social acceptance in the community.

In Luke 8:26–39, a demoniac is stark naked like an animal, a sign of his shame and abject spiritual state.

> As [Jesus] stepped out on land, a man of the city who had demons met him. For a long time he had worn no clothes, and he did not live in a house but in the tombs. (8:27)[3]

The demoniac is socially and spiritually dead. His home is a tomb, the place of the dead. After the demons are exorcised, Luke notes a striking change in the man's appearance and demeanor: he was "clothed and in his right mind" (8:35). The newfound clothes symbolize his social and spiritual regeneration and mark his transition from death to life, from alienation to restoration, from loss of his selfhood to a new identity.

In the parable of the prodigal son, clothing also marks an important transition in the younger son's social and spiritual status (15:11–32). When the prodigal returns home he receives the best robe,[4] a ring, and sandals for his feet (15:22), festive expressions of extravagant love pointing to his spiritual rebirth. The best robe (literally, "the first robe," i.e., a robe of first quality), sandals, and a ring are *not* the clothing of a day laborer but of an honored guest.[5] Clothing signals his transition from abject alienation to reconciliation: he was once dead and lost; now he is alive and found (15:24).[6]

A new garment also marks transition in the disciples' lives. After Jesus' ascension, they are clothed with "power from on high," the gift of the Spirit (cf. Acts 1:8).

> And see, I am sending upon you what my Father promised; so stay here in the city until you have been clothed[7] with power from on high. (24:49)

Three other times the same verb[8] for clothes is used in the Gospel: when the Gerasene demoniac is found without clothes (8:27), when the disciples are told not to worry about what they will wear (12:22), and when the prodigal returns home and is clothed with the best robe (15:22). Similar to the prodigal, whose new clothes represent rebirth, the disciples receive new "clothes," a spiritual empowerment from on high which fills their speech and actions with intelligence, authority, and purpose.[9]

Jesus' clothing signals important transitions in his life; his clothing is also a commentary on his inner nature or character. The first reference in the Gospel to Jesus' clothing is found in the infancy narrative:

> And she gave birth to her firstborn son and wrapped him in bands of cloth,[10] and laid him in a manger, because there was no place for them in the inn. (2:7)
> This will be a sign[11] for you: you will find a child wrapped in bands of cloth and lying in a manger. (2:12)

It is not unusual for a mother to wrap a baby in swaddling clothes (see Wis 7:4);[12] but it is strange to associate a few strips of cloth and a feeding trough for animals[13] with a felicitous sign. Fitzmyer notes the oddness of this event: "it is an unusual one, corresponding in *no way to the signs that one might have expected of a coming Messiah.*"[14] This, however, is precisely the point of entering the world in rags: Jesus comes into our world just as everyone else does. The new act of God's intervention in this world (the coming Messiah) is found in the everyday (a few strips of cloth); the "masks of the holy"[15] are a few strips of rags, not regal or arabesque garments. The simple garments demonstrate that the unusual—i.e., the coming of the promised Messiah—is to be found nowhere else than in the ordinary. The extraordinary is visible in the everyday; "the ordinary . . . evoke[s] the numinous."[16]

At the transfiguration, on the other hand, Jesus' clothing reveals his spectacular glory, his irreducible Otherness.[17]

> And while he was praying, the appearance of his face changed, and his clothes became dazzling white. (9:29)[18]

A "white" garment is one that is thoroughly washed and "fulled," i.e., bleached in a special clay to make it as white as possible. Fulled garments, which are costly and take a long time to process, would normally "have been the prerogative of priests and for contacts with the gods in general."[19] Slaves and common people, on the other hand, wore "unfulled" cloth, "that is, in its natural color, which was grey for linen and 'black' (i.e., dark), brown, or greyish to white for other materials."[20] White garments were easily soiled from dust from the road, spit from passers-by in crowded streets, contact with others, or one's work,[21] and, therefore, unsoiled, bleached garments were metonymic for undefiled behavior and moral and spiritual purity. In Revelation, bright, pure linen, representing the righteous deeds of the saints, is mandatory dress at the marriage feast of the Lamb (19:8). And in Rev 3:18, the Laodiceans are to purchase white robes from Christ to hide the shame of their nakedness. In the transfiguration account, Jesus' garments are not only "white," they also "flash or gleam like lightning."[22] His stunning transformation provides a glimpse into his inner character: his transcendent glory, his Otherness.

In Jesus' entrance into Jerusalem, cloaks are spread on his colt and placed at his feet, providing a prodigious "red carpet" reception.[23]

> Then they brought [the colt] to Jesus; and after throwing their cloaks on [it], they set Jesus on it. As he rode along, people kept spreading their cloaks on the road. (19:35–6)

The significance of this extraordinary reception is found in the disciples' voluntary surrender of their most prized possession. The cloak[24] was the outer garment made of thick material, usually wool, which also served as a blanket at night. It was an item of considerable value: bandits would steal it (e.g., 10:30), and it could be used as payment for debts and as collateral.[25] "The cloak was the most prized possession of many a man."[26] In laying their cloaks on the colt and spreading their garments on the road as Jesus passed by, the disciples[27] literally surrendered their most valuable possession to Jesus. A similar outpouring of prodigality occurred when Jehu became king in 2 Kgs 9:13. The people laid their garments on the bare steps, blew a trumpet, and proclaimed, "Jehu is king!" C. F. Evans suggests that "the garments represent the men themselves, and the piling of them to form a throne indicates submission to Jehu's authority."[28] The casting of garments at Jesus' feet is similar to the casting of crowns before the throne of God by the twenty-four elders in Rev 4:10. Although the disciples lack the expensive and elaborate headgear of the obeisant elders, they surrender their most valuable possession in a similar act of obeisance.

The remaining references to Jesus' clothing occur at his trial, crucifixion, and resurrection. In 23:11, Herod sends Jesus back to Pilate with "an elegant robe on him."[29] The significance of this act is unclear as is the type of robe Herod placed on Jesus. Hamel thinks that the cloak was "bright white," which signifies Jesus' innocence in a droll, ironic way.[30] But the word means "bright," "shining," or "radiant," not necessarily white.[31] What is certain is that the robe is no ordinary cloak; it is an elegant robe that gives Jesus the high social rank of a dignitary, perhaps even royal status. By placing an elegant robe on him, Herod heightens the carnivalesque atmosphere by making him into a mock king.[32] This startling act of gallows humor has a second level of meaning that is lost on Herod but not on the Gospel writer or reader: it is a poignant, powerful testimony to Jesus' true status as king.

The clearest example of clothing's marking a transition in the spiritual life occurs at the tomb. Jesus' discarded shroud marks his passage from death to life and signals death's defeat.

> Then [Joseph of Arimathea] took it down, wrapped it in a linen cloth,[33] and laid it in a rock-hewn tomb where no one had ever been laid. (23:53)

> But Peter got up and ran to the tomb; stooping and looking in, he
> saw the linen cloths[34] by themselves;[35] then he went home,
> amazed at what had happened. (24:12)[36]

At the beginning of the Gospel, Jesus is swaddled in strips of rags; at
the end, he is clothed with dignity. Linen is a fine garment worn by
the rich and by priests in their duty at the temple.[37] The rich man in
16:19, for example, wears fine linen.[38] Yet unlike the rich who parade
around in fine linen and find their identity in their clothing, Jesus'
linen cloths are thrown away. They are cast aside (24:12), no longer of
any use, marking the most important spiritual transition for humankind: death's certain defeat.

## Anxiety

The average American spends an inordinate amount of money
on clothing. Designer clothing and designer logos enhance one's
self-esteem and serve as indicators of social status.[39] Obsession with
clothing, however, may indicate a restless, inadequate faith or spiritual hunger—a desire to fill a vast, endless void in our lives.

Jesus associates fine clothing and an abundance of clothing
with the privileged lifestyle of the few. What they wear is a commentary on who they are.

> What then did you go out to see? Someone dressed in soft robes?[40]
> Look, those who put on fine clothing[41] and live in luxury are in royal
> palaces. (7:25)

Long robes made with expensive dyes and ornate hems are a
sign of wealth and status;[42] they also suggest an unctuous spirituality
that seeks reward in terms of public recognition. Jesus warns the
people of the scribes' consuming zeal for attention and draws attention to their elaborate cloaks and exhibitionist traits.

> Beware of the scribes, who like to walk around in long robes,[43] and
> love to be greeted with respect in the marketplaces, and to have the
> best seats in the synagogues and places of honor at banquets. (20:46)

Similarly, the rich man's raffish display of excess in the parable
of the Rich Man and Lazarus testifies to a self-serving spirituality

(16:19–31).[44] His fine clothing and decadent lifestyle stand in striking contrast to Lazarus's garment of shame: his sores.[45] The parallelism accents the extremes.

> There was a rich man
> > *who was dressed in purple and fine linen*
> > and who feasted sumptuously every day. (16:19)
> And at his gate lay a poor man named Lazarus,
> > *covered with sores.* (16:20)[46]

The rich man is clothed with "purple and fine linen," garments that were "so costly that normally only kings could afford them."[47] He has no desire that is unfilled. His affluence renders him independent; he needs neither God nor the outcast who lies at his gate longing for crumbs to satisfy his hunger. Lazarus, on the other hand, has nothing save the benefaction of others. His passive, wan posture magnifies his discarded state and underlines his total dependency. He is literally thrown down at the rich man's gate,[48] where he lies helplessly as dogs lick his sores (16:21), a rueful tribute to his less than human status. For Lazarus and the rich man, clothing describes their respective social and spiritual statuses. Lazarus, clothed with sores, is utterly dependent upon God and others; he is socially and spiritually abject. The rich man, clothed with the finest garments, is utterly independent of God and others; his independence testifies to a self-will that is socially and spiritually without need. The rich man's consolation is now; Lazarus's consolation is in the life to come (cf. 6:24).

Obsession with food and clothing is a sign of an anxious faith.[49] Jesus warns the disciples not to be anxious concerning what they wear.

> Therefore I tell you, do not worry about your life, what you will eat, or about your body, what you will wear. (12:22)
> For life is more than food, and the body more than clothing. (12:23)
> Consider the lilies, how they grow: they neither toil nor spin; yet I tell you, even Solomon in all his glory was not clothed like one of these. (12:27)
> But if God so clothes the grass of the field, which is alive today and tomorrow is thrown into the oven, how much more will he clothe you—you of little faith! (12:28)

Jesus uses a striking example to shock the disciples into a reality far different from the concerns of "the nations of the world" (12:30). The vehicle—birds and flowers—is low on the hierarchic scale of values. Precisely because they are least able to provide for themselves, lilies and ravens should be filled with anxiety. Birds "have neither store-house nor barn," and lilies "neither toil nor spin," and yet they are more resplendent than "Solomon in all his glory" (12:24, 27). Humans, by contrast, should be devoid of anxiety precisely because they can provide for themselves. They have storehouse and barn, and they toil and spin. Yet those least able to provide for themselves know no anxiety, while those most able to seek food and clothing are filled with angst. Jesus' illustration intends to shock the reader into a proper evaluation.[50] If God provides for birds and flowers, how much more will God provide for human creatures. In other words, anxiety about food, drink, and clothing is a sign of spiritual impoverishment and evidence of "little faith"[51] (12:28).

Therefore, Jesus requires the disciples to take modest clothing on their journeys. To the twelve, he allows one tunic.

> Take nothing for your journey, no staff, nor bag, nor bread, nor money—not even an extra tunic. (9:3)

And the seventy are forbidden to take sandals.[52]

> > Carry no purse, no bag, no sandals; and greet no one on the road. (10:4)
> > When I sent you out without a purse, bag, or sandals, did you lack anything? (22:35)[53]

The disciples' lack of clothing is a physically demanding condition. "To have only one tunic was to risk impurity through spots of various origins, and the impossibility to wash it without being put to shame."[54] It is also a "sign of wretchedness,"[55] for only the very poor lacked a change of clothes, and only the poor and slaves lacked sandals.[56]

Nolland suggests that the disciples' sparse clothing is a "pro-phetic sign of eschatological urgency."[57] Hamel, on the other hand, argues that their clothing symbolizes that each day is a sabbath day.[58] More likely, one tunic is a sign of total dependence on God.[59] If the rich and those of high social status have elaborate garments and an abundant change of clothing, the disciples "are to embody in themselves the extreme simplicity and detachment from the world that their eschatological message of the kingdom is to bring about."[60] The disciples' simple clothing reflects their detachment from the cares and concerns of this world and signifies trusting dependence on God.

Nowhere is this abnegation of worldly cares and concerns more startling than in Luke 6:29:

> If anyone strikes you on the cheek, offer the other also;
> and from anyone who takes away your coat[61] do not withhold even
> your shirt.[62]

Balanced reciprocity[63] requires that a person who takes your coat be sued for return of the garment or required to substitute something of equal value. If, in 6:29, the disciple is robbed,[64] balanced reciprocity requires the victim to foil the act of violence at the very least. But Jesus turns a seemingly sensible form of reciprocity on its head, advocating a system of generalized reciprocity,[65] which requires disciples not only to relinquish their cloaks but also their tunics. Hans Dieter Betz calls the disciple's action "an absurd exchange of gifts," which demonstrates "the even greater generosity" of the disciple.

> If the robber proves to be "generous," in that he is only after the victim's overcoat, he is outdone by the even greater generosity of the victim. . . . The paradoxical reaction of the victim counters the violence by making a gift, no doubt a challenge to respond in kind.[66]

In this example, clothing is a striking metaphor for "the paradoxical nature of Christian behavior,"[67] an ethic that is based not on normal human behavior, but modeled on God's vast, overflowing generosity. "Be merciful, just as your Father is merciful" (6:36). The disciples' command not to be concerned with clothing is emblematic of a spiritual life freed from anxiety.

## Temple Veil and Cloak of Darkness

The disrobing of the temple[68] and the cloaking of the earth with darkness also develop Luke's spiritual landscape. At the climactic moment before Jesus' death both garments are mentioned together.

> It was now about noon, and darkness came over the whole land until three in the afternoon, while the sun's light failed; and the curtain[69] of the temple was torn in two. (23:44–45)

Darkness covers the whole land like a giant cloak until three in the afternoon; the temple's clothing is also torn in two. The Lukan narrative repositions the torn veil from *after* Jesus' death to *before* his death (cf. Mark 15:38; Matt 27:51). Thus the two garments—darkness and curtain—contribute together to the Lukan spiritual landscape. Luke is the only synoptic writer to refer to the powers of darkness in the Passion Narrative. When Jesus says to the arresting posse, "this is your hour, and the power of darkness" (22:53), he is acknowledging the momentary triumph of darkness.[70] The cloak of darkness represents the hegemony of satanic activity at the death of Jesus. Light, by contrast, characterizes the coming of Jesus in this Gospel.

> By the tender mercy of our God, the *dawn from on high* will break upon us, to give *light* to those who sit in darkness and in the shadow of death. (1:78–79)

Thus the garment of darkness that cloaks the entire land at midday represents the momentary triumph of the powers of darkness, a symbolism that "should have been apparent to Luke's readers."[71]

The torn veil, on the other hand, offers no simple explanation.[72] It is uncertain whether Luke refers to the inner curtain that separated the holy of holies from the remainder of the temple or to the outer curtain that separated the temple from the outer court. The question is perhaps irresolvable, since he "writes about the temple as a whole instead of particular areas or parts of the temple. . . ."[73] Whether inner or outer veil, it is a garment that clothes the temple, a carapace separating holy space from profane space, and, therefore, the covering gives the temple (or sanctuary) special character and distinctiveness. The rending of the veil, then, is an act of disrobing the temple and removing its distinctiveness as sacred space precisely at the moment before Jesus dies. And if the temple no longer represents a *sui generis* arena in which God accomplishes God's purposes, then that uniqueness must be found elsewhere. The rent veil is not a judgment upon the temple, as in Mark,[74] but dissolution of the symbolic world surrounding the temple, which is replaced by Jesus and his death on the cross.[75] In disrobing the temple, God exposes[76] the temple as inadequate to accomplish God's purposes. And just as nakedness is a sign of spiritual poverty, representing a lethargic, abject spirituality, the disrobing of the temple unveils an inadequate spirituality that can no longer provide for the spiritual needs of a nation. With the rending of the veil and Jesus' death, the spiritual landscape of Israel is altered forever: God's purposes are now fulfilled in Jesus.

## Conclusion

Today, as well as in the New Testament, clothing is a marker of social status. Presidents, heads of states, CEOs, and others dress in manners appropriate to each one's status and office. In Luke, clothing marks important transitions in the spiritual life. The Gerasene demoniac appears stark naked (8:27), a sign of his social and spiritual abject state. He is out of touch with his social roots, with himself, and with God. After Jesus heals him, however, he is fully clothed and in his right mind, a sign of his spiritual and social renewal (8:35). The prodigal son's rebirth is announced with fine clothing: the best robe, a ring, and sandals for the feet (15:22). On the Mount of Transfiguration, Jesus' clothing is transformed, giving a glimpse of his numinousness. At the resurrection his earthly garment is discarded, a useless relic of a former age. The disciples are clothed with power on high, the Holy Spirit (Acts 1:8), as they enter a new stage in their lives.

Lavish clothing, however, may represent a solipsistic spiritual life. The parable of the Rich Man and Lazarus highlights the rich man's opulent clothing (16:19), a sign of his full material life but parsimonious spiritual life. The scribes like to parade in long robes (20:46), denoting an impoverished spiritual life that craves approbation from others. Anxiety concerning clothing is emblematic of a restless, inadequate faith, while simple clothing reflects simple, unadorned confidence that God provides abundantly.

   Like the social landscape of families, households, meals, and clothing, economic landscape is a mirror of the spiritual life. What we do with our possessions is a testimony to our spiritual values. The next chapter develops and elaborates the peril of plenty—immoderate accumulation and consumption—and its solution.

# Chapter
## 6

# Consumption:
# The Spiritual Life and Possessions

## Peril of Plenty

The peril of plenty is spiritual deprivation. Immoderate accumulation and consumption are quests for satisfaction and signs of spiritual hunger. Overwrought consumption comes at a costly price: the bankruptcy of the spiritual life.

Consumption or hyperconsumerism is a "quasi religion" in America. We make frequent "pilgrimages" to "cathedrals of consumption": shopping malls, fast food restaurants, cybermalls, superstores, Disney World, gambling casinos, cruise ships, gated luxury communities, to name a few.[1] Like temples, shopping malls are constructed with balance, symmetry, and order; the pleasant ambience of atriums with trees, flowers, and plants encourages community gathering and connectedness. Food courts are gathering places for joyous, ceremonial meals. The new "cathedrals" are designed to entice us to consume well beyond any reasonable level of consumption. Credit cards, debit cards, smart cards, and ATM (automated teller machine) cards enable us to support "cathedral budgets" and practice the religion of hyperconsumption. Instant availability of credit, higher credit limits with super low payments, and multiple credit cards increase "donations" to the maintenance and growth of even larger cathedrals.[2] Advertising entices us to buy things that we might not otherwise consume and "goods" we cannot afford. Symbols of this consumer religion include sport utility vehicles (SUVs), Rolex watches, designer clothing, trophy homes ("McMansions"), granite countertops, and conspicuous, one-carat diamonds.[3] Immoderate accumulation and consumption forces people to devote long hours to work and to take second and third jobs in order to pay for their ever-increasing debt load. "Competitive consumption"—the concept that "spending is in large part driven by a comparative or competitive process in which individuals try to keep up with the norms of the social group with which they identify"[4]—encourages people to buy more than they need, to pay higher prices than they should, and to spend more than they can afford. The purchase of a new home, for example, requires the purchase of new furniture, and new china requires new glass stemware, and so on and so forth. This "Diderot effect"[5] creates discomfort with our present surroundings so that we add to and upgrade the "stuff" in our lives. "Competitive consumption" contributes to disease, divorce, bankruptcy, and, in some cases, robbery and "sneaker murders."

Hyperconsumerism or "conspicuous consumption,"[6] however, is not a new phenomenon. In Luke 14:1–6, the man afflicted with dropsy[7] is the perfect metaphor for overwrought consumerism. Dropsy's distinguishing symptom is an unquenchable thirst for fluids in a body that is already swollen with excess fluids. The more the person drinks to alleviate thirst, the more the body bloats. Therefore, the craving for more fluids exacerbates rather than resolves the dropsical condition.

In *Feasting and Social Rhetoric in Luke* 14, Willi Braun shows that the Cynics employed dropsy as a metaphor for consuming passion.[8] Diogenes Laertius was one of the first writers to use dropsy as an image for insatiable greed.

> Diogenes compared money-lovers to dropsies: as dropsies, though filled with fluid, crave drink, so money-lovers, though loaded with money, crave more of it, yet both to their demise. . . . For, their desires increase the more they acquire the objects of their cravings.[9]

Plutarch, a contemporary of Luke, uses an unquenchable appetite as an image of hyperconsumerism.

> Those . . . who part with nothing, though they have great possessions, but always want greater, would strike one who remembers what Aristippus said as even more absurd. "If a man eats and drinks a great

deal," he used to say, "but is never filled, he sees a physician, inquires what ails him, what is wrong with his system, and how to rid himself of the disorder; but if the owner of five couches goes looking for ten, and the owner of ten tables buys up as many again, and though he has lands and money in plenty is not satisfied but bent on more, losing sleep and never sated by any amount, does he imagine that he does not need someone who will prescribe for him and point out the cause of his distress?"[10]

Dropsy is an ancient metaphor for a modern problem: the peril of plenty. Like dropsy, plenty does not alleviate or resolve the craving for more, but, paradoxically, feeds immoderate consumption.[11] The more we have, the more we want, and the more we want, the more we accumulate. Like dropsy, immoderate consumption is a vicious cycle that consumes the consumer. Bloated with excess, the consumer must build larger houses, buy more clothes, purchase larger vehicles, buy larger TVs, and so on. In 12:13–21, Luke addresses the peril of immoderate accumulation, and in 16:19–31, the peril of immoderate consumption.

## Immoderate Accumulation (Luke 12:13–21)

The parable of the Rich Farmer is a story of the impotence of abundance to provide an abundant life. The peril of immoderate accumulation is that it views the "storing up of treasures" on earth as a measure of a full life. It ignores or is oblivious to the true definition of life: pursuit of riches toward God.[12]

> Take care! Be on your guard against all kinds of greed;[13] for one's
>     life[14] does not consist in the abundance of possessions. (12:15)[15]
> So it is with those who store up treasures for themselves but are not
>     rich toward God. (12:21)

The farmer is deceived into believing that the stockpiling of possessions represents a full and rich life.[16] He mistakenly assumes that his life is his own, to do with as he pleases.[17]

The parable accents his excess: "a certain rich man" is not only rich with land but also with an abundant harvest.[18] Yet plenty creates it own set of problems, for he has nowhere to store his excess. An interior monologue, which is a tribute to his self-absorbed lifestyle, both highlights and resolves his dilemma. In the soliloquy, he is both the subject ("I" and "my") and the object ("soul" and "you") of the discourse—a clever narrative device that shows that the farmer is totally imprisoned within the self.[19]

> "What should I do, for I have no place to store *my* crops?" Then he said,
> "I will do this: I will pull down *my* barns and build larger ones, and
> there I will store all *my* grain and *my* goods. And I will say to *my* soul,
> 'Soul, you have ample goods laid up for many years; relax, eat, drink,
> be merry.'" (12:17–19)

The accumulation of first-person pronouns underscores his self-regarding, self-indulgent posture.[20] In the Greek, the first person appears no less than eleven times in a soliloquy of forty-eight words. If the self-address to the soul is included with its imperatives to the self,[21] six more occurrences could be added to the list. The asyndetic[22] imperatives, which have no conjunctions to slow down the pace, accentuate the farmer's plans. The grammar heaps up a list of self-absorbed pleasures with no breaks ("relax, eat, drink, be merry"); similarly, the farmer intends to lead a plentiful life of unbroken pleasure.

The farmer's self-congratulatory confidence, however, is a testimony to his foolishness, and God,[23] therefore, intervenes to awaken him to another reality.

> But God said to him, "You fool! This very night your life is being demanded of you. And the things you have prepared, whose will they be?" (12:20)

The farmer assumes that an economic future of excess secures life[24] and fails to consider that "life" is not guaranteed by material pursuits. The "many years" he planned on is interrupted by "this very night." And his grand plan to build larger barns to store all the grain is demolished by a single question that reveals the emptiness of his plans: "And the things you have prepared, whose will they be?" The farmer's tragic flaw is a failure to consider that his "destiny cannot be found with himself."[25] "Because he concentrated exclusively on increasing his material wealth, he now has nothing which he can truly call his own. He has nothing which is not taken away by death."[26] His shortsightedness is what makes him a fool.[27] "So it is with those who store up treasures for themselves but are not rich toward God" (12:21). If preoccupation with one's own material future is characteristic of a "fool" and evidence of spiritual poverty, then the opposite is also true; real wealth is paradoxically found in the abandonment of the desire to secure one's future with material possessions. Until this orientation is accepted, material goods will usurp God's "role as source and measure and guarantor of life."[28]

### Immoderate Consumption (Luke 16:19–31)

In the parable of the Rich Man and Lazarus, material wealth leaves the rich man spiritually poor. His well-stocked material life depletes his social and spiritual life; daily feasting starves him spiritually. Material extravagance leaves him spiritually deprived. Commentators typically focus on the reversal of fortunes in the next world, which parallels Luke 6:20, 24.[29] Richard Bauckham, for example, says: "The next world compensates for . . . inequality [in this world] by replacing it with a reverse inequality."[30] But the rich man's fate *in the next world* is actually a commentary on his spiritual deprivation *in this world*. The peril of plenty—immoderate consumption—soothes the self while starving the soul.

Luke highlights the rich man's spiritual deprivation in the following ways: 1) Chiasms underscore his reversed fate, as if to indicate that his immoderate consumption leaves him spiritually depleted. 2) Lazarus is a foil to underscore the social as well as spiritual implications of the rich man's material excess. 3) The account alternates between full and stark narration. While full narration amplifies the rich man's extravagant lifestyle, stark narration depicts his spiritual indigence.

In the introduction to the parable, the rich man's lifestyle is highlighted by an overfull description of his excess. The lengthy description (fourteen words in the Greek) parallels a full material life; his well-stocked material life is accented by a well-stocked narrative description.

> There was a rich man who was dressed in purple and fine linen
> and who feasted sumptuously[31] every day. (16:19)

Lavish clothing[32] and daily lavish banquets characterize his excess, and a gate fortifies his house (16:20), a tribute to his wealth and a boundary that isolates him from others such as the mendicant outside his gate.[33] The gate keeps him in while keeping others out.

By contrast, sparse narration (seven words in the Greek) describes the rich man's fate. The full narration that characterizes his earthly existence contrasts with the stark narration of his fate.

The rich man also died and was buried. (16:22b)

The bleak nakedness of 16:22b is even more striking when compared to the lavish, full description of Lazarus's death.[34]

And it happened that the poor man died and was carried by the angels into the bosom of Abraham. (16:22, author's translation)

The order of narration also underscores the reversal of status. In 16:19–20, the rich man is described first; Lazarus is described second. The rich man is thus given the privileged position in the narrative description on earth. Then Lazarus is given the privileged position in the narrative description of the afterlife (16:22). The rich man is "first" in this life, but "last" in the afterlife. Also by giving Lazarus a name (16:20), the narrative introduction sets him apart from the rich man. Materially indigent, Lazarus at least has the dignity of a name, while the rich man has no name and thus no individuality apart from his materialistic lifestyle. "The naming of the poor man while the rich man remains anonymous already anticipates the coming reversal by reversing the normal anonymity of poverty and the individuating significance of wealth."[35] A chiasm underscores the reversal of status:

A   a man
   B   was rich
   B'  a poor (man)
A'  by the name Lazarus

Lazarus is a foil for the rich man's arrogant solipsism. Lazarus's material indigence accents the rich man's life of immoderate consumption.

> And at his gate lay a poor man named Lazarus,
>> covered with sores,
>>> who longed to satisfy his hunger with what fell from the rich man's table;
>>> even the dogs would come and lick his sores. (16:20–21)

Instead of fine clothing, Lazarus is clothed with sores; instead of unending feasts, Lazarus starves. Lazarus is passive, unable to alter his lifestyle. He is thrown down[36] at the rich man's gate, unable to keep even the dogs at bay. On the other hand, the rich man is active; he is able to alter his lifestyle, but prefers a life of excess.

In Hades,[37] the landscape is a mirror image of earthly terrain. On earth, the rich man enjoyed a life of extravagance; in Hades, he lacks even water to ameliorate his suffering (16:24). His request for relief is small just as Lazarus's desire for scraps was minimal, and like Lazarus who received nothing in this lifetime, the rich man receives nothing in the next life. The man-made gate that kept Lazarus outside is now replaced by a divinely[38] fixed chasm that keeps the rich man outside (16:26). In place of misery on earth, Lazarus receives an honored position in the bosom[39] of Abraham.

The dialogue (16:24–31) provides a clarifying commentary on the narrative description (16:19–23); it elaborates the rich man's parsimonious spirituality. His request to Abraham is an indictment of his selfish ways, for not only was he aware of the propinquity of the poor man, he even knew Lazarus's name![40]

> Father Abraham, have mercy on me, and send *Lazarus* to dip the tip of his finger in water and cool my tongue; for I am in agony in these flames. (16:24)

Abraham's explanation of the rich man's torment joins together the material and the spiritual. Like two sides of the same coin, the outer parameters of the chiasm in 16:25 link "good things" with "pain."

> A   Child, remember that *you* received *your good things* in *your* life,
>> B   and Lazarus likewise *evil things*;
>> B'  but now *he* is *comforted* here,
> A'  and *you* are in *pain* (author's translation).

His choice of "good things" is not merely a material choice; it is also a spiritual decision. The rich man had a choice, *"your good things in your life,"* but the decision starved him spiritually. Lazarus, on the other hand, did not have the same choice. It is not *"his evil things;"* it is simply *"evil things,"* a state of affairs *he* had no control over. Ironically, the outcome could have been different if the rich man bridged the chasm between Lazarus and himself during his lifetime.[41] Instead, immoderate consumption starved the rich man spiritually; his well-stocked material life depleted his spiritual and social life.

# Dispossession

## Luke 19:1–10

The story of Zacchaeus shows a way out of the peril of plenty:[42] the dispossession of wealth.[43] Zacchaeus is rich; yet, unlike the rich farmer, he finds "life" in the dispossession of his plenty.

A tax or toll collector was an entrepreneurial and often dishonest person who worked for a foreign government—in this instance Rome—and exploited the system of taxation for his own gain. Zacchaeus is not merely a toll collector; he is a "chief tax collector," a supervisor of several toll collectors.[44] He is also rich, which is highlighted as a separate item in Luke's annotation: "He was a chief tax collector and *was rich*" (19:2).[45] Thus Zacchaeus is oriented to the accumulation of wealth, which in Luke is routinely criticized (cf. 6:24; 12:16–21; 16:19–31; 18:18–23) as a formidable (though not impossible) barrier for those who want to enter the kingdom of God (18:24–25).

Zacchaeus is also at the margins of society, "a sinner" (19:7), whose venal self-interest increased the poverty of others (19:8).[46] Two barriers magnify his separation from Jesus and others: 1) his height, and 2) an imposing crowd, which pushes him to the margins and prevents him from seeing Jesus. The barricade of people adds to the indignity of his short stature.[47] Zacchaeus is indeed "lost" (19:10). Yet the tax collector reverses his marginalization. Neither his height nor the impassable crowd prevents him from "seeing" Jesus. Although he is "lowly," he refuses to remain low. He climbs[48] the tree (the lowly going high) only to find that he must come down[49] to find what he wants (the lofty being brought low: 19:5; cf. 1:52).

> So he ran ahead and climbed a sycamore tree to see him, because he was going to pass that way. (19:4)
>
> "Zacchaeus hurry and come down; for I must[50] stay at your house today." [51] So he hurried down and was happy[52] to welcome him. (19:5–6)

Jesus' acceptance of Zacchaeus brings the tax collector from the margins to the foreground. "In the eyes of men Zacchaeus is to be rejected as a sinner. Jesus, on the other hand, singles him out for favor."[53] In response, Zacchaeus willingly shares Jesus' values ("welcomed him joyfully [NRSV: happy]") by placing his wealth in the service of the poor and making right the wrongs he has committed.

> Look, half of my possessions, Lord, I will give[54] to the poor; and if I have defrauded anyone of anything I will pay back[55] four times as much. (19:8)[56]

Zacchaeus was lost: at the margins of society, a "sinner," a Dives whose spiritual values were oriented to the self, not to the kingdom. His impoverished spirituality was determined by material values that placed him at odds with his community and with the ethics of the kingdom of God. Unlike the rich farmer who defined his life in terms of accumulation of possessions, Zacchaeus relinquishes control of his wealth and abandons the dropsical drive to accumulate. Jesus approves of his choice.

> Today salvation has come to this house, because he too is a son of Abraham. For the Son of Man came to seek out and to save the lost. (19:9–10)

## Luke 18:18–27

By contrast, the story of the Rich Ruler shows the consuming power of plenty. When offered the opportunity to follow Jesus, the ruler chooses to follow wealth, demonstrating his fidelity to money, to Mammon: the fleeting security of possessions becomes his god. In

18:18, the ruler asks, "What must I do to inherit eternal life?" Jesus requires him to give up control of his wealth and to give it to the poor. "Sell *all* [57] that you own and distribute the money to the poor, and you will have treasure in heaven; then come, follow me" (18:22). But the ruler is morose[58] because he was "extremely rich."[59] The pull of the material is stronger than the call of discipleship.

To receive the treasure he wants, the ruler must give up the treasure he has. The choice is not easy.

> Indeed, it is easier for a camel *to go through*[60] *the eye of a needle* than
> for someone who is rich *to enter*[61] *the kingdom of God*. (18:25)

The parallel phrases, "to enter the kingdom of God" and "to enter the eye of a needle"[62] underscore the dilemma of the wealthy: the sheer pull of possessions sets up an impossible situation that cannot be overcome apart from the grace of God (18:27). The required conversion calls the ruler to adopt a "generalized reciprocity" in which he redistributes his wealth to the poor. His decision not to control wealth by disbursing it to the poor means that wealth continues to control him. His choice not only distances him from the poor[63] but also separates him from God. Despite the ruler's failed quest,[64] others do abandon the securities of this world to follow Jesus. Peter, for instance, demonstrates that the tug of the material is not greater than the desire to follow: "Look, we have left our homes[65] and followed you" (18:28).

## Luke 16:1–13

The parable of the Unjust Steward (16:1–8a)[66] and the accompanying sayings (16:8b–13) underscore the controlling power of wealth: either a person controls wealth or wealth controls the person. Unless one subjects wealth to servitude, he or she becomes enslaved to wealth; either a person makes friends by means of wealth or else wealth, like a seductive master or mistress, becomes an alluring, irresistible force that controls us.[67]

The parable cannot be properly interpreted apart from the commentary in 16:8b–13;[68] the descriptive term "dishonest"[69] links the parable proper with the sayings in 16:9–13.

And his master[70] commended *the dishonest manager*[71] because he had
   acted shrewdly. (16:8a)

And I tell you, make friends for yourselves by means of *dishonest wealth*.
   (16:9)[72]

Whoever is faithful in a very little is faithful also in much; and whoever is *dishonest*[73] in a very little is *dishonest*[74] also in much. (16:10)

If then you have not been faithful with *the dishonest wealth*,[75] who will
   entrust to you the true riches? (16:11)

The word "to receive, welcome, or take"[76] binds the actions of
the steward with the desired actions of Christians (16:4, 6, 7, 9).

The parable of the Unjust Steward is a story of a manager who is
accused of squandering[77] his master's property and is required to
give an account of his management. Like the rich farmer who says,
"What shall I do?" (12:17), the steward ponders his dilemma, rules
out undesirable options, and crafts a plan to ingratiate himself to the
master's debtors.

What will I do, now that my master is taking the position away from
me? I am not strong enough to dig, and I am ashamed to beg. I have
decided what to do so that, when I am dismissed as manager, people
may welcome into their homes. (16:3–4)

The course of action the steward decides on is to "make friends . . . by
means of dishonest wealth" (16:9), which the following parallelism
clarifies.[78]

I have decided what to do *so that, when* I am dismissed as manager,
   *people [they] may welcome me into their homes.* (16:4)[79]

And I tell you, make friends for yourselves by means of dishonest
   wealth *so that when* it is gone, *they may welcome you into the eternal
   homes.* (16:9)[80]

He gives the debtors something they need,[81] and, correspond-
ingly, they give him something he needs: a guaranteed future.[82] By
canceling a portion of their promissory notes, he makes friends by
means of dishonest wealth—a shrewd decision because his act assures that the debtors will befriend him in his need. Thus both the

steward and debtors benefit from the disposition of money, a point underscored by the repeated usage of *dexomai* ("receive, take, or welcome"). The debtors "receive" a discount on their bill, and the steward "receives" a place to go in his unemployment.

> I have decided what to do so that, when I am dismissed as manager, people *may welcome*[83] me into their homes. (16:4)
>
> So, summoning his master's debtors one by one, he asked the first, "How much do you owe my master?" He answered, "A hundred jugs of olive oil." He said to him, *"Take*[84] your bill, sit down quickly, and make it fifty." (16:5–6)
>
> Then he asked another, "And how much do you owe?" He replied, "A hundred containers of wheat." He said to him, *"Take*[85] your bill and make it eighty." (16:7)
>
> And I tell you, make friends for yourselves by means of dishonest wealth so that when it is gone, *they may welcome*[86] you into the eternal homes.[87] (16:9)

Halvor Moxnes asserts that the steward's action hovers between balanced reciprocity ("business deals with specific and quick equal returns") and general reciprocity ("close social relations with deferred expectations of return").[88] The servant understands that possessions are correctly used to make friends. Similarly, Christians are to deal with wealth as did the steward: they are to "make friends" with wealth, which in Luke means to give alms to the needy. Luke 12:33 is the clarifying commentary on 16:9.[89]

> Sell your possessions, and give alms.
> > *Make for yourselves*[90] purses that do not wear out,
> > a treasure *unfailing*[91] in heaven. (12:33, author's translation)
> And I tell you,
> > *for yourselves make*[92] friends by means of dishonest wealth
> > so that when *it fails*,[93] they may welcome you into the eternal
> > homes. (16:9, author's translation)

By giving away wealth, Christians take control of wealth and use it for the benefit of others; if they do not use wealth for a greater need, wealth subjects the self to baser needs.[94] This latter possibility is stated forthrightly in 16:13: "You cannot serve God and wealth."

The enslaving power of mammon is seen in the rich farmer whose unrestrained avidity leaves him spiritually poor (12:16–21), in the rich man whose immoderate consumption bankrupts him spiritually (16:19–31), and in the religious leaders whose rapacity increases spiritual indigence (11:39).[95] But the enslaving power of wealth is broken when it is used to make friends by giving it to the poor and dispossessed. Mammon has no place in the age to come, for it will fail;[96] yet it can be used properly in this age to make friends so that when it fails, "they[97] may welcome you into the eternal homes" (16:9).[98] If mammon is used for self-aggrandizing purposes and not to benefit others ("to make friends"), it becomes a lord that competes with God. "Those who allow mammon to control them render service to it and thereby exclude service to God."[99] Its idolatrous power, however, is broken when used to benefit the poor and those in need.

## Conclusion

Hyperconsumerism stems from a relentless desire for satisfaction. It demonstrates spiritual hunger. Dropsy, an unquenchable thirst for fluids in a body that is already swollen with excess liquids, is an ancient metaphor for a modern problem. Far from resolving the problem, additional drink aggravates the condition so that the person drowns in his excess fluids. The drive to consume is insatiable; it consumes the person who is driven. It causes people to increase debt beyond reasonable limits, their own ruin. Immoderate consumption causes people to overeat, to feast when they should fast, to develop health problems: obesity, heart problems, cirrhosis, and so forth. It leads to the break-up of marriages and emotional problems. Overwrought consumerism gives the appearance of health: nice clothing, gourmet foods, big houses, expensive cars, an increasing gross national product. But it is symptomatic of a deeper spiritual hunger both in individuals and in a consumerist society.

The rich farmer of Luke 12 equated life with the accumulation of possessions. Preening success and gloating dissipation, however, left him poor toward God. Conspicuous consumption did not fill his spiritual hunger; instead, it left him empty. The more he accumulated, the more he wanted. And the more he wanted, the more he accumulated. In the vicious cycle of accumulation and consumption there was no room for God. Similarly, the well-stocked material life of the rich man in the parable of Luke 16 was a sign of spiritual indigence.

Luke offers a way out of the cycle of plenty and consumption. Zacchaeus discovered that life is not found in the accumulation of possessions but in the dispossession of his abundance. Before he met Jesus, his material values determined his spirituality; after Jesus, his spiritual values determined his material values. He placed his wealth in the service of the poor and made right the wrongs he had committed. The rich ruler (18:18–24), on the other hand, decided that the allure of riches was stronger than the call of discipleship. One decision liberates; the other enslaves.

# Conclusion

In Luke, *the spiritual life is a journey, an exodus to a new promised land, the kingdom of God*. It begins at the Jordan, a threshold experience that marks a radical break with past ways and a complete surrender to God's new aims. At the Jordan, we assess where we have come from and where we are going. Luke calls this threshold experience a "baptism of repentance for the forgiveness of sins" (3:3). Self-protective modes of social intercourse are abandoned (3:10–14); manipulative self-aggrandizement loses its appeal. The follower with two coats shares with the one who has none; those who have food share with those who are hungry, and the ones who misappropriate, defraud, or overcharge through threats and false accusations abandon their wrongful practices.

The journey also includes *tests of spiritual integrity*. The desert is not only the necessary way to spiritual growth but also the desired way to spiritual development. In this untamed space, we face our own limitations. Life's choices are clearest in the vast starkness of desert waste. The desert takes us to the edges of life where we realize what is important in life and what is irrelevant, and it is at the edges that we learn to set our priorities straight and to rely upon divine solace. The desert is where God's unsayable grace and divine succor turn a wildness of empty space into an empyrean of spiritual and physical nourishment.

With unrelenting fierceness our integrity is tested in the austere, feral desert. Satan, the consummate artist of the material, offers Jesus *this world and all its allure* in the desert. But the price is too high and the rewards are too fleeting. Jesus rejects the material. It is as empty as desert waste, for it cannot satisfy spiritual hunger. In their desert test, the disciples learn to rely upon God's uncommon grace. There we also confront our limitations and learn to depend wholly upon God.

The journey includes *spiritual awakenings* to God's infinite power and our own spiritual poverty. The lake clarifies not only the limits of human endeavor but also our need to rely fully on God. In Peter's spiritual awakening, he recognizes the bankruptcy of the self and the plenitude that Jesus offers (5:1–11). Peter decides to follow the One who turns failure into success. The other disciples also are awakened to their spiritual poverty on the lake. The tempest on the lake stirs up an inner tempest (8:22–25). The inner storm is a fragile faith; the disciples, however, awake to the comforting realization that Jesus controls life's uncertainties, tames the unpredictable, and quells life's troubles.

The *itinerary of this journey is spiritual formation*. God initiates the journey and becomes our traveling companion. Like the two on the Emmaus road, we cannot fathom God's inscrutable ways in this world. God's way are not our ways; God, therefore, comes alongside us with a clarifying word and a clarifying act to open our eyes. Jesus leads, we follow. He travels the difficult road to humiliation and rejection, to suffering and death, to resurrection and glorification. The hard road is the way the disciples travel also.

On this journey we learn to relinquish control over the securities of this world and "set *our* faces" towards the destination, the kingdom of God. Obligations that are important for survival in this world pale in comparison with the invitation to follow Jesus. In Luke's spirituality of brokenness family ties may be left behind (14:26). The securities of this world are broken so that the disciples are freed to follow Jesus with singleness of purpose. The decision of discipleship may tear apart the fabric of the traditional family: father against son, son against father, and so forth (12:52–53). Yet Jesus provides a new spiritual family: those who hear and do God's word (8:21). On the journey, we learn to abandon our tenacious grip on the self and possessions. There is no ladder of personal success to climb, no competitive acts of one-upmanship, no presumption of self-sufficiency, no self-seeking actions to bolster self-worth, and no resources that we can bring on this exodus. Money, accomplishments, and self-importance are not only inadequate for the journey; they get in the way.

The *models for spiritual development* are the marginalized and vulnerable, the destitute and unseen: slaves, children, and widows. Religious leaders are too ensconced in self-regarding, protective behaviors to serve as positive models. Their itinerary is one of self-promotion, not inward change; outward appearance, not inward integrity; one-upmanship, not self-effacement; comfortable smugness, not sincerity of heart. On the other hand, the marginalized have no pretensions at greatness. They are ideal models for the spiritual life. Children have no need to bolster their self-worth with an endless array of self-promoting activities. They are unencumbered by the accoutrements of success, society, and experience. Slaves are benefactors that do not serve themselves. They serve for the benefit of others. Their acts of service do not gain rewards or enhance their prestige. They also are ideal models. Widows are among the weak and vulnerable members of society, yet they are models of uncommon strength and self-giving. Their courageous acts of self-giving shame both the rich and the powerful.

Table fellowship mirrors the landscape of the kingdom. Our decision to eat or not eat with someone reflects our social and spiritual values. Jesus eats with the marginalized: the tax collector and sinner, the unclean and the waif, the disenfranchised and the stigmatized. Similarly, we are to invite to the table those who cannot reciprocate: the socially and morally marginalized, including the poor, the crippled, the lame, and the blind (14:12–14). *Generalized reciprocity*—hospitality to "the other"—replaces *balanced reciprocity*—hospitality to well-positioned friends, neighbors, the rich, and so forth. Altruism and generosity are hallmarks of the new spiritual landscape.

The *spiritual distractions* of the journey include anxiety, indolence, and consumerism, to name a few. Luke uses the imagery of clothing and food to describe anxiety. Anxiety—concerning what we wear, for instance—is emblematic of a restless, inadequate faith: "If God so clothes the grass of the field, which is alive today and tomorrow is thrown into the oven, how much more will he clothe you—you of little faith" (12:28). Martha represents the angst of a divided spiritual life (10:38–42). She is a follower of Jesus and her orientation is toward the kingdom of God, but her anxiety concerning the cares and concerns of this world erodes the unifying center. Martha is the model of the modern-day Christian: the busyness of the everyday erodes the unifying center found in Christ.

Clothing represents another spiritual distraction: indolence. Girded garments reflect spiritual readiness, a state of mind and heart that is not overburdened with the distractions of this life; ungirded garments suggest indolence. Luke uses the image of slaves whose master goes to a wedding banquet and returns in the middle of the night or near dawn (12:35–38). The slaves' task is to stay alert, fight off fatigue, and open the door upon the master's return. Indolence, however, sets in when life's distractions are too great or too many. A spiritual life characterized by attentiveness (vigilance and wakefulness) and indifference (detachment) separates essential tasks and obligations from the unessential—difficult to do in a society in which the unessential appears essential.

Immoderate accumulation and immoderate consumption are also distractions to the spiritual life. Modern society regards consumerism as neutral or even positive; it is necessary for the material health and well-being of a nation. Luke, on the other hand, regards consumerism as a measure of one's spiritual vitality. Immoderate consumption is a defiant, belligerent act of self-sufficiency that makes it impossible to travel the hard road of this exodus. Immoderate accumulation defines life in terms of "abundance of possessions" and the "storing up treasures" for oneself (12:15, 21); it attempts to secure life by stockpiling possessions. The act of stockpiling "goods" becomes life's goal and life's god; material goods usurp the role of God. The more we want, the more we accumulate, and the more we accumulate, the more we want. Luke, however, promotes dispossession as the way to break the vicious cycle of desire and chimerical satisfaction. The rich ruler, for instance, decided that wealth was more important than spiritual health and, therefore, decided not to join the exodus. Zacchaeus, on the other hand, adopted a spirituality of economic justice and almsgiving (19:8). He gave half of his possessions to the poor and paid back fourfold to persons he defrauded. When used to benefit the poor and those in need, the false gods of consumption and possessions are deprived of their insatiable consuming power.

The *spiritual disciplines* of the journey include prayer, almsgiving, economic justice, and fasting. The mountain is a place of prayer where we draw closer to God. The noise of the everyday is silenced and we can hear God's clarifying word for us, and on this stark terrain, suspended between earth and sky, we realize the limits of human resources. The mountain is where our self-will is tamed and where God's will emerges with striking clarity.

Jesus' prayer on the Mount of Olives is a model for *spiritual fitness*. Like an athlete preparing for the contest of his life, Jesus struggles with the divine; the disciples, on the other hand, fall fast asleep. His request to remove the cup is a model for Christian prayer: "Father, if *you* are willing, remove this cup from *me*; yet, not *my* will but *yours* be done" (22:42). The second-person singular (*you and yours*) brackets the first person (*me and my*). In this way, the will of the self rests entirely within the will of the Father. Conformity to God's will comes through earnest, submissive, intense prayer in contrast to another form of prayer that is merely a tribute to the self. "God, I thank you that I am not like other people: thieves, rogues, adulterers, or even like this tax collector. I fast twice a week; I give a tenth of all *my* income" (18:11–12). The two prayers represent the two spiritualities of Luke's Gospel: the one directed to the self, the other to God.

# Notes

## Notes to Introduction

1. Alister E. McGrath, *Christian Spirituality: An Introduction* (Oxford: Blackwell, 1999), 88.

2. The literature on spirituality is immense. See Alister McGrath's bibliography in *Christian Spirituality*, 198–201, and Eugene H. Peterson, *Take and Read, Spiritual Reading: An Annotated List* (Grand Rapids: Eerdmans, 1996). The literature on Lucan spirituality is sparse. See Stephen C. Barton, *The Spirituality of the Gospels* (Peabody, Mass.: Hendrickson, 1992), 71–112; Charles H. Talbert, "The Way of the Lukan Jesus: Dimensions of Lukan Spirituality," *PRSt* 9 (1982): 237–49; Paul J. Bernadicou, "The Spirituality of Luke's Travel Narrative," *Review for Religious* 36 (1977): 455–66. For Mark, see Eugene H. Peterson, *Subversive Spirituality* (Grand Rapids: Eerdmans, 1997), 3–15; Mitzi Minor, *The Spirituality of Mark: Responding to God* (Louisville: Westminster John Knox, 1996).

3. See Barton, *Spirituality*, 71–112 for a different definition of spirituality in Luke.

4. ἔξοδος. Only Luke refers to the journey to Jerusalem as an exodus.

5. Joel Green, *The Theology of the Gospel of Luke* (Cambridge: Cambridge University Press, 1995), 148.

6. See Halvor Moxnes, *The Economy of the Kingdom: Social Conflict and Economic Relations in Luke's Gospel* (Philadelphia: Fortress, 1988), 34–35, 129–34, 174. Reciprocity is the relationship between two parties that have distinct socioeconomic interests. Moxnes (p. 34) offers the following definitions: (1) "Generalized reciprocity . . . is the 'solidarity extreme.' This form for exchange covers transactions that are altruistic; the ideal form is the 'pure gift.'" (2) "Balanced reciprocity . . . attempts to reach near-equivalence in goods and services. Within this form of exchange relationships between people can be disrupted if there is a failure to reciprocate for a gift

received." (3) "Negative reciprocity . . . is the 'unsocial extreme.' It designates attempts to 'get something for nothing,' and the ways to get it may vary from nonviolent to violent."

7. See, for example, Alfred Plummer, *A Critical and Exegetical Commentary on the Gospel According to S. Luke* (Edinburgh: T&T Clark, 1922), xlv–xlvi; Allison A. Trites, "The Prayer Motif in Luke-Acts," in *Perspectives on Luke-Acts* (ed. Charles Talbert; Edinburgh: T&T Clark, 1978), 168–86; Wilhelm Ott, *Gebet und Heil: Die Bedeutung der Gebetsparänese in der lukanischen Theologie* (Munich: Kösel, 1965); P. T. O'Brien, "Prayer in Luke-Acts," *TynBul* 24 (1973): 111–27; Walter L. Liefeld, "Parables on Prayer (Luke 11:5–13; 18:1–14)," in *The Challenge of Jesus' Parables* (ed. Richard N. Longenecker; Grand Rapids: Eerdmans, 2000), 240–62; Steven F. Plymale, *The Prayer Texts of Luke-Acts* (New York: Peter Lang, 1991); David Crump, *Jesus the Intercessor: Prayer and Christology in Luke-Acts* (Grand Rapids: Baker, 1999); John Navone, *Themes of St. Luke* (Rome: Gregorian University, 1970), 118–31; Stephen S. Smalley, "Spirit, Kingdom and Prayer in Luke-Acts," *NovT* 15 (1973): 59–71; Barbara E. Reid, "Prayer and the Face of the Transfigured Jesus," in *The Lord's Prayer and Other Prayer Texts from the Greco-Roman Era* (ed. James H. Charlesworth; Valley Forge, Pa.: Trinity Press International, 1994), 39–53; Kyu Sam Han, "Theology of Prayer in the Gospel of Luke," *JETS* 43 (2000): 675–93.

8. Plummer, *Luke*, xlv; Trites, "Prayer," 172.

9. For an introduction to narrative criticism see Mark Allan Powell, *What is Narrative Criticism?* (Minneapolis: Fortress, 1990); James L. Resseguie, *Revelation Unsealed: A Narrative Critical Approach to John's Apocalypse* (Leiden: Brill, 1998), 1–31; idem, "New Testament as Literature," *EDB* 815–17. See also the handbooks of literature for definition of terms, such as C. Hugh Holman, *A Handbook to Literature* (4th ed., Indianapolis: ITT Bobbs-Merrill, 1980); M. H. Abrams, *A Glossary of Literary Terms* (6th ed., Forth Worth: Harcourt Brace College Publishers, 1993); Roger Fowler, *A Dictionary of Modern Critical Terms* (rev. ed., London: Routledge & Kegan Paul, 1987). Stephen D. Moore, *Literary Criticism and the Gospels: The Theoretical Challenge* (New Haven: Yale University Press, 1989), 179–83, provides a helpful glossary of terms.

10. Holman, *Handbook*, 413.

11. Seymour Chatman, *Story and Discourse: Narrative Structure in Fiction and Film* (Ithaca: Cornell University Press, 1978), 141–45.

12. Two other landscapes, which are not considered in this book, are also maps of the spiritual life: architectural (temple, tomb, synagogue) and political (Roman Empire, kingdom of God).

# Notes to Chapter 1, Topography

1. The description is from Belden C. Lane, *The Solace of Fierce Landscapes: Exploring Desert and Mountain Spirituality* (New York: Oxford University Press, 1998).

2. Henry O. Thompson, "Jordan River," ABD 3:953–58; David Rhoads, Joanna Dewey, Donald Michie, *Mark as Story: An Introduction to the Narrative of a Gospel* (2d ed., Minneapolis: Fortress, 1999), 69; on the Jordan in OT and Jewish literature see K. Rengstorf, "ποταμός κτλ," TDNT 6:595–623, 608–23.

3. Luke uses the "people" (λαοί) in 3:15, which typically refers to the people of God in Luke. See Paul S. Minear, "Jesus' Audiences, according to Luke," *NovT* 16 (1974): 81–109. In 3:21, ἅπαντα τὸν λαόν, found only in Luke, underscores the formative nature of this event. It may mean "all of Israel" or "all from Israel who responded," but in either case Israel (the λαός) once more returns to the Jordan.

4. Joel B. Green, *The Gospel of Luke* (Grand Rapids: Eerdmans, 1997), 164.

5. There are two references to the Jordan in Luke: 3:3; 4:1.

6. See Resseguie, *Revelation Unsealed*, 43–44.

7. The usage of Psalm 2 in 3:22 reinforces Jesus as the Lord's anointed. See Green, *Luke*, 186.

8. ἔρημος occurs in 1:80; 3:2, 4; 4:1, 42; 5:16; 7:24; 8:29; 9:12; 15:4. On the desert in the Gospels see Ulrich W. Mauser, *Christ in the Wilderness: The Wilderness Theme in the Second Gospel and Its Basis in the Biblical Tradition* (London: SCM, 1963); Elizabeth Struthers Malbon, *Narrative Space and Mythic Meaning in Mark* (San Francisco: Harper & Row, 1986), 72–75; G. Kittel, " ἔρημος κτλ," TDNT 2:657–60; W. Radl, " ἔρημος," EDNT 2:51–52; Edmund Leach, "Fishing for Men on the Edge of the Wilderness," in *The Literary Guide to the Bible* (ed. Robert Alter and Frank Kermode; Cambridge: Belknap, 1987), 579–99. For a balanced discussion of the desert in the Old Testament see Shemaryahu Talmon, "The 'Desert Motif' in the Bible and in Qumran Literature," in *Biblical Motifs: Origins and Transformations* (ed. A. Altmann; Cambridge: Harvard University Press, 1966), 31–63.

9. Mauser, *Wilderness*, 37 n. 2, lists OT references to wild animals associated with the wilderness. He includes fiery serpents, fiery scorpions, hawk (?), porcupine, owl (?), raven, jackals, ostriches, hyena, satyr, hag, vulture (?), hedgehog, wild beasts.

10. Richard Bauckham, "Jesus and the Wild Animals (Mark 1:13): A Christological Image for an Ecological Age," in *Jesus of Nazareth: Lord and Christ: Essays on the Historical Jesus and New Testament Christology* (ed. Joel Green and Max Turner; Grand Rapids: Eerdmans, 1994), 3–21, at 8.

11. Resseguie, *Revelation Unsealed*, 80–81.

12. Lane, *Fierce Landscapes*, 38.

13. Green, *Luke*, 170.

14. Ibid., 172; Darrell L. Bock, *Luke*, 2 vols. (Grand Rapids: Baker, 1994, 1996), 1:290–96; Mark Allan Powell, "Narrative Criticism," *Hearing the New Testament: Strategies for Interpretation* (ed. Joel B. Green; Grand Rapids: Eerdmans, 1995), 239–55, at 249: "Luke's readers are invited to consider what, for them, constitute the valleys, mountains, crooked places, or rough ways that need to be transformed."

15. On a material point of view see James L. Resseguie, *The Strange Gospel: Narrative Design and Point of View in John* (Leiden: Brill, 2001). A material point of view is literal, concrete, and superficial.

16. Green, *Luke*, 192, conveniently lists the parallels between the testing of Israel in the wilderness and Jesus' testing; cf. also Jacques Dupont, "L'arrière-fond biblique du récit des tentations de Jésus," NTS 3 (1956–1957): 287–304.

17. Luke's account is even more striking when compared to the parallel in Matt 4:9: "All these I will give you, if you will fall down and worship me."

18. δώσω; θέλω; δίδωμι.

19. ἐμοί; ἐμοῦ.

20. ὁ ἄνθρωπος = "humankind."

21. There are also parallels to Israel's complaining at Rephidim (Exod 17:2–7). See Robert L. Brawley, *Text to Text Pours Forth Speech: Voices of Scripture in Luke-Acts* (Bloomington: Indiana University Press, 1995), 23.

22. The pronoun "you" (ὑμεῖς) is emphatic. Plummer, *Luke*, 244, translates: "Ye are to find food for them, not they." Commentators regularly note the parallels with Elisha's servant in 2 Kgs 4:42–44.

23. The narrative aside in 9:14 places the solution outside a material, logical solution. See Steven Sheeley, *Narrative Asides in Luke-Acts* (Sheffield: JSOT Press, 1992), 101.

24. εἰ μήτι.

25. Bread as a commodity distinguishes Pharaoh's household from God's household where bread is a gift. See M. Douglas Meeks, *God the Economist: The Doctrine of God and Political Economy* (Minneapolis: Fortress, 1989), 78–92.

26. The imperfect tense is used, ἐδίδου ("went on giving it"), with progressive force. See Maximilian Zerwick, *Biblical Greek: Illustrated by Examples* (Rome: Scripta Pontificii Instituti Biblici, 1963), § 271.

27. πάντες is in an emphatic position; it emphasizes that "they were satisfied, *all*."

28. ἐχορτάσθησαν. The same verb is used in 6:21.

29. Twelve is a symbolic number of completeness in the New Testament. See Resseguie, *Revelation Unsealed*, 48–69; Adela Yarbro Collins, "Numerical Symbolism in Jewish and Early Christian Apocalyptic Literature," ANRW 21.2:1221–87; M. H. Pope, "Number, Numbering, Numbers," IDB 3:561–67.

30. Sharon H. Ringe, *Luke* (Philadelphia: Westminster John Knox, 1995), 133; John Paul Heil, *The Meal Scenes in Luke-Acts: An Audience-Oriented Approach* (Atlanta: Society of Biblical Literature, 1999), 62; Joel Marcus, *Mark 1–8: A New Translation with Introduction and Commentary* (New York: Doubleday, 2000), 411.

31. Lake, λίμνη, occurs in 5:1, 2; 8:22, 23, 33. Sea, θάλασσα, occurs in 17:2, 6; 21:25.

32. On the sea or lake in biblical narratives see Malbon, *Narrative Space*, 76–79; idem, "The Jesus of Mark and the Sea of Galilee," *JBL* 103 (1984): 363–77; John Paul Heil, *Jesus Walking on the Sea: Meaning and Gospel Functions of Matt 14:22–33; Mark 6:45–52 and John 6:15b–21* (Rome: Biblical Institute, 1981); R. Kratz, "θάλασσα," *EDNT* 2:127–28.

33. See Malbon, "The Jesus of Mark," 375.

34. A similar narrative, however, is found in John 21:1–11.

35. John Nolland, *Luke* (3 vols.; Dallas: Word, 1989, 1993), 1:221.

36. Here and 6:14 are the only places Luke uses the double name. For a study of Simon's name in the New Testament see J. K. Elliott, "Κηφᾶς: Σίμων Πέτρος: ὁ Πέτρος: An Examination of New Testament Usage," *NovT* 14 (1972): 241–56. Elliott considers 5:8 to be secondary; yet the textual evidence is strong for its inclusion.

37. κύριε.

38. Green, *Luke*, 233; Nolland, *Luke*, 1:222.

39. According to Henry J. Cadbury, *The Making of Luke-Acts* (London: SPCK, 1958), 258, Luke uses the word "sinners" more than all the other evangelists together. For the meaning of sinner in Luke, see David A. Neale, *None But the Sinners: Religious Categories in the Gospel of Luke* (Sheffield: JSOT Press, 1991), 69–97.

40. This is a further indication of an encounter with the divine; see 1:13, 30.

41. ἀπὸ τοῦ νῦν; the expression is found also in 1:48; 12:52; 22:18, 69.

42. I. Howard Marshall, *The Gospel of Luke: A Commentary on the Greek Text* (Grand Rapids: Eerdmans, 1978), 205, says it is "the new stage that begins a man's life when he meets Jesus." Cf. also Nolland, *Luke*, 1:223.

43. Marcus, *Mark*, 339.

44. Robert C. Tannehill, *The Narrative Unity of Luke-Acts: A Literary Interpretation* (2 vols.; Philadelphia: Fortress, 1986, 1990), 1:213.

45. ἐπετίμησεν is used in exorcisms (cf. 4:35). Some commentators (e.g., Green, *Luke*, 333) conclude that the sea is portrayed as a demonic power in Luke. This theme, however, is stronger in Mark 4:39 than in Luke.

46. BDAG, "λαῖλαψ," 581.

47. NRSV, which has "the boat was filling with water," does not capture this nuance.

48. ἐπιστάτης occurs only in Luke (5:5; 8:24, 45; 9:33, 49; 17:13) and always in the vocative as a title addressed to Jesus, almost always by the disciples.

49. Marshall, *Luke*, 334; François Bovon, *Luke 1: A Commentary on the Gospel of Luke 1:1–9:50* (Minneapolis: Fortress, 2002), 318.

50. E.g., Luke 1:13, 30; 5:10. Cf. Plummer, *Luke*, 227: "The fear which accompanies this question or exclamation is not that which the storm produced, but that which was caused by a sudden recognition of the presence of supernatural power of a kind that was new to them."

51. Green, *Luke*, 334.

52. Joseph A. Fitzmyer, *The Gospel according to Luke: Introduction, Translation, and Notes* (2 vols., Garden City, N.Y.: Doubleday, 1981, 1985), 1:730.

53. Cf. C. F. Evans, *Saint Luke* (Philadelphia: Trinity Press International, 1990), 381: "the story from the first [is] a paradigm of the religious truth that Jesus is the saviour of those who are perishing. . . ."

54. McGrath, *Christian Spirituality*, 103.

55. ὄρος occurs in 3:5; 4:29; 6:12; 8:32; 9:28, 37; 19:29, 37; 21:21, 37; 22:39; 23:30.

56. Malbon, *Narrative Space*, 84; W. Foerster, "ὄρος," TDNT 5:475–87. See Robert L. Cohn, *The Shape of Sacred Space: Four Biblical Studies* (Chico, Calif.: Scholars Press, 1981), 25–41 on the mountain motif in biblical literature.

57. McGrath, *Christian Spirituality*, 103.

58. διανυκτερεύω, found only here in the NT, indicates that Jesus spent the entire night in prayer. See BDAG, "διανυκτερεύω," 234.

59. Evans, *Luke*, 319; Tannehill, *Narrative Unity*, 1:205.

60. προσευχῇ τοῦ θεοῦ, "prayer of God," is an objective genitive meaning "prayer to God."

61. However, he does not go far enough in his interpretation; Crump, *Jesus the Intercessor*, 44–48. Green, *Luke*, 377 rightly sees the relationship between hearing and seeing in this narrative.

62. See Resseguie, *Revelation Unsealed*, 33–37; J. P. M. Sweet, *Revelation* (Philadelphia: Westminster, 1979), 125–27.

63. "Making strange" (*ostranenie* in Russian) is the creative distortion of familiar assumptions or objects to make them seem strange and unfamiliar. See J. L. Resseguie, "Automatization and Defamiliarization in Luke 7:36–50," LitTh 5 (1991): 137–50; idem, "Defamiliarization in the Gospels," *Mosaic: A Journal for the Interdisciplinary Study of Literature* 21 (1988): 25–35; idem, "Defamiliarization and the Gospels," BTB 20 (1990): 147–53; idem, "Reader-Response Criticism and the Synoptic Gospels," JAAR 52 (1984): 307–24.

64. τὸ εἶδος.

65. καὶ ἰδού.

66. οἱ ὀφθέντες.

67. εἶδον.

68. ἑώρακαν.

69. Clothing is a potential indicator of one's inner character or nature; see chapter 5.

70. "Listen to him!" is an allusion to the prophet like Moses in Deut 18:15.

71. ἔξοδος occurs only three times in the NT (2 Pet 1:15; Heb 11:22; Luke 9:31). On the exodus theme in Luke see Sharon H. Ringe, "Luke 9:28–36: The Beginning of an Exodus," *Semeia* 28 (1983): 83–99; J. Mánek, "The New Exodus in the Book of Luke," NovT 2 (1958): 8–23.

72. αὐτοῦ ἀκούετε in Luke 9:35 follows the LXX order of Deut 18:15 (αὐτοῦ ἀκούσεσθε). Those who note this connection include: H. Schürmann, *Das Lukasevangelium* (Freiburg: Herder, 1969), 1:562; Fitzmyer, *Luke*, 1:803; Mark L. Strauss, *The Davidic Messiah in Luke-Acts: The Promise and Its Fulfillment in Lucan Christology* (Sheffield: JSOT Press, 1995), 270–71.

73. See Susan Garrett, "Exodus from Bondage: Luke 9:31 and Acts 12:1–24," CBQ 52 (1990): 656–80; Strauss, *Davidic Messiah*, 285–305; David P. Moessner, *Lord of the Banquet: The Literary and Theological Significance of the Lukan Travel Narrative* (Minneapolis: Fortress, 1989), 60–69.

74. Crump, *Jesus the Intercessor*, 48.

75. The verb ἀκολουθέω has both meanings in several passages in Luke, including this one. See Fitzmyer, *Luke*, 1:241–43.

76. The imperfect is used, προσηύχετο, emphasizing the duration of the prayer, "he kept praying."

77. On the similarities between the Mount of Olives prayer and the Lord's Prayer see Anthony Kenny, "The Transfiguration and the Agony in the Garden," CBQ 19 (1957): 444–52, at 450–52; Raymond Brown, *The Death of the Messiah: From Gethsemane to the Grave* (2 vols.; New York: Doubleday, 1994), 1:175–78.

78. Luke 22:43–44 is omitted by 𝔓[69vid] 𝔓[75] ℵ[1] A B N T W among others. It is included by ℵ[*, 2] D K L et. al. Bart D. Ehrman and Mark A. Plunkett, "The Angel and the Agony: The Textual Problem of Luke 22:43–44," CBQ 45 (1983): 401–16, exclude the verses. Several, however, hold to its authenticity, including Lyder Brun, "Engel und Blutschweiss Lc 22,43–44," ZNW 32 (1933): 265–76; Gerhard Schneider, "Engel und Blutschweiss (Lk 22, 43–44): 'Redaktionsgeschichte' im Dienste der Textkritik," BZ 20 (1976): 112–16. See Brown, *Death of the Messiah*, 1:180–86 for a full discussion that favors authenticity. Crump, *Jesus the Intercessor*, 116 n. 25, provides a list of supporters for and against authenticity. Eduard Schweizer, *The Good News according to Luke* (Atlanta: John Knox, 1984), 343, offers a plausible reason for their omission: "Without these verses the passage would have no real point; later copyists probably found them too human."

79. BDAG, "ἐκτενῶς," 310.

80. R. S. Barbour, "Gethsemane in the Tradition of the Passion," NTS 16 (1969–70); 231–51, at 240, notes that "Satan's testing of Jesus is repulsed by Jesus' prayer." Cf. also Crump, *Jesus the Intercessor*, 166–70; Joel Green, "Jesus on the Mount of Olives (Luke 22.39–46): Tradition and Theology," JSNT 26 (1986): 29–48, at 38.

81. Green, *Luke*, 781.

82. ἀναστὰς ἀπὸ τῆς προσευχῆς. Crump, *Jesus the Intercessor*, 169: "Luke's statement that Jesus 'stood up from (his) prayer' . . . may well convey an important symbolic, as well as literal sense, due to the ambiguity of the preposition ἀπό. Jesus literally stood up 'from' prayer and returned to the disciples,

but he was also now able to stand in the face of his trial 'because of' (ἀπό) this prayer."

83. Crump, *Jesus the Intercessor*, 170.

84. ἀπὸ τῆς λύπης. BDAG, "λύπη," 605, translates it "from sorrow."

85. Brian E. Beck, "'Imitatio Christi' and the Lucan Passion Narrative," in *Suffering and Martyrdom in the New Testament: Studies Presented to G. M. Styler by the Cambridge New Testament Seminar* (ed. William Horbury and Brian McNeil; Cambridge: Cambridge University Press, 1981), 28–47, at 39–40. Cf. also Green, "Mount of Olives," 36–37.

86. ἐν ἀγωνίᾳ. Jerome Neyrey, *The Passion According to Luke: A Redaction Study of Luke's Soteriology* (New York: Paulist, 1985), 58–62, makes the case for ἀγωνία as a victorious struggle. Brown, *Death of the Messiah*, 1:189, likens the imagery to a runner at the starting line who is tensed up and begins to sweat profusely. Jesus' trial resembles an athletic contest in which the strengthening angel is like a trainer who readies the athlete for the contest.

87. Green, "Mount of Olives," 39.

88. Schweizer, *Luke*, 343.

89. Nolland, *Luke*, 3:1085.

## Notes to Chapter 2, Journeys

1. Cf. B. P. Robinson, "The Place of the Emmaus Story in Luke-Acts," *NTS* 30 (1984): 481–97, at 482: "Whatever else he is doing in the Emmaus story, Luke is surely using the journey as an image of the Christian life, and indicating how the latter ought to be viewed—not as a solitary, melancholy progress, but as a following of Christ, in full assurance that he has not abandoned his own but will lead them through grief to glory." The emphasis on recognition underscores the spiritual awakening: 1) "from recognizing him" (μὴ ἐπιγνῶναι αὐτὸν, 24:16); 2) "and they recognized him" (καὶ ἐπέγνωσεν αὐτόν, 24:31); 3) "but they did not see him" (αὐτὸν δὲ οὐκ εἶδον, 24:24); 4) "how he had been made known to them" (ὡς ἐγνώσθη αὐτοῖς, 24:35).

2. The kingdom of God is both present in Jesus' earthly ministry (e.g., 4:43; 6:20; 8:1; 9:2; 10:9–11; 11:20; 12:32; 17:20–21) and revealed at a future consummation (e.g., 11:2; 14:15; 19:11; 21:31; 22:16). On the kingdom of God in Luke see Michael Wolter, "'Reich Gottes' bei Lukas," *NTS* 41 (1995): 541–63; Robert F. O'Toole, "The Kingdom of God in Luke-Acts," *The Kingdom of God in 20th-Century Interpretation* (ed. Wendell Willis; Peabody, Mass.: Hendrickson, 1987), 147–62; Otto Merk, "Das Reich Gottes in den lukanischen Schriften," in *Jesus und Paulus: Festschrift für Werner Georg Kümmel* (ed. E. Earle Ellis and E. Grässer; Göttingen: Vandenheock und Ruprecht, 1975), 201–20; Halvor Moxnes, "Kingdom Takes Place: Transformation of Place and Power in the Kingdom of God in the Gospel of Luke," in *Social Scientific Models for Interpreting the Bible: Essays by the Context Group in Honor of Bruce J.*

Malina (ed. John J. Pilch; Leiden: Brill, 2000), 176–209; E. Earle Ellis, "Present and Future Eschatology in Luke," NTS 12 (1965–66): 27–41; idem, *Eschatology in Luke* (Philadelphia: Fortress, 1972); Robert Maddox, *The Purpose of Luke-Acts* (Edinburgh: T&T Clark, 1982), 100–157.

3. The Lucan vocabulary for journeying includes the following: ὁδός ("way"); ἔξοδος ("departure, path, course"); ἀκολουθέω ("to follow"); πορεύομαι ("to go, to travel"). Luke uses ἡ ὁδός ("the way") in Acts 9:2; 19:23; 22:4; 24:14, 22 to denote Christianity.

4. On the journey motif in Mark see Rhoads, Dewey, and Michie, *Mark as Story*, 66–69, 71–72.

5. The majority of manuscripts have sixty stadia.

6. ἦσαν πορευόμενοι εἰς κώμην.

7. ὡμίλουν.

8. The Greek is emphatic: αὐτὸς Ἰησοῦς.

9. συνεπορεύετο αὐτοῖς.

10. περιπατοῦντες.

11. ἐκρατοῦντο.

12. διηνοίχθησαν.

13. Geoffrey F. Nuttall, *The Moment of Recognition: Luke as Story-Teller* (London: Athlone, 1978).

14. Marshall, *Luke*, 893; Richard J. Dillon, *From Eye-Witnesses to Ministers of the Word: Tradition and Composition in Luke 24* (Rome: Biblical Institute, 1978), 104–5; Bock, *Luke*, 2:1909–10; Arthur A. Just Jr., *The Ongoing Feast: Table Fellowship and Eschatology at Emmaus* (Collegeville, Minn.: Liturgical, 1993), 67; Plummer, *Luke*, 552, 557; Evans, *Luke*, 905.

15. Nolland, *Luke*, 3:1201, 1206

16. Green, *Luke*, 845; Fitzmyer, *Luke*, 2:1558.

17. Tannehill, *Narrative Unity*, 1:282.

18. σκυθρωποί. means "pert. to having a look suggestive of gloom or sadness, *sad, gloomy, sullen, dark*": BDAG, "σκυθρωπός," 932–33.

19. ἀνόητοι. signifies "unintelligent, foolish, dull-witted": BDAG, "ἀνόητος," 84.

20. βραδεῖς τῇ καρδίᾳ. According to BDAG, 183, "βραδύς" refers to mental and spiritual dullness; "too dull to believe."

21. Dillon, *Eye-Witnesses*, 111: "the *totality of facts* is developed in ironic counterpart to their *total incomprehension* by those who experience and recount them" (Dillon's emphasis).

22. D. C. Muecke, *The Compass of Irony* (London: Methuen & Co., 1970), 19, refers to a double-layered or two-story phenomenon of irony.

23. An emphatic expression is used: "Jesus *himself* (αὐτὸς Ἰησοῦς) came near and went with them."

24. Nuttall, *Moment of Recognition*, 9.

25. τὰ γενόμενα.

26. σὺ μόνος. NRSV translates "Are *you* the *only* stranger."

27. BDAG, "παροικέω," 779.2b: "a stranger." Other possibilities include "only one living near Jerusalem" or "inhabit, live in" without connotation of stranger.

28. ἡμεῖς.

29. Cadbury, *Making of Luke-Acts*, 237.

30. λυτρόω means "set free, rescue, redeem." See BDAG, "λυτρόω," 606.2.

31. Fitzmyer, *Luke*, 2:1564.

32. οὐχὶ ἔδει. οὐχί expects a positive reply.

33. See Charles H. Cosgrove, "The Divine ΔΕΙ in Luke-Acts: Investigations into the Lukan Understanding of God's Providence," *NovT* 26 (1984): 168–90, 174; Paul Schubert, "The Structure and Significance of Luke 24," in *Neutestamentliche Studien für Rudolf Bultmann* (2d ed.; ed. W. Eltester; Berlin: Alfred Töpelmann, 1957), 165–86, for the meaning of δεῖ.

34. Several commentators see Jesus as present in the Eucharist. See, for example, Just, *Ongoing Feast*, 219–61; Fitzmyer, *Luke*, 2:1559. On the other hand, B. P. Robinson, "The Emmaus Story," 487–93, argues that Luke "has no discernable interest in the Eucharist." Crump, *Jesus the Intercessor*, 101–4 provides a thorough critique of the eucharistic interpretation of the Emmaus meal.

35. James E. Loder, *The Transforming Moment: Understanding Convictional Experiences* (New York: Harper & Row, 1981), 103.

36. Karl Ludwig Schmidt, *Der Rahmen der Geschichte Jesu: Literakritische Untersuchungen zur ältsten Jesusüberlieferung* (Berlin: Trowitzsch und Sohn, 1919), 269.

37. Hans Conzelmann, *The Theology of St. Luke* (trans. G. Buswell; New York: Harper & Row, 1960), 63 n. 6.

38. Although there is no doubt that 9:51 is the beginning of the journey, there is little agreement concerning its end. (1) A number of scholars accept 18:14 as the conclusion, including J. Blinzler, "Die literarische Eigenart des sogenannten Reiseberichts im Lukasevangelium," in *Synoptische Studien* (ed. J. Schmid and A. Vögtle; Munich: Karl Zink, 1953), 20–52, at 20; Erich Klostermann, *Das Lukasevangelium* (2d ed.; Tübingen: J. C. B. Mohr [Paul Siebeck], 1929), 110; C. F. Evans, "The Central Section of St. Luke's Gospel," in *Studies in the Gospels: Essays in Memory of R. H. Lightfoot* (ed. D. E. Nineham; Oxford: Basil Blackwell, 1955), 37–53, at 40. Luke 18:14, however, is not the appropriate point to end this section, even though Luke's narrative rejoins Mark's at this point, for the destination, Jerusalem, is not yet reached. (2) Several others extend the section to 19:27 or 28. For example, Walter Grundmann, "Fragen der Komposition des lukanischen 'Reiseberichts'," *ZNW* 50 (1959): 252–70, at 254; J. Schneider, "Zur Analyse des lukanischen Reiseberichtes," in Schmid and Vögtle, eds., *Synoptische Studien* 207–29, at 211; W. Gasse, "Zum Reisebericht des Lukas," *ZNW* 34 (1935): 293–99, at 298; George Ogg, "The Central Section of the

Gospel according to St Luke," NTS 18 (1971): 39–53; Frederick W. Danker, *Jesus and the New Age According to St. Luke: A Commentary on the Third Gospel* (St. Louis: Clayton, 1972), 123; G. W. Trompf, "La Section Médiane de L'Évangile de Luc: L'Organisation des Documents," RHPR 53 (1973): 141–54, at 141; G. B. Caird, *The Gospel of St. Luke* (Baltimore: Penguin Books, 1963), 139; Conzelmann, *Luke*, 63–64; Ringe, *Luke*, 147. In favor of ending the section at 19:27 is the narrator's annotation in 19:11 that Jesus is "near Jerusalem." Conzelmann notes that Jesus does not arrive at Jerusalem until 19:28. But in 19:38, 44 Jesus is still outside the city. 3) Others conclude the section at 19:44: see James L. Resseguie, "Interpretation of Luke's Central Section (Luke 9:51–19:44) Since 1856," StBTh 5 (1975): 3–36; E. Earle Ellis, *The Gospel of Luke* (rev. ed.; London: Oliphants, 1974), 223; Peter von der Osten-Sacken, "Zur Christologie des lukanischen Reiseberichts," EvT 33 (1973): 476–96, at 476 n. 2; David Gill, "Observations on the Lukan Travel Narrative and Some Related Passages," HTR 63 (1970): 199–221, at 199; Norval Geldenhuys, *Commentary on the Gospel of Luke: The English Text with Introduction, Exposition and Notes* (Grand Rapids: Eerdmans, 1951), 291; Arland J. Hultgren, "Interpreting the Gospel of Luke," Int 30 (1976): 353–65, at 359; Moessner, *Lord of the Banquet*, 33 n. 3. The reason for extending the section to 19:44 is that Jesus is still en route to Jerusalem and does not enter the temple until 19:45, which begins a new section. 4) Frank J. Matera, "Jesus' Journey to Jerusalem (Luke 9:51–19:46): A Conflict with Israel," JSNT 51 (1993): 57–77; Jack Dean Kingsbury, *Conflict in Luke: Jesus, Authorities, Disciples* (Minneapolis: Fortress, 1991), 150 n. 158; and Paul Kariamadam, "The Composition and Meaning of the Lucan Travel Narrative (Lk. 9,51–19,46), BiBh 13 (1987): 179–98, locate the end at 19:46. 5) A few extend the central section to 19:48: J. M. Creed, *The Gospel according to St. Luke: The Greek Text with Introduction, Notes, and Indices* (London: Macmillan, 1930), 139; Green, *Luke*, 294; H. L. Egelkraut, *Jesus' Mission to Jerusalem: A Redaction Critical Study of the Travel Narrative in the Gospel of Luke, Lk 9:51–19:48* (Frankfurt am Main: Peter Lang, 1976).

39. What should this section be called? D. R. Wickes, *The Sources of Luke's Perean Section* (Chicago: University of Chicago, 1912), calls it "the Perean Section." But L. C. Girard, *L'Évangile des voyages de Jésus, Ou la section 9:51–18:14 de saint Luc* (Paris: J. Gabalda, 1951), 55, considers it inadequate because Luke never envisions Jesus journeying through Perea; Luke 9:51, for example, lacks Mark's phrase in 10:1, "beyond the Jordan," and thus shows no interest in the route Jesus takes. R. H. Lightfoot, *Locality and Doctrine in the Gospels* (London: Hodder and Stoughton, 1938), 137–39, and E. Lohse, "Missionarisches Handeln Jesu nach dem Evangelium des Lukas," TZ 10 (1954): 1–13, refer to the section as "the Samaritan Section." However, C. C. McCown, "The Geography of Luke's Central Section," JBL 57 (1938): 51–66, at 57, notes several events that are practically impossible within Samaria. Two other titles used are: "the Great Insertion" and "the Travel

Document." "The Great Insertion" is inadequate since it assumes that this section ends at 18:14. B. H. Streeter, *The Four Gospels: A Study of Origins* (London: Macmillan, 1924), 203, notes that "the Travel Document" is dangerously misleading, for it implies that the section existed as a separate document. Simply "the Travel Narrative" may be used, but technically Jesus is travelling from 4:42–44 onwards, and, therefore, the designation seems inadequate. McCown seems to be correct; the "Central Section" is "the only satisfactory title to apply"; "Geography," 65. As Streeter says, it "states a fact but begs no questions"; *Four Gospels*, 203.

40. See Moessner, *Lord of the Banquet*, 1–44.

41. See Luke 9:52, 56; 10:1, 38; 11:1; 13:10, 22; 14:1; 17:11, 12.

42. See Luke 9:51, 57; 10:1, 21, 38; 11:1, 14, 29, 37, 53; 12:1; 13:1, 10, 31, 33; 14:1; 17:12, 18:35; 19:5, 7, 11, 28, 29, 41.

43. Schneider, "Analyse," 217.

44. The literary model considered here is the correspondence between the central section and the book of Deuteronomy. Some follow a different literary model, namely, a chiastic structure. See M. D. Goulder, "The Chiastic Structure of the Lucan Journey," SE II (ed. F. L. Cross; Berlin: Akademie-Verlag, 1964), 195–202; idem, *Type and History in Acts* (London: SPCK, 1964), 132–42; Kenneth E. Bailey, *Poet and Peasant: A Literary Cultural Approach to the Parables in Luke* (Grand Rapids: Eerdmans, 1976), 79–85; Charles H. Talbert, *Reading Luke: A Literary and Theological Commentary on the Third Gospel* (New York: Crossroad, 1982), 111–13; Charles Talbert, *Literary Patterns, Theological Themes, and the Genre of Luke-Acts* (Missoula, Mont.: Scholars Press, 1974), 51–56; Craig L. Blomberg, "Midrash, Chiasmus, and the Outline of Luke's Central Section," *Gospel Perspectives III: Studies in Midrash and Historiography* (ed. R. T. France and D. Wenham; Sheffield: JSOT Press, 1983), 217–61; Kariamadam, "Lucan Travel Narrative," 179–98. For chiasm to be an effective literary device, it must be fairly obvious. But in four hundred and twenty-three verses or more, it is only with concerted effort that one can spot the inverted outline. In many instances the chiasms are forced. Interestingly, M. D. Goulder, who was one of the first to suggest a chiastic structure for the central section, abandoned the hypothesis in *Midrash and Lection in Matthew* (London: SPCK, 1974), where he revives C. F. Evans' hypothesis.

45. Evans, "Central Section," 37–53. See the criticisms of Evans in C. H. Cave, "Lazarus and the Lukan Deuteronomy," NTS 15 (1968–69); 319–25, at 319; Goulder, *Midrash and Lection*, 466; Blomberg, "Midrash," 221–28; J. W. Wenham, "Synoptic Independence and the Origin of Luke's Travel Narrative," NTS 27 (1981): 507–15, at 509–10.

46. Moessner, *Lord of the Banquet*; idem, "Luke 9:1–50: Luke's Preview of the Journey of the Prophet like Moses of Deuteronomy," JBL 102 (1983): 575–605.

47. Moessner, *Lord of the Banquet*, 323.

48. See the critique by Strauss, *Davidic Messiah*, 275–85.

49. Ibid., 285–305.

50. Moessner, "Luke 9:1–50," 603.

51. Conzelmann, *Luke*, 65.

52. Ibid., 197.

53. "Fragen," 252–70.

54. "*Lehrer im Angesicht des Todes*"; Grundmann, "Fragen," 259.

55. Osten-Sacken, "Zur Chistologie," 495.

56. "Analyse," 220.

57. "Instruction and Discussion in the Travel Narrative," SE I (Berlin: Akademie-Verlag, 1959), 206–16; see Resseguie, "Instruction and Discussion," 180–91 for a critique of Reicke.

58. Green, *Luke*, 399, does not argue for a spiritual journey, but he comes close: "The 'journey' in which Luke is interested is not about narrative structure or travel itinerary; rather it concerns the fulfillment of God's redemptive purpose together with the thematization of the formation of a people who will hear and obey the word of God." Also Green, *Theology of Luke*, 104–5, and Brian E. Beck, *Christian Character in the Gospel of Luke* (London: Epworth, 1989), 97: "The literal journey is a parable of the metaphorical journey which discipleship involves, and its destination, regularly stressed, points to the end to which it leads: it is the way of the cross."

59. Cf. also James M. Dawsey, "Jesus' Pilgrimage to Jerusalem," PRSt 14 (1987): 217–32 who views the Lukan pilgrimage as a new exodus to the kingdom.

60. Gill, "Observations," 214.

61. Schubert, "Structure and Significance," 183. Luke's hand is indelibly stamped on this verse. The use of ἐγένετο δὲ ἐν τῷ plus an infinitive is an "Indiz für Lk-Redaktion." So Albert Fuchs, *Sprachliche Untersuchungen zu Matthäus und Lukas: Ein Beitrag zur Quellenkritik* (Rome: Biblical Institute Press, 1971), 185; cf. also C. F. D. Moule, *An Idiom Book of New Testament Greek* (2d ed.; Cambridge: Cambridge University Press, 1959), 76, and Gerhard Sellin, "Komposition, Quellen und Funktion des lukanischen Reiseberichtes (Lk. 9.51–19.28)," NovT 20 (1976): 100–35, 102 n. 7. The verb, "to draw near" or "to fulfill" (συμπληρόω) is found only in Luke (8:23, 9:51; Acts 2:1). The noun, "to be taken up" (ἀνάλημψις) is found only here in the NT; the cognate verb, ἀναλαμβάνω, is found in Acts 1:2, 11, 22.

62. Wesley A. Kort, *Story, Text, and Scripture: Literary Interests in Biblical Narrative* (University Park: Pennsylvania State University Press, 1988), 17, defines atmosphere as "the element that establishes the boundaries enclosing the narrative's world. These limits are secured by the sense of what might be expected to occur, of what is and what is not possible. . . . In addition to determining the boundaries of what is possible, atmosphere establishes the conditions affecting the narrative world, whether negatively or positively. Atmosphere is, therefore, tied to 'setting,' but it is a more inclusive and precise term than setting."

63. τὸ πρόσωπον ἐστήρισεν.

64. E.g., Ezek 6:2; 13:17; 14:8; 15:7; 20:46; 21:2; 25:2; 28:21; 29:2; 38:2.

65. Jer 21:10.

66. Plummer, *Luke*, 263. J. H. Davies, "The Purpose of the Central Section of St. Luke's Gospel," SE II (Berlin: Akademie-Verlag, 1964), 164–69, suggests that the phrase also implies hostility; but the LXX includes the preposition ἐπί when hostility is implied and this preposition is conspicuously absent in 9:51. More recently, Craig A. Evans, "'He Set His Face': A Note on Luke 9,51," Bib 63 (1982): 545–48; idem "'He Set His Face': Luke 9,51 Once Again," Bib 68 (1987): 80–4, idem, *Luke* (Peabody, Mass.: Hendrickson, 1990), 161, argues unconvincingly for a hostile connotation. See the criticism of Evans in C. H. Giblin, *The Destruction of Jerusalem according to Luke's Gospel: A Historical-Typological Moral* (Rome: Biblical Institute, 1985), 31–32. J. Starcky, "Obfirmavit faciem suam ut iret Jerusalem: Sens et portée de Luc ix, 51," RSR 39 (1951): 197–202, at 199, claims that the phrase is similar to Isa 50:7 (ἔθηκα τὸ πρόσωπόν μου ὡς στερεὰν πέτραν) where the notion of firm resolution of purpose is implied.

67. ἀνάλημψις. Since this is a hapax legomenon in the Greek Bible, the precise meaning is uncertain. Josef Schmid, *Das Evangelium nach Lukas* (4th ed.; Regensburg: Pustet, 1960), 176, and Gerhard Friedrich, "Lk 9,51 und die Entrückungschristologie des Lukas," in *Orientierung an Jesus: Zur Theologie der Synoptiker für Josef Schmid* (ed. Paul Hoffmann, et. al.; Freiburg: Herder, 1973), 48–77, at 48–52, claim that Jesus' "death" is the primary meaning here. Schmid cites PsSol.4:18 where ἀνάλημψις means "death." Others claim that it refers to Jesus' "ascension," e.g., Plummer, *Luke*, 262; A. R. C. Leaney, *A Commentary on the Gospel according to St. Luke* (2d ed.; London: Black, 1966), 172; Helmut Flender, *St. Luke: Theologian of Redemptive History* (London: SPCK, 1967), 33. For other supporters of this position see Friedrich, "Lk 9,51," 48 n. 2. Still others interpret ἀνάλημψις as a reference to the entire chain of events (death, resurrection, ascension); see Resseguie, "Interpretation," 30 n. 156, for a list of supporters and Mikeal Parson, *The Departure of Jesus in Luke-Acts: The Ascension Narratives in Context* (Sheffield: JSOT Press, 1987), 130–33, for a discussion of the word.

68. The verb, "to draw near" (συμπληρόω), which Evans, *Luke*, 435, calls a "lame rendering" of the verb "to be fulfilled," indicates that the journey is entirely within God's saving will. See G. Delling, "συμπληρόω," TDNT 6:308–9.

69. Conzelmann, *Luke*, 68.

70. The δεῖ indicates divine necessity. See Cosgrove, "Divine ΔΕΙ," 174; Walter Grundmann, "δεῖ κτλ," TDNT 2:21–25, at 22; and Schubert, "Structure and Significance," 181: "In most cases, Luke's δεῖ has fully technical, theological denotations and connotations." On a broader scale, see the study of John T. Squires, *The Plan of God in Luke-Acts* (Cambridge: Cambridge University Press, 1993).

71. Nolland, *Luke*, 2:465.

72. The verb, τελέω, in Luke has the sense of "fulfill" (cf. 12:50; 22:37; Ac 13:29). See BDAG, "τελέω," 997–98. It is a divine passive, according to Fitzmyer, *Luke*, 2:1209.

73. καὶ πορευομένων αὐτῶν ἐν τῇ ὁδῷ is Lukan. See Siegfried Schulz, *Q: Die Spruchquelle der Evangelisten* (Zürich: Theologischer Verlag, 1972), 434; Michi Miyoshi, *Der Anfang des Reiseberichts Lk 9,51–10,24: Eine redaktions-geschichtliche Untersuchung* (Rome: Biblical Institute Press, 1974), 34–36.

74. The reading has the support of 𝔓⁷⁵ and B and with minor variations ℵ.

75. On the Son of Man title see the excursus in W. D. Davies and Dale C. Allison, Jr., *A Critical and Exegetical Commentary on the Gospel According to Saint Matthew* (3 vols.; Edinburgh: T&T Clark, 1988, 1991, 1997), 2:43–52.

76. See Robert C. Tannehill, *The Sword of His Mouth: Forceful and Imaginative Language in Synoptic Sayings* (Philadelphia: Fortress, 1975), 161–62.

77. E.g., Bock, *Luke*, 2:979.

78. Although κύριε is present in 𝔓⁴⁵, 𝔓⁷⁵, ℵ, it is omitted by B* and D. UBSGNT 4th revised edition puts it in brackets.

79. Steven C. Barton, *Discipleship and Family Ties in Mark and Matthew* (Cambridge: Cambridge University Press, 1994), 149.

80. E.g., Kenneth E. Bailey, *Through Peasant Eyes: More Lucan Parables, Their Culture and Style* (Grand Rapids: Eerdmans, 1980), 26, unnecessarily blunts the force of Jesus' aphorism.

81. See Martin Hengel, *The Charismatic Leader and His Followers* (Edinburgh: T&T Clark, 1981), 3–14.

82. Only Luke has the words, "but as for you, go, and proclaim the kingdom of God" (cf. Matt 8:21). Hengel, *Charismatic Leader*, 4, labels it a typically Lukan formula. See also Miyoshi, *Anfang*, 39–40; Schulz, *Q*, 435; Rudolf Bultmann, *The History of the Synoptic Tradition* (trans. John Marsh; 2d ed.; New York: Harper & Row, 1968), 90.

83. Tannehill, *Sword*, 163; cf. also Hengel's conclusion in *Charismatic Leader*, 14, and Craig S. Keener, *A Commentary on the Gospel of Matthew* (Grand Rapids: Eerdmans, 1999), 277.

84. Talbert, *Reading Luke*, 118; Joachim Jeremias, *The Parables of Jesus* (rev. ed.; New York: Charles Scribner's Sons, 1963), 195, describes the "dexterity and concentrated attention" needed to use the Palestinian plough.

85. The aorist is used to describe the action of taking hold of the plow (ἐπιβαλών), while the present describes his looking back (βλέπων). This reading has the support of B and A among others; some manuscripts (viz., 𝔓⁴⁵ᵛⁱᵈ, D) have present participles in both instances.

86. Other sayings and narratives concerning possessions are dealt with in chapter 6.

87. For an analysis of the meaning of ὄχλοι in Luke's central section see Minear, "Jesus' Audiences," 81–109. According to Minear, the ὄχλοι in Matthew and Mark are treated as followers of Jesus, but in Luke the ὄχλοι

form a more neutral category which, unlike ὁ λάος, has no theological significance on its own. The ὄχλοι come to hear the word and to see signs ( 4:42; 5:1, 15; 7:9; 8:8). They are distinguished from the disciples (9:10f., 18f., 37f.; 12:1). Occasionally the ὄχλοι are opponents (22:47; 23:4). Cf. also G. Lohfink, *Die Sammlung Israels: Eine Untersuchung zur lukanishcen Ekklesiologie* (Munich: Kösel, 1975), 35; C. E. Carlston, *The Parables of the Triple Tradition* (Philadelphia: Fortress, 1975), 67.

88. συνεπορεύοντο. This is a past continuous tense, emphasizing the continuation of the (spiritual) journey.

89. BDAG, "ἀποτάσσω," 123.

90. ἀποτάσσεται.

91. Thomas E. Schmidt, *Hostility to Wealth in the Synoptic Gospels* (Sheffield: JSOT Press, 1987), 152, prefers to see ἀποτάσσεται as an "aoristic present." But if this verse in any way recalls Luke 9:61–2, where ἀποτάσσω also occurs, "looking behind" is a destructive action of the spiritual life that is always possible. Green, *Luke*, 567 n. 185, understands the present tense rightly: "Luke's usage of the present indicative here . . . comports well with his overall portrait of discipleship as necessitating a particular and ongoing orientation with respect to 'all one has.'"

92. Marshall, *Luke*, 591.

93. Schmidt, *Hostility to Wealth*, 150.

94. Ibid., 150–51.

95. οὐ δύναται εἶναί μου μαθητής.

96. οὐ δύναται εἶναί μου μαθητής.

97. οὐχὶ ... ... ... εἰ δυνατός ἐστιν.

98. οὐ δύναται εἶναί μου μαθητής.

99. Cf. Martin Hengel, *The Cross of the Son of God* (SCM Press, 1986), 182: "The theological reasoning of our time shows very clearly that the particular form of the death of Jesus, the man and the messiah, represents a scandal which people would like to blunt, remove or domesticate in any way possible."

100. Marshall, *Luke*, 373 (emphasis Marshall's).

101. Gerald O'Collins, "Crucifixion," ABD 1:1207–10; Hengel, *Cross*, 91–185.

102. βαστάζει.

103. Cf. Donald R. Fletcher, "Condemned to Die: The Logion on Cross-Bearing: What Does It Mean?" *Int* 18 (1954): 156–64, at 163–64: "The condemned man on his way to execution is one for whom all the ordinary concerns, all the familiar goods of life have ceased to hold meaning."

104. Cf. Robert Tannehill, "The Lukan Discourse on Invitations (Luke 14, 7–24)," in *The Four Gospels 1992: Festschrift Frans Neirynck* (Leuven: University Press, 1992), 2:1603–1616, at 1606; Mark Allan Powell, "The Religious Leaders in Luke: A Literary-Critical Study," *JBL* 109 (1990): 93–110, at 109; Beck, *Christian Character*, 131: "The Pharisees express in concrete terms the

nature of an influence which Christians have to resist if they are to be true disciples."

105. On the scribes and Pharisees see Marcus, *Mark*, 519–27. Several scholars see the Pharisees as a literary construction. Willi Braun, *Feasting and Social Rhetoric in Luke* 14 (Cambridge: Cambridge University Press, 1995), 27–28, claims that they represent "a configuration of what Luke thinks to be objectionable moral and social values." Carolyn Osiek and David L. Balch, *Families in the New Testament World: Households and House Churches* (Louisville: Westminster John Knox, 1997), 141, argue that the Pharisees have little to do with the historical Jewish sect in Israel; rather they are a symbol for the wealthy in Luke's own culture. Also Powell, "Leaders," 93, warns against the "referential fallacy." There can be little doubt that "the NT authors use the Pharisees mainly as a negative foil for Jesus" (Steve Mason, "Pharisees," EDB, 1043–44, at 1043). There appears to be no agreement among scholars concerning the portrait of the Pharisees in Luke-Acts. Some regard Luke's presentation of the Pharisees as at least partially favorable (e.g., J. A. Ziesler, "Luke and the Pharisees," NTS 25 [1978–79] 146–57) while others view it as negative (e.g., Kingsbury). See the discussion in J. D. Kingsbury, "The Pharisees in Luke-Acts," *The Four Gospels* 1992, 2:1497–1512; David B. Gowler, *Host, Guest, Enemy and Friend: Portraits of the Pharisees in Luke and Acts* (New York: Peter Lang, 1991); Joseph B. Tyson, *Luke-Acts and the Jewish People: Eight Critical Perspectives* (Minneapolis: Augsburg, 1988); Eric Franklin, *Luke: Interpreter of Paul, Critic of Matthew* (Sheffield: JSOT Press, 1994), 174–97. Gowler concludes that the portrayal of the Pharisees in Luke-Acts is "relatively complex," 313. He criticizes Powell for tending to lump together Pharisees with other religious leaders in Luke. The position taken in this work is that the Pharisees are representative of a hidebound, pious conservatism that results in a formulaic spirituality.

106. See chapter 4 for a close reading of Luke 11:37–54 and a development of the spiritual life of the religious authorities.

107. H. Windisch, "ζύμη κτλ," TDNT 2:902–6.

108. "ὑπόκρισις," BDAG, 1038. Other definitions include: "play-acting, pretense, outward show, dissembling."

109. Contra Green, *Luke*, 480–81, who argues that play-acting is not the point of Jesus' invective: "Jesus' point is not that they are play-acting, but that Jesus regards them as misdirected in their fundamental understanding of God's purpose and, therefore, unable to present anything other than the impression of piety." But that is play-acting.

110. Powell, "Leaders," 95, identifies the two principal attributes of the Pharisees as "self-righteous" and "unloving."

111. See chapter 4 for a close reading of Luke 14.

112. "βδέλυγμα," BDAG, 172, defines βδέλυγμα as a "loathsome, detestable thing" in the sight of God.

113. φιλάργυροι occurs only in Luke as a characteristic of the Pharisees. This has spurred much debate as to its historical validity. See Moxnes, *Economy*, 1–9.

114. Moxnes, *Economy*, 1–9.

115. Ibid., 168–69.

# Notes to Chapter 3, Families and Households

1. McGrath, *Christian Spirituality*, 109.

2. S. Scott Bartchy, "Slavery (Greco-Roman)," ABD 6:65–73, at 66. For a definition of "slave" see Yvon Thébert, "The Slave," in *The Romans* (ed. Andrea Giardina; Chicago: University of Chicago Press, 1993), 138–74. See also the discussion of slavery and the bibliography of relevant sources in Warren Carter, *Households and Discipleship: A Study of Matthew 19–20* (Sheffield: JSOT Press, 1994), 175–89, esp. 176 nn. 1–3.

3. K. H. Rengstorf, "δοῦλος κτλ," TDNT 2:261–80; see 268 where δοῦλος is an honorary title given to Moses, Joshua, Abraham, David, Isaac, the prophets, and Jacob = Israel as the people of God.

4. κυριεύω. Peter K. Nelson, *Leadership and Discipleship: A Study of Luke 22:24–30* (Atlanta: Scholars Press, 1994), 148–50, argues that κυριεύω is not used negatively ("lord over" as in NRSV) but neutrally ("rule over").

5. εὐεργεταί. See Frederick W. Danker, *Benefactor: Epigraphic Study of a Graeco-Roman and New Testament Semantic Field* (St. Louis: Clayton, 1982), on benefaction in the ancient world.

6. Carolyn Osiek and David L. Balch, *Families in the New Testament World: Households and House Churches* (Louisville: Westminster John Knox, 1997), 205.

7. Luke uses ὁ διακονῶν ("the one who serves") for table servant, which raises the question whether a "servant" is different from a "slave" (δοῦλος). Nelson, *Leadership*, 40–44, argues that servanthood and slavery "come together to a degree" and that no "bold line" should be drawn between servant and slave. Mary Ann Beavis, "Ancient Slavery as an Interpretive Context for the New Testament Servant Parables with Special Reference to the Unjust Steward (Luke 16:1–8)," JBL 111 (1992): 37–54, at 40, makes the point that δοῦλος in the NT should be translated as "slave" and not "servant." Arland J. Hultgren, *The Parables of Jesus: A Commentary* (Grand Rapids: Eerdmans, 2000), 474, concludes: "In spite of the risks of using the term 'slave' as a translation for the Greek term in a North American context, it is, in the end, preferable to the term 'servant' in the case of the parables."

8. Cf. Moxnes, *Economy*, 158.

9. This diagram is found in Nelson, *Leadership*, 133; idem, "The Flow of Thought in Luke 22:24–27," JSNT 43 (1991): 113–221, at 117; and Osiek and Balch, *Families*, 205.

10. καλοῦνται may be either passive (as NRSV) or middle. See arguments in Nelson, *Leadership*, 153–54. Green, *Luke*, 768 and Nolland, *Luke*, 3:1064,

prefer the middle ("call themselves benefactors" or "let themselves be called" or "have themselves called").

11. Contra David J. Lull, "The Servant-Benefactor as a Model of Greatness (Luke 22:24–30)," NovT 28 (1986): 289–305, who argues that the disciples are in fact to follow the positive example of benefactors. Nelson, Leadership, 132–36, offers a critique of Lull's position.

12. ὁ νεώτερος has the force of the superlative; the youngest is obliged to perform the lowliest service (cf. Acts 5:6). See BDAG, "νέος," 669.

13. Green, Luke, 769. On the role of the young and servants see Nelson, Leadership, 36–44, 155–58.

14. οὐχί expects a positive response.

15. Hermann W. Beyer, "διακονέω κτλ," TDNT 2:81–93, at 84.

16. Moxnes, Economy, 158: "Greatness is not to be transformed into privilege and power."

17. Ibid., 158–59; Carter. Households, 189–92, emphasizes the egalitarian aspects of "voluntary marginality" (i.e., slavery).

18. David L. Tiede, "The Kings of the Gentiles and the Leader Who Serves: Luke 22:24–30," WW 12 (1992): 23–28, offers a commentary on this passage for the modern, Western context.

19. Lane, Solace of Fierce Landscapes, 188–89. See also Harvey D. Egan, "Indifference," in A Dictionary of Christian Spirituality (ed. Gordon S. Wakefield; London: SCM, 1983), 211–13; George E. Ganss, "Detachment," in The New Dictionary of Catholic Spirituality (Collegeville, Minn.: Liturgical, 1993), 269–70; Michael Casey, "Apatheia," in The New Dictionary of Catholic Spirituality (Collegeville, Minn.: Liturgical, 1993), 50–51.

20. περιεζωσμέναι. The perfect participle implies a state of continual preparation.

21. H. Seesemann, "ὀσφύς," TDNT 5:496–97, at 496; Evald Lövestam, Spiritual Wakefulness in the New Testament (Lund: GWK Gleerup, 1963), 93–94.

22. On clothing as a metaphor for one's spiritual state see chapter 5.

23. ὑμῶν.

24. Plummer, Luke, 330.

25. In Mark 13:33–37, the doorkeeper is to stay awake whereas Luke envisions all the slaves waiting for the master to return.

26. A. J. Mattill Jr., Luke and the Last Things: A Perspective for the Understanding of Lukan Thought (Dillsboro, N.C.: Western North Carolina Press, 1979), 87. J. Dominic Crossan, In Parables: The Challenge of the Historical Jesus (New York: Harper & Row, 1973), 99, finds the setting "mildly humorous." "There is the inference that the returning master will need even more assistance, and, therefore, preparatory watchfulness, the later the hour at which he seeks to find the door, or the house, or maybe even the village."

27. Lövestam, Spiritual Wakefulness, 135, draws a similar conclusion: "The believers stand perpetually in danger of being spiritually weighed down in this age, of being weakened in their obedience and their eschatological

expectation, of concentrating themselves on the present and being stifled in their spiritual life (in Christ), of 'going to sleep' in 'the night.'"

28. Alfons Weiser, *Die Knechtsgleichnisse der synoptischen Evangelien* (Munich: Kösel, 1971), 219, believes that Luke changed δοῦλος in Q (cf. Matt 24:45) to οἰκονόμος. In this way, the parable is directed to the leaders of the community. Cf. also Ellis, *Luke*, 181; Dale B. Martin, *Slavery as Salvation: The Metaphor of Slavery in Pauline Christianity* (New Haven; Yale University Press, 1990), 53.

29. διχοτομέω. Only here and in the parallel passage in Matt 24:51.

30. Fitzmyer, *Luke*, 2:986.

31. δοῦλον.

32. Weiser, *Knechtsgleichnisse*, 108–10, views, 17:8 as editorial.

33. περιζωσάμενος.

34. Beavis, "Ancient Slavery," 41. The question, "which of you . . ." expects a negative answer. See Crossan, *Parables*, 107.

35. The NRSV translate ἀχρεῖος as "worthless," i.e., of no use or profit. However, a better translation is "unworthy," i.e., being unworthy of any praise. The slave is useful but not worthy of special favor or praise. See BDAG, "ἀχρεῖος," 160.

36. Michael P. Knowles, "'Everyone Who Hears These Words of Mine': Parables on Discipleship (Matt 7:24–27//Luke 6:47–49; Luke 14:28–33; Luke 17:7–10; Matt 20:1–16)," in *The Challenge of Jesus' Parables* (ed. Richard N. Longenecker; Grand Rapids: Eerdmans, 2000), 286–305, at 295. By assuming that 17:10 is secondary, Paul S. Minear, "A Note on Luke 17:7–10," JBL 93 (1974): 82–7, misses the unexpected twist of the parable.

37. Jeremias, *Parables*, 193; Marshall, *Luke*, 645; Green, *Luke*, 614–15.

38. In 17:1, the disciples are addressed while in 17:5 the apostles are spoken to. These are not identical groups in Luke. (I am indebted to Weiser, *Knechtsgleichnisse*, 118–19, for the following summary.) The ἀπόστολοι are selected out of the group of disciples (6:13) and they represent an inner group of disciples (9:10; 22:14; 24:10) with the exception of 11:49. The μαθηταί can refer to (1) all those who follow Jesus or are closely connected with him (6:17; 19:37, 39); (2) an inner circle of disciples who may be identical with the apostles (so perhaps 8:9, 22; 9:14, 16, 18, 40, 43, 54; 10:23 [?]; 18:15; 19:29) or they may be different from the apostles (so perhaps 6:20; 20:45) or the relation with the apostles may be ambiguous (so perhaps 5:30; 6:1; 7:11; 11:1; 12:1, 22; 14:26, 27, 33; 16:1; 17:22); (3) a circle that is expressly different from the disciples (6:13; 17:5); (4) the inner group of disciples, the apostles (22:11, 39, 45). Cf. also Minear, "A Note," 83, on the audiences.

39. This is a reworking of Knowles, "Everyone," 297, concerning Israel.

40. μνᾶ, equivalent to 100 drachmas, was about three months' wages for a laborer.

41. πραγματεύσασθε, a NT *hapax legomenon*, implies that the slaves are to trade with the one pound while the nobleman is absent. See BDAG, "πραγματεύομαι," 859.

42. William R. Herzog II, *Parables as Subversive Speech: Jesus as Pedagogue of the Oppressed* (Louisville: Westminster John Knox, 1994), 167.

43. πονηρὲ δοῦλε. He is wicked because of his disobedience; Fitzmyer, *Luke*, 2:1237.

44. Scott, *Hear*, 234.

45. Nolland, *Luke*, 3:919.

46. James H. Moulton and George Milligan, *The Vocabulary of the Greek New Testament: Illustrated from the Papyri and Other Non-Literary Sources* (Grand Rapids: Eerdmans, 1930), "αὐστηρός," 93. BDAG, "αὐστηρός," 151–2: the "imagery of a tough uncompromising, punctilious financier."

47. Dan O. Via Jr., *The Parables: Their Literary and Existential Dimension* (Philadelphia: Fortress, 1967), 118–19: "In the fear of the one-talent man we see the anxiety of one who will not step into the unknown. He will not risk trying to fulfill his own possibilities; therefore, his existence is circumscribed in the narrowest kind of way. Action is paralyzed by anxiety, and the self of our protagonist is only a shadow of what it potentially is."

48. Fred B. Craddock, *Luke: Interpretation, A Bible Commentary for Teaching and Preaching* (Louisville: John Knox, 1990), 223, identifies the pound or talent as the spread of the word.

49. E.g., Carter, *Households*, 90–114, at 97.

50. Fitzmyer, *Luke*, 2:1193.

51. Thomas Wiedemann, *Adults and Children in the Roman Empire* (New Haven: Yale University Press, 1989), 176: "Classical society relegated children, together with women, old men, and slaves, to the margins of community life." See also the discussion of children in Carter, *Households*, 95–113; A. Oepke, "παῖς κτλ," TDNT 5:636–54; G. Braumann and C. Brown, "Child," NIDNTT 1:280–85; Joseph A. Grassi, "Child, Children," ABD 1:904–7, at 905; Beryl Rawson, "Children in the Roman Familia," in *The Family in Ancient Rome: New Perspectives* (Ithaca: Cornell University Press, 1986), 170–200; idem, "Adult-Child Relationships in Roman Society," in *Marriage, Divorce, and Children in Ancient Rome* (Oxford: Oxford University Press, 1991), 7–30; J. Kodell, "Luke and the Children: The Beginning and End of the Great Interpolation (Luke 9:46–56; 18:9–23)," CBQ 49 (1987): 415–30; James Francis, "Children and Childhood in the New Testament," in *The Family in Theological Perspective* (ed. Stephen Barton; Edinburgh: T & T Clark, 1996), 65–85; Keener, *Gospel of Matthew*, 448.

52. On this practice see Rawson, "Children," 172.

53. τὰ βρέφη. In 18:16 Jesus calls them τὰ παιδία, "little children."

54. Evans, *Luke*, 647.

55. The kingdom belongs to τῶν τοιούτων, "such ones as these," which implies that the children are representatives of those to whom the kingdom belongs.

56. ὡς παιδίον.

57. See Green, *Luke*, 651 n. 131, for the following interpretations.

58. νήπιοι. See Bernadicou, "Spirituality," 460–63, on Luke 10:21–24.

59. Evans, *Luke*, 648.

60. Fitzmyer, *Luke* 1:817.

61. Luke has one woe and five stories that involve widows: 20:47 (par. Mark 12:40), 21:1–4 (par. Mark 12:41–44), 2:25–26, 4:25–26, 7:11–17, 18:1–8.

62. Kathleen S. Nash, "Widow," EDB, 1377–78, at 1377.

63. See Deut 10:18; 24:17; 27:19; Ps 146:9; Isa 10:2; cf. G. Stählin, "χήρα," TDNT 9:440–65, at 445.

64. Ringe, *Luke*, 250. Cf. also Addison G. Wright, "The Widow's Mites: Praise or Lament?—A Matter of Context," CBQ 44 (1982): 256–65; Green, *Luke*, 728–29; Fitzmyer, *Luke*, 2:1320–21; S. John Roth, *The Blind, the Lame, and the Poor: Character Types in Luke-Acts* (Sheffield: JSOT Press, 1997), 202–5; Joel Green, "Good News to Whom? Jesus and the 'Poor' in the Gospel of Luke," in *Jesus of Nazareth: Lord and Christ: Essays on the Historical Jesus and New Testament Christology* (ed. by Joel B. Green and Max Turner; Grand Rapids: Eerdmans, 1994), 59–74, at 67.

65. Elizabeth Struthers Malbon, *In the Company of Jesus: Character in Mark's Gospel* (Louisville: Westminster John Knox, 2000), 176, concludes that Wright's interpretation is "more ingenious than convincing."

66. Roth, *Blind, Lame, Poor*, 205 (emphasis mine). Nolland, *Luke*, 3:979, provides several other reasons for rejecting Wright's interpretation: 1) other traditions (Greek, Jewish, Buddhist) have stories that valorize the small gift of the poor over the extravagant gifts of the rich; 2) the Lukan Jesus is in favor of the temple and its worship (see Anna, 2:36–8); and 3) the *corban* tradition, though in Mark, is not found in Luke.

67. Turid Karlsen Seim, *The Double Message: Patterns of Gender in Luke-Acts* (Nashville: Abingdon, 1994), 245.

68. πάντα τὸν βίον in 21:4 Noted by Malbon, *In the Company of Jesus*, 176, although Mark 12:44 is slightly different: ὅλον τὸν βίον αὐτῆς.

69. The word for poverty, ὑστέρημα, is used in contrast to abundance and means "need, want, deficiency." See BDAG, "ὑστέρημα," 1044.

70. Either she is 84 years old or she has been a widow for 84 years; if the latter, she would be approximately the same age as Judith (105 in Jdt 16:23). For 84 years as a widow, see J. K. Elliott, "Anna's Age (Luke2: 36–37)," NovT 30 (1988): 100–102.

71. Anna is often compared with Judith, whose long widowhood was dedicated to God (Jdt 11:17).

72. For fasting as a plea to God in the OT, see Ezra 8:21–23; Dan 9:3; 6:16–24. See the section in chapter 4 on "fast."

73. See the section in this chapter on "children."

74. Luke 18:6 characterizes him as "the judge of unrighteousness" (ὁ κριτὴς τῆς ἀδικίας).

75. These are most likely negative, not positive characteristics. See Edwin D. Freed, "The Parable of the Judge and the Widow (Luke 18.1–8)," NTS 33 (1987): 38–60, at 42; Ben Witherington III, *Women in the Ministry of Jesus: A Study of Jesus' Attitudes to Women and their Roles as Reflected in His Earthly Life* (Cambridge: Cambridge University Press, 1984), 37. Hedrick, *Parables*, 187–207, attempts to find redeeming characteristics in the judge, but his ironic reading of the parable is unconvincing. He makes this "thoroughly honest," "impartial" judge the victim and the widow an "aggressive" abuser who physically threatens to beat him up. The fear of violence (ὑπωπιάζω = "to give a black eye" in 18:5) is the judge's assessment, not necessarily the woman's intent. Hedricks's interpretation, like Roth's victimization of the widow in Luke 21, places the widow in the role of abuser rather than abused.

76. Cf. Stählin, "χήρα," 450 n. 86.

77. Luise Schottroff, *Lydia's Impatient Sisters: A Feminist Social History of Early Christianity* (trans. Barbara and Martin Rumscheidt; Louisville: Westminster John Knox, 1995), 101–4.

78. See Herzog, *Parables*, 225, for other OT passages with similar concerns.

79. Herzog, *Parables*, 230, also sees her as "active and aggressive"; Freed, "Judge and Widow," 51, sees the unrighteous judge as a foil to underscore the persistence of the widow, who is the main character in the story.

80. ἐπὶ χρόνον answers the questions, "How long?" See BDAG, "ἐπί," 363 §18c.

81. Freed, "Judge and Widow," 50, notes that εἰς τέλος can be translated "in the end," "finally," "decisively," "completely," "forever," "continually," "to the end." The present tenses—"keep bothering" and "wear out"—"imply the meaning 'continually' in the sense of a repeated action." So also BDF §207.3.

82. BDAG, "ὑπωπιάζω," 1043.1. Stählin, "χήρα," 450 n. 88, favors this translation. J. Duncan M. Derrett, "Law in the New Testament: The Parable of the Unjust Judge," in *Studies in the New Testament*, (2 vols.; Leiden: Brill, 1977, 1978), 1:32–47, at 43–5, argues that it means "to blacken the face," "to disgrace." Ringe, *Luke*, 224; Nolland, *Luke*, 2:868; and Marshall, *Luke*, 673, adopt this interpretation. However, a sense of shame is an unlikely nuance because the judge demonstrates no concern for others and, therefore, is unlikely to be concerned with the loss of reputation.

83. Scott, *Hear*, 183, notes that she does not address him as "Sir."

84. Ibid.

85. ἐκδίκησόν με. Luke follows the forensic usage: to "procure justice." G. Schrenk, "ἐδικέω κτλ," TDNT 2:442–46, at 444.

86. Freed, "Judge and Widow," 45; Fitzmyer, *Luke*, 2:1179; ἤρχετο is an iterative imperfect that is translated in NRSV as "she kept coming."

87. *qal wahomer* or *a minori ad maius*.

88. Bailey, *Through Peasant Eyes*, 137, draws the wrong conclusion from the *a fortiori* argument: "If this woman's needs are met, *how much more* the needs of the pious who pray not to a harsh judge but to a loving Father." Cf. Seim, *Double Message*, 244 n. 177: "Even if an inference *a minore ad maius* is to be drawn from the unworthy judge to the much greater, that is God, this does not necessarily imply a similar inference from the widow to the disciples. . . ."

89. Hultgren, *Parables*, 258.

90. Cf. John R. Donahue, *The Gospel in Parable: Metaphor, Narrative, and Theology in the Synoptic Gospels* (Philadelphia: Fortress, 1988), 184: "This parable is rife with reversal and paradox. The widow, who from the OT evokes the image of the powerless and vulnerable victim of more powerful people, while here a subject of injustice, is hardly powerless and vulnerable."

91. Herzog, *Parables*, 228; Green, *Luke*, 640; Bailey, *Through Peasant Eyes*, 134–35.

92. Osiek and Balch, *Families*, 136, 143.

93. Moxnes, *Kingdom Takes Place*, 201.

94. Ibid., Luke's is the only Gospel to emphasize that leaving behind family structures is for the sake of the kingdom of God.

95. Tannehill, *Sword*, 146.

96. Marshall, *Luke*, 549.

97. Tannehill, *Sword*, 146.

98. Cf. Dennis M. Sweetland, *Our Journey with Jesus: Discipleship according to Luke-Acts* (Collegeville, Minn.: Liturgical, 1990), 144: "The radical nature of Christian discipleship demands that no thing or person, or even one's spouse, be allowed to stand in one's way of allegiance to Jesus. It is not inevitable that this will happen, as elsewhere the Lukan Jesus speaks about the permanency of marriage (Luke 16:18), but should it happen one's relationship to Jesus must be preferred."

99. Parataxis is a style in which members within a sentence or a sequence of complete sentences are put together with "and." See Abrams, *Glossary*, 204.

100. μισέω.

101. E.g., Robert H. Stein, "Luke 14:26 and the Question of Authenticity," *Forum* 5 (1989): 187–92, at 188; T. W. Manson, *The Sayings of Jesus: As Recorded in the Gospels according to St. Matthew and St. Luke Arranged with Introduction and Commentary* (London; SCM Press, 1949), 131: "In the Old Testament (e.g. Gen 29:31ff.; Dt. 21:15ff.) 'love' and 'hate' stand side by side in contexts where it is obvious that 'hate' is not to be taken in the literal sense, but in the sense 'love less.'" BDAG, "μισέω," 652.2 translates it as "disfavor, disregard in contrast to preferential treatment (Gn 29:31; Dt 21:15, 16)," but "leave behind" is closer to the meaning in 14:26 and 16:13. See the argument in Schmidt, *Hostility to Wealth*, 126–27. Schmidt cites Prov 1:29–30 where "hate" means "to reject": "Because they hated knowledge and did not choose the fear of the Lord, would have none of my counsel, and despised all my reproof."

102. Discussed in Schmidt, *Hostility to Wealth*, 126–27.

103. Otto Michel, "μισέω," TDNT 4:683–94, at 690–91.

104. Mark 10:30: "houses and brothers and sisters and mothers and children and lands. . . ."

105. πολλαπλασίονα means "many times as much, manifold." So BDAG, "πολλαπλασίων," 846.

106. Frank Kermode, *The Sense of an Ending: Studies in the Theory of Fiction with a New Epilogue* (New York: Oxford University Press, 2000).

107. Kermode, *Sense*, 44–45.

108. Kermode, *Sense*, 45.

109. See Tannehill, *Sword*, 118–22.

110. The parallel passage in Matt 24:37–39 lacks the rhythmic cadences of asyndeton.

111. Seim, *Double Message*, 209.

112. Tannehill, *Sword*, 121.

113. Seim, *Double Message*, 209.

114. See Barton, *Discipleship and Family Ties*, 78–79; Philip F. Esler, *Community and Gospel in Luke-Acts: The Social and Political Motivations of Lucan Theology* (Cambridge: Cambridge University Press, 1987), 118; Seim, *Double Message*, 66–67. Raymond Brown, *Mary in the New Testament* (Philadelphia: Fortress, 1978), 168, translates "those" resumptively: "My mother and my brothers—these are the ones who hear the word of God and do it." So also Fitzmyer, *Luke*, 1:722–25. Although it is a possible translation, Tannehill, *Narrative Unity*, 1:212–13, gives reasons for rejecting it.

115. Beverly Roberts Gaventa, *Mary: Glimpses of the Mother of Jesus* (Columbia, S.C.: University of South Carolina Press, 1995), 71. Brown, *Mary*, 168, sees Jesus' mother and brothers as meeting the criterion for inclusion in the spiritual family, but the text is ambiguous.

116. The adversative conjunction μενοῦν is used to correct or modify a foregoing statement. See BDF §450 (4); Moule, *Idiom Book*, 163, translates it as "Nay rather . . ." On the other hand, Brown, *Mary*, 171, understands it as "Yes, but even more." But the contrast is not between Mary as mother and Mary as model disciple, for the plural is used in 11:28. See Tannehill, *Narrative Unity*, 1:213.

117. Green, *Luke*, 461.

118. Nolland, *Luke*, 2:821–22; Marshall, *Luke*, 631; Bock, *Luke*, 2:1357.

119. Seim, *Double Message*, 223.

120. Ibid., 224.

# Notes to Chapter 4, Meals

1. Dennis E. Smith, "Table Fellowship as a Literary Motif in the Gospel of Luke," JBL 106 (1987): 613–38, at 633. On meals see also Dennis E. Smith,

"Table Fellowship," ABD 6:302–4; Moxnes, *Economy*, 127–38; Jerome H. Neyrey, "Ceremonies in Luke-Acts: The Case of Meals and Table Fellowship," in *The Social World of Luke-Acts: Models for Interpretation* (ed. Jerome H. Neyrey; Peabody, Mass.: Hendrickson, 1991), 361–87; Robert J. Karris, *Luke: Artist and Theologian: Luke's Passion Account as Literature* (New York: Paulist, 1985), 47–78; Heil, *Meal Scenes*; Just, *Ongoing Feast*; Esler, *Community and Gospel*, 71–109; Osiek and Balch, *Families*, 45–46; Nelson, *Leadership*, 62–74; Navone, *Themes*, 11–37.

2. On joy as a distinctive theme in Lucan spirituality see William Morrice, *Joy in the New Testament* (Exeter: Paternoster, 1984); Navone, *Themes*, 71–87; Robert F. O'Toole, *The Unity of Luke's Theology: An Analysis of Luke-Acts* (Wilmington, Del.: Michael Glazier, 1984), 225–60. Barton, *Spirituality*, 74, calls joy "one of the most distinctive aspects of Lucan spirituality."

3. Halvor Moxnes, "Meals and the New Community in Luke," SEÅ 51 (1986): 158–67, at 162.

4. On tax collectors see Otto Michel, "τελώνης," TDNT 8:88–105; St-B 1:378–79; John R. Donahue, "Tax Collectors and Sinners: An Attempt at Identification," CBQ 33 (1971): 39–61; Fritz Herrenbrück, *Jesus und die Zöllner: Historische und neutestamentlich-exegetische Untersuchungen* (Tübingen: J. C. B. Mohr [Paul Siebeck], 1990).

5. δοχὴν μεγάλην. Cf. also in Luke 14:13.

6. ἐγόγγυζον. A cognate verb (διαγογγύζειν) is used in 15:2; 19:7.

7. K. H. Rengstorf, "ἁμαρτωλός κτλ," TDNT 1:317–35, at 327–28.

8. Green, *Luke*, 247; Neale, *None But the Sinners*, 127, makes the point that the text does not tell us why the Pharisees were offended.

9. For a close reading of this narrative, see Resseguie, "Automatization and Defamiliarization," 137–50. For alternative perspectives see Judith K. Applegate, "'And She Wet His Feet with Her Tears': A Feminist Interpretation of Luke 7.36–50," in *Escaping Eden: New Feminist Perspectives on the Bible* (ed. Harold C. Washington, Susan Lochrie Graham and Pamela Thimmes; New York: New York University Press, 1999), 69–90, and Teresa J. Hornsby, "Why Is She Crying? A Feminist Interpretation of Luke 7.36–50," in ibid., 91–103.

10. For an extended discussion of "sinner," see Neale, *None but the Sinners*, 68–97; Kathleen E. Corley, *Public Women, Public Meals: Social Conflict in the Synoptic Tradition* (Peabody, Mass.: Hendrickson, 1993), 89–93.

11. James Malcolm Arlandson, *Women, Class, and Society in Early Christianity: Models from Luke-Acts* (Peabody, Mass.: Hendrickson, 1997), 162.

12. κατεφίλει.

13. ἤλειφεν.

14. αὕτη δέ.

15. Although it was not essential for a host to provide water, oil, and a kiss, these acts would be especially welcomed after a long journey. Simon's failure is not that he acted discourteously, but that he extended no *especial* acts of hospitality to Jesus. Clearly, Jesus expected more (7:44–46) than

Simon offered. See L. Goppelt, "ὕδωρ," TDNT 8:314–33, at 323–24; Bruce J. Malina, "Hospitality," HBD, 408–9; Seim, *Double Message*, 94.

16. The pronoun is in the emphatic position (though not an emphatic pronoun). Jesus says, "I entered into *your* house" (εἰσῆλθόν σου εἰς τὴν οἰκίαν), 7:44. See Gowler, *Host, Guest, Enemy*, 225.

17. John A. Darr, *On Character Building: The Reader and the Rhetoric of Characterization in Luke-Acts* (Louisville: Westminster John Knox, 1992), 102, refers to Simon's "grudging treatment of Jesus" as "spiritual blindness caused by religious bigotry. . . ."

18. οὗτος is contemptuous. See Plummer, *Luke*, 211.

19. Barbara E. Reid, *Choosing the Better Part? Women in the Gospel of Luke* (Collegeville, Minn.: Liturgical, 1996), 107–23.

20. Ibid., 123: "In the narrative, Simon's ability to perceive Jesus correctly rested on his ability to change how he saw the woman."

21. Green, *Luke*, 312–13.

22. στραφεὶς πρὸς τὴν γυναῖκα. Green, *Luke*, 288, notes that "Luke generally speaks of Jesus' 'turning' to speak in order to add emphasis to Jesus' statement." He cites as examples 7:9, 44; 9:55; 10:23; (22:61?); 23:38.

23. στᾶσα ὀπίσω in 7:38.

24. Contra Green, *Luke*, 312, who views the turning as "momentarily reduc[ing] her [i.e., the woman] from the role of central actor to that of object lesson." On the contrary, Jesus' turning recognizes her as a person in her own right.

25. How should ὅτι be translated? If it is translated as "because" then the woman's love is the basis of forgiveness; if it is translated as "hence" or "for," then the woman's love is evidence of her forgiveness. With most modern commentators, I understand ὅτι to be evidential, not causal. For a discussion of 7:47 see Fitzmyer, *Luke*, 1:692; John J. Kilgallen, "John the Baptist, the Sinful Woman, and the Pharisee," JBL 104 (1985): 675–79; Nolland, *Luke*, 1:358–59; Zerwick, *Biblical Greek*, §422; John J. Donahue, "The Penitent Woman and the Pharisee: Luke 7:36–50," *American Ecclesiastical Review* 142 (1960): 414–21 argues that her actions are the condition of her pardon; also Joël Delobel, "Lk 7,47 in its Context: An Old Crux Revisited," in *The Four Gospels 1992: Festschrift Franz Neirynck* (Leuvan: University Press, 1992), 2:1581–90. Witherington, *Women*, 56, follows Moule and argues that ὅτι may be causal if it modifies λέγω and not ἀφέωνται. The translation would be: "I can say with confidence that her sins are forgiven, *because* her love is evidence of it." See the discussion in Moule, *Idiom Book*, 147.

26. E. Springs Steele, "Luke 11:37–54—A Modified Hellenistic Symposium?" JBL 103 (1984): 379–94 argues that 11:37–54, like Luke 7:36–50 and 14:1–24, is modeled on a Hellenistic symposium.

27. Cf. Osiek and Balch, *Families*, 141, on this issue: "Modern Christians must deplore that the author chose the Pharisees as a negative model

of leadership, a choice that has had utterly disastrous consequences over centuries for how Christians have understood and treated Jews. Historically, the Pharisees represent Christian leaders in Luke's own churches (see, e.g., Acts 15:5), but the literary choice has had lethal consequences for Jews in subsequent centuries."

28. On the custom of washing of hands before and after meals see Str-B 1:695–704. However, handwashing is not a biblical requirement. See E. P. Sanders, *Jewish Law from Jesus to the Mishnah: Five Studies* (Philadelphia: Trinity Press International, 1990), 203–4, and 228–31.

29. BDAG, "ἁρπαγή," 133, translates ἁρπαγή as "rapacity."

30. Cf. Darr, *Characterization*, 104: "Their unhealthy preoccupation with 'how things look' is exactly the cause of their inability to *see* things for what they actually are."

31. Green, *Luke*, 469; Gowler, *Host, Guest, Enemy*, 234–35.

32. John H. Elliott, "Temple versus Household in Luke-Acts: A Contrast in Social Institutions," in *The Social World of Luke-Acts: Models for Interpretation* (Peabody, Mass.: Hendrickson, 1991), 211–40, at 221–22.

33. See Bruce J. Malina and Richard L. Rohrbaugh, *Social-Science Commentary on the Synoptic Gospels* (Minneapolis: Fortress, 1992), 318–20.

34. Moxnes, *Economy*, 111; David B. Gowler, "Hospitality and Characterization in Luke 11:37–54: A Socio-Narratological Approach," *Semeia* 64 (1993): 213–51, at 230.

35. πονηρία.

36. πονηρός.

37. See Susan R. Garrett, "'Lest the Light in You Be Darkness': Luke 11:33–36 and the Question of Commitment," JBL 110 (1991): 93–105, at 103.

38. Moxnes, *Economy*, 34–35.

39. τὰ ἐνόντα. Does this refer to the inside of vessels, or rapacity and wickedness? It makes more sense to take the referent as rapacity and wickedness.

40. Moxnes, *Economy*, 114; cf. also David P. Seccombe, *Possessions and the Poor in Luke-Acts* (Linz: Fuchs, 1983), 182–86.

41. Green, *Luke*, 471; idem, *Theology of Luke*, 114.

42. More specifically, Gowler, "Hospitality and Characterization," 232, refers to it as "vertical generalized reciprocity," "a redistribution from the advantaged to the disadvantaged that expects nothing in return."

43. On Luke 14 as a symposium see Smith, "Table Fellowship," 617–20; X. de Meeûs, "Composition de Lc., XIV et genre symposiaque,' ETL 37 (1961): 847–70; Willi Braun, *Feasting and Social Rhetoric*. On the ideological point of view of Luke 14 see James L. Resseguie, "Point of View in the Central Section of Luke (9:51–19:44)," JETS 25 (1982): 41–47.

44. Literally, the "first seat" (πρωτοκλισίαν).

45. The use of the divine passive (ταπεινωθήσεται, ὑψωθήσεται) indicates that God does the action of exalting and humbling in 14:11.

46. It is not just a characteristic of the Pharisees. Braun, *Feasting and Social Rhetoric*, 45–46, shows the widespread concern with seating arrangements in ancient Near Eastern, Greek, and Roman societies.

47. ἀνταπόδομα.

48. ἀνταποδοῦναι.

49. ἀνταποδοθήσεται.

50. Moxnes, "Meals," 164. Roth, *Blind, Lame, Poor*, 181, notes that Jesus applies only one character trait in this parable to the poor, maimed, and blind: "they lack the capacity to reciprocate generosity (14:14)."

51. Navone, *Themes*, 30, refers to the feasts as the world's banquet and the heavenly banquet.

52. The expectation of an end-time feast is well documented in the OT. See Isa 25:6–8; 55:1–2; 65:13–14; cf. 1 Enoch 62:14; 25:5; 2 Baruch 29:4–8. Str-B 4:1145–46, 1163, cite rabbinic passages.

53. BDF §241 (6) suggests that ἀπὸ μιᾶς means "unanimously, with one accord."

54. Some note the similarity between the excuses and the excuses for conscription for war in Deut 20:5–7; 24:5. See J. Duncan M. Derrett, *Law in the New Testament* (London: Darton, Longman & Todd, 1970), 126–55; Evans, *Luke*, 574; Paul H. Ballard, "Reasons for Refusing the Great Supper," *JTS* 23 (1972): 341–50; J. A. Sanders, "The Ethic of Election in Luke's Great Banquet Parable," in *Essays in Old Testament Ethics* (ed. J. L. Crenshaw and J. T. Willis; New York: KTAV, 1974), 245–71. Humphrey Palmer, "Just Married, Cannot Come," *NovT* 18 (1976): 241–57, notes that the connection, if it exists, is humorous: in battles people are killed whereas people usually survive dinner parties.

55. ὀργισθείς, 14:21.

56. Cf. Richard L. Rohrbaugh, "The Pre-Industrial City in Luke-Acts: Urban Social Relations," in *The Social World of Luke-Acts: Models for Interpretation* (ed. Jerome H. Neyrey; Peabody, Mass.: Hendrickson, 1991), 125–49, at 144–45: "These final guests are not, as is frequently assumed, country people. . . . Instead, those just outside the walls usually included ethnic groups, tanners, and traders (along with the more commonly noted beggars and prostitutes), many of whom would have had business in the city (serving the needs of the elite) that required proximity to it. But they were not allowed to live inside the city walls."

57. ἀνάγκασον εἰσελθεῖν.

58. Braun, *Feasting and Social Rhetoric*, 98–131.

59. Ibid., 130.

60. Ibid., 131.

61. E.g., Green, *Luke*, 554–63; Heil, *Meal Scenes*, 106–111. Also see the favorable reviews of Steven Muir in *NovT* 38 (1996): 408–9; Maureen Moran in *BibInt* 71 (1999): 450–53; and Robert Tannehill in *Bib* 77(1996): 564–67.

62. See the critique by Robert O'Toole in *CBQ* 59 (1997): 149–50.

63. Robert H. Stein, *An Introduction to the Parables of Jesus* (Philadelphia: Westminster, 1981), 83–84 places the stress on the banquet itself, but this is hardly illuminating.

64. Green, *Luke*, 557, attempts to shift the question to "who will be repaid at the resurrection?" But that is a different question answered in another parable (Luke 14:12–14).

65. Green, *Luke*, 559. To various degrees this is also the view of Gowler, *Host, Guest, Enemy*, 247; Braun, *Feasting and Social Rhetoric*, 75–80; Rohrbaugh, "The Pre-Industrial City," 142–43.

66. Gowler, *Host, Guest, Enemy*, 247.

67. John O. York, *The Last Shall Be First: The Rhetoric of Reversal in Luke* (Sheffield: JSOT Press, 1991), 142; Nolland, *Luke*, 2:758: "These people have the kind of preoccupations with the material affairs of life that, in Luke's view, can be a most serious trap . . . , or the kind of attachment to family relationships that cripples the possibility of any costly, committed stance. . . ."

68. Esler, *Community and Gospel*, 179.

69. Ringe, *Luke*, 199.

70. The poor, crippled, blind, and lame are not invited (καλέω) but brought in (εἰσάγω), and those outside the city are actually compelled (ἀναγκάζω).

71. Nolland, *Luke*, 3:1054–55; Green, *Luke*, 762.

72. On the salvific significance of this meal see Heil, *Meal Scenes*, 165–98; Green, *Luke*, 761–64.

73. This is one of the few places where the term "apostles," not "disciples," is used in Luke (cf. also Luke 6:13; 9:10; [11:49]; 17:5; 24:10). See also chapter 3, note 38.

74. Luke 19b–20 is omitted by D. For arguments supporting the longer reading see Kobus Petzer, "Style and Text in the Lucan Narrative of the Institution of the Lord's Supper (Luke 22.19b–20)," NTS 37 (1991): 113–29.

75. See chapter 3, pp. 46–48 for a discussion of Luke 22:24–27.

76. Green *Luke*, 762.

77. Malina and Rohrbaugh, *Social-Science Commentary*, 318. On fasting in the New Testament see Joseph F. Wimmer, *Fasting in the New Testament: A Study in Biblical Theology* (New York: Paulist, 1982); John Muddiman, "Fast, Fasting," ABD 2:773–76; Daniel L. Smith-Christopher, "Fasting," EDB, 456.

78. Malina and Rohrbaugh, *Social-Science Commentary*, 318.

79. Green, *Luke*, 151.

80. Moxnes, "Meals," 161.

81. Bruce J. Malina, *Christian Origins and Cultural Anthropology: Practical Models for Biblical Interpretation* (Atlanta: John Knox, 1986), 200.

82. It is not certain who these critics are since Luke says, "they said to him." Tannehill, *Narrative Unity*, 1:174, believes that the critics are the scribes and Pharisees mentioned in 5:30.

83. Cf. Manson, *Sayings*, 255: "Jesus [in 5:39] says that a great obstacle to the reception of new revelation is the *pietas* of religious people." Cf. also Plummer, *Luke*, 164; Fitzmyer, *Luke*, 1:597.

84. Green, *Luke*, 250, sees Jesus as the one who brings the old wine and not the new. See also Talbert, *Reading Luke*, 65; R. S. Good, "Jesus, Protagonist of the Old, in Lk 5:33–39," *NovT* 25 (1983): 19–36; David Flusser, "Do You Prefer New Wine? *Immanuel* 9 (1979): 26–31; A. H. Mead, "Old and New Wine: St Luke 5:39," *ExpT* 99 (1988): 234–35. However, Nolland, *Luke*, 1:244, notes that the inappropriate behavior in 5:33 and 37–39 involves a preference for the old, not the new.

85. Although omitted by D and other Western manuscripts, it is included in a wide distribution of texts.

86. These new expressions of spirituality take the form of table fellowship with "tax collectors and sinners."

87. Alistair Kee, "The Old Coat and the New Wine: A Parable of Repentance," *NovT* 12 (1970): 13–21, argues that the point of the parable is the danger of loss.

88. Fitzmyer, *Luke*, 1:601.

89. Elizabeth Schüssler Fiorenza, "A Feminist Critical Interpretation for Liberation: Martha and Mary: Lk. 10:38–42," *Religion and Intellectual Life* 3 (1986): 21–36, at 32, concludes that "Lk. 10:38–40 pits the apostolic women of the Jesus movement against each other and appeals to the revelatory word of the resurrected Lord in order to silence women leaders of housechurches who like Martha might have protested, and at the same time to extol the silent and subordinate behavior of Mary." A similar interpretation is adopted by Robert M. Price, *The Widow Traditions in Luke-Acts: A Feminist-Critical Scrutiny* (Atlanta: Scholars Press, 1997), 175–90. But see the responses to Schüssler Fiorenza in *Center for Hermeneutical Studies in Hellenistic and Modern Culture* 53 (1986): 13–38.

90. The reading εἰς τὴν οἰκίαν or εἰς τὸν οἶκον is not adopted in the UBSGNT, 4th rev. ed. However, it is clear that Jesus enters the house of the sisters. See Seim, *Double Message*, 98.

91. ὑποδέχομαι means to "entertain as a guest." See BDAG, "ὑποδέχομαι," 1037.

92. The word is Warren Carter's. See "Getting Martha out of the Kitchen: Luke 10:38–42 Again," *CBQ* 58 (1996): 264–80, at 276.

93. περὶ πολλήν.

94. περὶ πολλά.

95. The verse is textually uncertain but the case for "one" (ἐνός) is strong in terms of intrinsic and external evidence. See Marshall, *Luke*, 453; Bruce M. Metzger, *Textual Commentary on the Greek New Testament* (2d ed.; New York: United Bible Societies, 1994), 129. Gordon D. Fee, " 'One Thing is Needful', Luke 10:42," in *New Testament Textual Criticism: Its Significance*

*for Exegesis* (ed. Eldon J. Epp and Gordon D. Fee; Oxford: Clarendon, 1981), 61–75, argues for a longer reading: "a few things are necessary or one."

96. Twice used by the narrator (10:39, 41) and once by Martha (10:41).

97. Jutta Brutscheck, *Die Maria-Marta-Erzählung: Eine redaktionskritische Untersuchung zu Lk 10,38–42* (Frankfurt am Mein: Peter Hanstein, 1986), 42–43, notes the alliteration, ἀδελφή μου; μόνην με; μοι, which emphasizes her self-absorbed posture.

98. Cf. Green, *Luke*, 437: "Though she refers to him as 'Lord,' she is concerned to engage his assistance in her plans, not to learn from his."

99. μεριμνᾷς and θορυβάζῃ. BDAG, "θορυβάζω," 458 translates as "be troubled/distracted."

100. The doubling of vocatives is characteristic of Luke. He doubles, "Master, Master"; "Simon, Simon"; "crucify, crucify him." See Cadbury, *Making of Luke-Acts*, 218.

101. Heil, *Meal Scenes*, 75–76 notes the alliteration.

102. BDAG, "περισπάω," 804.2 translates as "to have one's attention directed from one thing to another, *become or be distracted, quite busy, overburdened.*"

103. μεριμνῶν.

104. μεριμνᾶτε.

105. μερίμναις.

106. Alliteration reinforces Mary's choice: Μαριὰμ . . . μερίδα.

107. Green, *Luke*, 437.

# Notes to Chapter 5, Clothing

1. Luke has several words for clothing: ἱματισμός ("clothing"), in 7:25; 9:29; ἱμάτιον ("cloak, robe, clothing," the most common word for clothing), in 5:36; 6:29; 7:25; 8:27, 44; 19:35, 36; 22:36; 23:34; ἐσθής ("clothing"), in 23:11; 24:4; χιτών ("tunic, shirt"), in 3:11; 6:29; 9:3; σινδών ("linen cloth"), in 23:53; and βύσσος ("fine linen"), in 16:19.

2. On clothing in the ancient world see Douglas R. Edwards, "Dress and Ornamentation," ABD 2:232–38; Gildas Hamel, *Poverty and Charity in Roman Palestine, First Three Centuries* C.E. (Berkeley: University of California Press, 1990), chapter 2; Jerome H. Neyrey, "The Symbolic Universe of Luke-Acts: 'They Turn the World Upside Down,'" in *The Social World of Luke-Acts: Models for Interpretation* (ed. Jerome H. Neyrey; Peabody, Mass.: Hendrickson, 1991), 271–304, at 283–85; Karris, *Luke: Artist and Theologian*, 85–87; Barbara E. Reid, *The Transfiguration: A Source- and Redaction-Critical Study of Luke 9:28–36* (Paris: J. Gabalda, 1993), 112–15; Edgar Haulotte, *Symbolique du Vêtement selon la Bible* (Paris: Aubier, 1966); J. M. Myers, "Dress and Ornaments," IDB 1:869–71; Joseph E. Jensen, "Clothing," EDB, 265–66. On clothing in the book of Revelation, see Resseguie, *Revelation Unsealed*, 41–42.

3. Only Luke notes that the man had no clothes (cf. Mark 5:2–3; Matt 8:28).

4. στολὴν τὴν πρώτην.

5. Fitzmyer, *Luke*, 2:1090; U. Wilckens, "στολή," TDNT 7:687–91, at 690.

6. Green, *Luke*, 583, recognizes that the clothing signifies "honorable restoration to the family he had snubbed and abandoned," but fails to see the spiritual significance of the father's lavish gifts.

7. ἐνδύσησθε.

8. ἐνδύειν.

9. Evans, *Luke*, 926: it "inspires their intelligent and confident speech (Acts 4:8, 31, 33; 5:32; 6:5, 10; 7:55), invests them with divine authority (Acts 5:3, 9; 8:14ff.; 15:28), and directs their purposeful movements (Acts 8:29; 10:19f.; 11:24f.; 13:2–4; 16:6–7; 20:22f.)."

10. ἐσπαργάνωσεν.

11. τὸ σημεῖον.

12. On the practice of wrapping a baby in swaddling clothes see Malina and Rohrbaugh, *Social-Science Commentary*, 296–97.

13. φάτνη is a feeding trough, not a stall. See M. Hengel, "φάτνη," TDNT 9:49–55.

14. Fitzmyer, *Luke*, 1:410 (emphasis mine).

15. Belden C. Lane, *Landscapes of the Sacred: Geography and Narrative in American Spirituality* (New York: Paulist, 1988), 39.

16. Lane, *Landscapes of the Sacred*, 39.

17. Green, *Luke*, 380.

18. λευκὸς ἐξαστράπτων.

19. Hamel, *Poverty and Charity*, 81.

20. Ibid.

21. Ibid., 84.

22. BDAG, "ἐξαστράπτω," 346. Mark 9:3 has "his clothes became dazzling white, such as not one on earth could bleach them." Matt 17:2 has "his clothes became dazzling white." A related word, ἀστράπτω, occurs in Luke 24:4 to describe the "dazzling white" garments of the two men at the tomb.

23. Luke uses a continuous tense (ὑπεστρώννυον) to emphasize the ongoing reception by the disciples.

24. τὸ ἱμάτιον.

25. Hamel, *Poverty and Charity*, 71.

26. Ibid.

27. The NRSV adds "people," presumably referring to the large group of disciples that traveled with Jesus.

28. Evans, *Luke*, 679.

29. ἐσθῆτα λαμπράν.

30. Hamel, *Poverty and Charity*, 86; also Evans, *Luke*, 853; Fitzmyer, *Luke*, 2:1482.

31. BDAG, "λαμπρός," 585.3.

32. On the carnivalesque attitude in general see Mikhail Bakhtin, *Problems of Dostoevsky's Poetics* (Minneapolis: University of Minnesota Press, 1984), 122–25; on the carnivalesque scene in Luke see Brawley, *Text to Text*, 42–60.

33. σινδών.

34. τὰ οθόνια.

35. μόνα.

36. Although D omits this verse, 𝔓⁷⁵ and ℵ include it.

37. Hamel, *Poverty and Charity*, 79.

38. Luke uses βύσσος, not σινδών, to describe his inner garment.

39. On the social significance of clothing for Americans' identity see Jenna Weissman Joselit, *A Perfect Fit: Clothes, Character, and the Promise of America* (New York: Metropolitan/Henry Holt, 2001). See also Alison Lurie, *The Language of Clothes* (New York: Random House, 1981); Anne Hollander, *Seeing Through Clothes* (New York: Viking, 1978).

40. ἐν μαλακοῖς ἱματίοις.

41. ἐν ἱματισμῷ.

42. Hamel, *Poverty and Charity*, 76–78; Green, "Good News to Whom?" 67.

43. ἐν στολαῖς.

44. For a close reading of this parable see chapter 6.

45. Scott, *Hear*, 150.

46. εἰλκωμένος.

47. Hamel, *Poverty and Charity*, 64.

48. ἐβέβλητο.

49. Luke uses a continuous tense, μὴ ζητεῖτε, "do not keep striving" (12:29), when he warns the disciples against anxiety.

50. See Tannehill, *Sword*, 60–67.

51. ὀλιγόπιστοι.

52. Cf. Luke 15:22; Hamel, *Poverty and Charity*, 75–76.

53. Although this is addressed to the disciples, it was originally for the seventy.

54. Hamel, *Poverty and Charity*, 68.

55. Ibid., 76.

56. Ibid., 68.

57. Nolland, *Luke*, 1:427.

58. Hamel, *Poverty and Charity*, 69.

59. Green, *Luke*, 359; Fitzmyer, *Luke*, 1:752.

60. Evans, *Luke*, 396.

61. τὸ ἱμάτιον.

62. τὸν χιτῶνα.

63. Moxnes, *Economy*, 34–35; 127–38; 174; Neyrey, "Ceremonies in Luke-Acts," 372; Green, *Luke*, 202, 270.

64. BDAG, "ἱμάτιον," 475.2; Hans Dieter Betz, *The Sermon on the Mount: A Commentary on the Sermon on the Mount, including the Sermon on the Plain* (Minneapolis: Fortress, 1995), 597.

65. Moxnes, *Economy,* 34–35; 127–38; 174; Neyrey, "Ceremonies in Luke-Acts," 372; Green, *Luke,* 202, 270.

66. Betz, *Sermon on the Mount,* 597.

67. Ibid.,

68. For the importance of the temple in Luke, see Klaus Baltzer, "The Meaning of the Temple in Lukan Writings," HTR 58 (1965): 263–77; Francis D. Weinert, "The Meaning of the Temple in Luke-Acts," BTB 11 (1981): 85–89; Michael Bachmann, *Jerusalem und der Tempel: Die geographisch-theologischen Elemente in der lukanischen Sicht des jüdischen Kultzentrums* (Stuttgart: W. Kohlhammer, 1980); Esler, *Community and Gospel,* 131–63.

69. κατεπέτασμα.

70. Cf. Green, *Luke,* 825; Nolland, *Luke,* 3:1156.

71. Brown, *Death of the Messiah,* 2:1042.

72. See, for example, Dennis D. Sylva, "The Temple Curtain and Jesus' Death in the Gospel of Luke," JBL 105 (1986): 239–50; Nolland, *Luke,* 3:1157–58, catalogs the various interpretations. For a refutation of Sylva's position, see Brown, *Death of the Messiah,* 2:1104–6; Joel B. Green, "The Death of Jesus and the Rending of the Temple Veil (Luke 23:44–49): A Window into Luke's Understanding of Jesus and the Temple," *in* SBLSP (Atlanta: Scholars Press, 1991), 543–57.

73. Sylva, "The Temple Curtain," 239 n. 2.

74. Luke does not have Mark 14:58: "I will destroy this temple that is made with hands, and in three days I will build another, not made with hands."

75. See Green, *Luke,* 826.

76. The divine passive is used ("was torn"), indicating that God is doing the action.

## Notes to Chapter 6, Consumption

1. George Ritzer, *Enchanting a Disenchanted World: Revolutionizing the Means of Consumption* (Thousand Oaks, Calif.: Pine Forge, 1999), x; idem, *The McDonaldization of Society* (Thousand Oaks, Calif.: Pine Forge, 2000). For a thoroughgoing critique of consumerism in America see Juliet B. Schor, *The Overspent American: Upscaling, Downshifting, and the New Consumer* (New York: Basic, 1998); idem, "Do Americans Shop Too Much?" (Boston: Beacon, 2000). I am indebted to Ritzer and Schor for the rest of this chapter.

2. See Robert D. Manning, *Credit Card Nation: The Consequences of America's Addiction to Credit* (New York: Basic, 2000).

3. Schor, "Shop," 9.

4. Ibid., 8.

5. The "Diderot effect" is named after an eighteenth-century French philosopher, Denis Diderot, who wrote an essay in 1772, "Regrets on Parting With My Old Dressing Gown." Diderot was given a new, elegant scarlet robe

that clashed with the shabby surroundings of his study, destroying the pleasant harmony of his study. "The harmony is destroyed. Now there is no more consistency, no more unity, and no more beauty" (311). To make his surroundings conform to "the imperious scarlet robe," he replaced his rough wooden table with an "expensive and pretentious desk"; his cheap Bergamo tapestry with new damask wall covering; his old straw chair with an armchair covered with Morocco leather, and so forth. The "Diderot effect" is thus an academic, if not marketing, term for the creation of a constellation of desire that feeds and supports consumption. See Denis Diderot, "Regrets On Parting with My Old Dressing Gown," in *Rameau's Nephew and Other Works* (trans. Jacques Barzun and Ralph H. Bowen; Indianapolis: Bobbs-Merrill, 1964); cf. also James B. Twitchell, *Lead Us into Temptation: The Triumph of American Materialism* (New York: Columbia University Press, 1999), 198–200.

6. The phrase "conspicuous consumption" was coined over a century ago by Thorstein Veblen, *The Theory of the Leisure Class* (1899; repr., Amherst, N.Y.: Prometheus, 1998). See Meeks, *God the Economist*, 157–80, for a response to the "joylessness" of conspicuous consumption and the "harriedness" of today's leisure class.

7. ὑδρωπικός is a *hapax legomenon*.

8. Braun, *Feasting and Social Rhetoric*, 30–8.

9. Storbaeus, *Florilegium* 3.10.45; cited by Braun, *Feasting and Social Rhetoric*, 34.

10. Plutarch, *Moralia* 524A-D; cited by Braun, *Feasting and Social Rhetoric*, 35.

11. This is not to say that Luke intended the dropsical man as a symbol of avarice, as Braun contends. I only suggest that dropsy is an appropriate metaphor for excessive consumption.

12. Cf. Schmidt, *Hostility to Wealth*, 146.

13. BDAG, "πλεονεξία," 824: "the state of desiring to have more than one's due, *greediness, insatiableness, avarice, covetousness.*"

14. Life is ζωή. Green, *Luke*, 486 n.26, says it refers "generally to the human being as a holistic entity and qualitatively to the human being with respect to his or her relationship to God."

15. Luke 12:15b is obscure, but the general sense is that possessions and life stand in opposition.

16. For the social implications of the farmer's decision see Green, *Luke*, 490–91. See also Bruce J. Malina, *The New Testament World: Insights from Cultural Anthropology* (3d ed., Louisville: Westminster John Knox, 2001), 81–107, on the concept of "limited good."

17. Cf. Meeks, *God the Economist*, 176: "He . . . falsely assumed that his property was meant to fulfill his own needs, thereby violating God's lordship and his own role as a responsible steward."

18. εὐφορέω, (Luke 12:16, *hapax legomenon*, means "to produce unusually well, bear good crops, yield well, be fruitful." See BDAG, "εὐφορέω," 414.

19. Scott, *Hear*, 135, interprets differently: "The rich man usurps the narrator's control of the story, replacing him in the story. The rich man now fully controls his own narrative. He not only is the subject of the narration but is also the narrator."

20. Charles Hedrick, *Parables as Poetic Fictions: The Creative Voice of Jesus* (Peabody, Mass.: Hendrickson, 1994), 159, dismisses the accumulation of first person possessives as "quite natural in the context of a soliloquy." However, he misses the importance of a soliloquy versus other types of narration: interior dialogue brings the self to the foreground and makes for "a more memorable psychological portrait." See Philip Sellew, "Interior Monologue as a Narrative Device in the Parables of Luke," JBL 111 (1992): 239–53, at 245.

21. All are second-person singular imperatives.

22. Asyndeton is the omission of conjunctions that ordinarily join coordinate words or clauses.

23. This is the only parable in which God enters directly as a character.

24. Nolland, *Luke*, 2:688.

25. Herman Hendrickx, *The Parables of Jesus* (San Francisco: Harper & Row, 1986), 106.

26. Ibid., 104

27. Commentators frequently refer to the LXX definition of fool as one who denies the existence of God (cf. Ps 14:1).

28. Sondra Ely Wheeler, *Wealth as Peril and Obligation: The New Testament on Possessions* (Grand Rapids: Eerdmans, 1995), 71.

29. E.g., Marshall, *Luke*, 632–39.

30. Richard Bauckham, "The Rich Man and Lazarus: The Parable and the Parallels," NTS 37 (1991): 225–46, at 232.

31. λαμπρῶς, a *hapax legomenon*, which BDAG, "λαμπρῶς," 585, translates as "splendidly" or "sumptuously" every day.

32. See chapter 5 on clothing as a potential indicator of one's spiritual condition.

33. Cf. Herzog, *Parables* , 121: "The gate clearly functions in the opening scene as a boundary marker; it shuts out Lazarus and symbolizes the social barrier between the elites and the expendables."

34. Bernard Brandon Scott, *Hear Then the Parable: A Commentary on the Parables of Jesus* (Minneapolis: Fortress, 1989), 152.

35. Nolland, *Luke*, 2:828.

36. ἐβέβλητο is pluperfect passive.

37. Hades (Sheol) is the abode of the dead. See BDAG, "ᾅδης," 19; Joachim Jeremias, "ᾅδης," TDNT 1:146–49, at 148.

38. Luke uses the divine passive: "has been fixed (ἐστήρικται)."

39. κόλπος suggests a place of intimacy or a place of honor for a guest at a banquet (see John 13:23). See Rudolf Meyer, "κόλπος," TDNT 3:824–26; Str-B 2:225–27. Herzog, *Parables*, 121, offers other suggestions.

40. Herzog, *Parables*, 123.

41. Contra Herzog, *Parables*, 120, who contends that "Lazarus was beyond redemption through patronage."

42. The theme of rich and poor is well covered territory in Luke. For literature see John R. Donahue, "Two Decades of Research on the Rich and Poor in Luke-Acts," in *Justice and the Holy: Essays in Honor of Walter Harrelson* (ed. Douglas A. Knight and Peter J. Paris; Atlanta: Scholars Press, 1989), 129–44, and the annotated bibliography in John Gillman, *Possessions and the Life of Faith: A Reading of Luke-Acts* (Collegeville, Minn.: Liturgical, 1991), 118–20. See Mark Allan Powell, *What Are They Saying About Luke?* (New York: Paulist, 1989), 97–101, for a summary of several views on rich and poor in Luke. Powell concludes from his survey of works by Hans Degenhardt, Luke Johnson, Walter Pilgrim, and David Seccombe that the consensus among scholars is that "Luke's concern over the use of possessions is just that: a concern," but he "does not provide a specific agenda for its resolution" (David P. Seccombe, *Possessions and the Poor in Luke-Acts* [Linz: Fuchs, 1983], 100–101).

43. For a modern-day appeal to frugality see James A. Nash, "On the Subversive Virtue: Frugality," *Ethics of Consumption: The Good Life, Justice, and Global Stewardship* (ed. David A. Crocker and Toby Linden; New York: Rowman & Littlefield, 1998), 416–36.

44. ἀρχιτελώνης is found only here in Greek literature, which complicates its meaning. Gillman, *Possessions*, 89, suggests that Zacchaeus "was probably the district manager responsible for collecting taxes for a geographical area with assistant tax collectors working under him."

45. καὶ ἦν αὐτὸς ἀρχιτελώνης καὶ αὐτὸς πλούσιος. See Robert C. Tannehill, "The Story of Zacchaeus as Rhetoric: Luke 19:1–10," *Semeia* 64 (1994): 201–11.

46. Alan C. Mitchell, "Zacchaeus Revisited: Luke 19,8 as a Defense," *Bib* 71 (1990): 153–76, argues that Zacchaeus may have extorted some inadvertently, but Dennis Hamm, "Zacchaeus Revisited Once More: A Story of Vindication or Conversion?" *Bib* 72 (1991): 249–52, at 249, wonders how extortion can be an inadvertent act. Marshall, *Luke*, 698, translates the conditional, "from whomsoever I have wrongfully exacted anything."

47. τῇ ἡλικίᾳ μικρὸς ἦν.

48. ἀνέβη.

49. κατέβη.

50. δεῖ indicates the necessity of staying at Zacchaeus's house in order to fulfill Jesus' mission to save the lost. See Cosgrove, "The Divine ΔΕΙ," 168–90.

51. σήμερον in Luke indicates the immediacy of salvation (cf. 2:11; 4:21).

52. χαίρων.

53. William P. Loewe, "Towards an Interpretation of 19:1–10," CBQ 36 (1974): 321–31, at 330.

54. This is a *crux interpretum* of the story. The NRSV translates as a futuristic present, indicating a present resolve, δίδωμι, "I will give." Those who interpret the verb as a customary present, "I give (as is my custom)" include D. A. S. Ravens, "Zacchaeus: The Final Part of a Lucan Triptych?" JSNT 41 (1991): 19–32; Mitchell, "Zacchaeus Revisited," 153–76; Fitzmyer, *Luke*, 2:1221, 1225; Green, *Luke*, 671–72; Richard C. White, "Vindication for Zacchaeus?" *ExpT* 91 (1979–80) 21; idem, "A Good Word for Zacchaeus? Exegetical Comment on Luke 19:1–10," LTQ 14 (1979): 89–96; Gillman, *Possessions*, 90. Those who argue for a futuristic present include Neale, *None but the Sinners*, 187; Hamm, "Zacchaeus Revisited," 249–52; idem, "Luke 19:8 Once Again: Does Zacchaeus Defend or Resolve?" JBL 107 (1988): 431–37; Tannehill, "Story of Zacchaeus," 203. Hamm has effectively refuted the points of those who favor a customary present.

55. Also considered by many to be a futuristic present or present resolve, ἀποδίδωμι, "I will pay back."

56. Cf. Green, *Luke*, 671 n. 208: "Fourfold restitution is by almost any reckoning excessive; cf. Exod 22:1; Lev 6:5; Num 5:6–7; 2 Sam 12:6"; cf. also "τετραπλοῦς," EDNT 3:353.

57. Neither Mark 10:21 nor Matt 19:21 has Luke's "all" (πάντα).

58. περίλυπος means "very sad, deeply grieved"; BDAG, "περίλυπος," 802.

59. πλούσιος σφόδρα. Cf. Evans, *Luke*, 652: "The man's upset was the greater in proportion to the greatness of his wealth."

60. εἰσελθεῖν.

61. εἰσελθεῖν.

62. Bailey, *Through Peasant Eyes*, 165–66, provides arguments against the attenuation of the camel/needle comparison.

63. Moxnes, *Economy*, 119.

64. Tannehill, *Narrative Unity*, 1:120–22, refers to it as a "quest story."

65. τὰ ἴδια is literally "(our) own things."

66. The literature on this parable is staggering. For histories of interpretation see Douglas M. Parrott, "The Dishonest Steward (Luke 16:1–8a) and Luke's Special Parable Collection," NTS 37 (1991): 499–515; William Loader, "Jesus and the Rogue in Luke 16,1–8a: The Parable of the Unjust Steward," RB 96 (1989): 518–32; Dennis J. Ireland, *Stewardship and the Kingdom of God: An Historical, Exegetical, and Contextual Study of the Parable of the Unjust Steward in Luke 16:1–13* (Leiden: Brill, 1992), 5–47; M. Krämer, *Das Rätsel der Parabel vom ungerechten Verwalter, Lk 16,1–13* (Zurich: PAS, 1972).

67. Cf. Walter E. Pilgrim, *Good News to the Poor: Wealth and Poverty in Luke-Acts* (Minneapolis: Augsburg, 1981), 129: "We conclude that the parable of the Dishonest Steward and its sequel are interpreted by Luke as a summons to free oneself from the bondage of mammon and to participate boldly in

the worldly service of making friends with your wealth." Cf. also Green, *Luke*, 229: "Wealth masters if it is not mastered," and idem, *Theology of Luke*, 148.

68. Herzog, *Parables*, 236; Jeremias, *Parables*, 45–8. Evans, *Luke*, 597, argues that the unit should be interpreted backwards, starting with 16:13.

69. "Dishonest" is a characteristic of this age in contrast to the age to come. Wealth is dishonest because it has the allure of this age and the power to turn one away from God. The "iniquitous seduction of mammon . . . enslave[s] those who pursue it and leads to forms of dishonesty": So Fitzmyer, *Luke*, 2:1109. See also Green, *Luke*, 593, and Seccombe, *Possessions*, 163–69.

70. The Greek has only "the master," not "his master." But the NRSV has correctly interpreted ὁ κύριος in 16:8a as a reference to the steward's master and not to Jesus himself. See Manson, *Sayings of Jesus*, 292; J. Fitzmyer, "The Story of the Dishonest Manager (Lk 16:1–13)," TS 25 (1964): 23–42, at 27–28.

71. τὸν οἰκονόμον τῆς ἀδικίας.

72. ἐκ τοῦ μαμωνᾶ τῆς ἀδικίας. μαμωνᾶς is an Aramaic word for wealth or property: BDAG, "μαμωνᾶς," 614. Of the word's four NT occurrences, three are found in this parable (16:9, 11, 13).

73. ἄδικος.

74. ἄδικος.

75. ἐν τῷ ἀδίκῳ μαμωνᾷ.

76. δέχομαι; Green, *Luke*, 591.

77. διασκορπίζω, also found in Luke 15:13, means "waste, squander": BDAG, "διασκορπίζω," 236.

78. Noted by Richard H. Hiers, "Friends by Unrighteous Mammon: The Eschatological Proletariat (Luke 16:9),"JAAR 38 (1970): 30–36, at 32. John S. Kloppenborg, "The Dishonoured Master (Luke 16,1–8a)," Bib 70 (1989): 474–94, at 475, also considers 16:9 to be a commentary on the steward's plan in 16:4; cf. also Seccombe, *Possessions*, 163.

79. ἵνα ὅταν . . . δέξωνταί με εἰς τοὺς οἴκους αὐτῶν.

80. ἵνα ὅταν . . . δέξωνται ὑμᾶς εἰς τὰς αἰωνίους σκηνάς.

81. How is the steward able to cancel a portion of the farmers' bill? J. Duncan M. Derrett, "The Parable of the Unjust Steward," in *Law in the New Testament* (London: Darton, Longman & Todd, 1970), 48–77, argues that the steward made usurious loans to the clients and when he was to be dismissed, he rebated the debtors the interest on the loans. Fitzmyer, "The Story of the Dishonest Manager," 23–42, argues somewhat the same. However, the interest on the loans was the steward's own commission which he cancelled. Green, *Luke*, 592 n. 272, provides reasons why Derrett's and Fitzmyer's interpretations are implausible. Kloppenborg, "The Dishonoured Master," 481–86, offers additional arguments against Derrett and Fitzmyer.

82. Moxnes, *Economy*, 141–42.

83. δέξωνται.

84. δέξαι.

85. δέξαι.

86. δέξωνται.

87. "Eternal dwellings," αἱ αἰώνιοι σκηναί, appears to be used positively as the ultimate home of the righteous rather than in a negative way as the abode of the unrighteous. See Hiers, "Friends," 31.

88. Moxnes, *Economy*, 142.

89. Hiers, "Friends," 33, shows the parallelisms between 16:9 and 12:33, and even considers 12:33 "a variant rescension [sic]" of 16:9. L. John Topel, "On the Injustice of the Unjust Steward: Lk 16:1–13," CBQ 37 (1975): 216–27, at 220–21, also argues that giving alms to the poor is the proper interpretation. Donald R. Fletcher, "The Riddle of the Unjust Steward: Is Irony the Key?" JBL 82 (1963): 15–30, at 25 calls the steward's actions "self-interested philanthropy [that] stands in jarring contrast to the general tone of Jesus' teaching." It is doubtful, however, that giving alms can be consider "self-interested philanthropy" when the only options available to an individual are either to control wealth or be controlled by wealth. If one wants to serve God, then wealth must be dethroned.

90. ποιήσατε ἑαυτοῖς.

91. ἀνέκλειπτον.

92. ἑαυτοῖς ποιήσατε.

93. ἐκλίπῃ.

94. Kyoung-Jin Kim, *Stewardship and Almsgiving in Luke's Theology* (Sheffield: JSOT Press, 1998), 155–56.

95. Moxnes, *Economy*, 146.

96. The NRSV translates it as "when it is gone." BDAG, "ἐκλείπω," 306.3, translates it as "fail, die out."

97. It is uncertain who "they" are. They may be: 1) the angels, as a circumlocution for God (Marshall, *Luke*, 621–22); 2) the recipients of the alms (Hiers, "Friends," 34–36; or 3) almsdeeds personified (Francis E. Williams, "Is Almsgiving the Point of the 'Unjust Steward'?" JBL 83 (1964): 293–97, at 295).

98. Fletcher, "Riddle," 29, reads 16:9 as an ironical saying of Jesus: "'Make friends for yourselves,' he seems to taunt; 'imitate the example of the steward; use the unrighteous mammon; surround yourselves with the type of insincere, self-interested friendship it can buy; how far will this carry you when the end comes and you are finally dismissed?'" However, for irony to work, there must be clues in the text that the saying is to be taken ironically. Fletcher offers no satisfactory clues.

99. Hendrickx, *Parables*, 194. Cf. also Luke T. Johnson, *Sharing Possessions: Mandate and Symbol of Faith* (Philadelphia: Fortress, 1981), 64: "It is the self-aggrandizing use of money which renders it idolatrous."

# Bibliography

Abrams, M. H. A *Glossary of Literary Terms*. 6th ed. Fort Worth: Harcourt Brace College Publishers, 1993.

Applegate, Judith K. "'And She Wet His Feet with Her Tears': A Feminist Interpretation of Luke 7.36–50." Pages 69–90 in *Escaping Eden: New Feminist Perspectives on the Bible*. Edited by Harold C. Washington, Susan Lochrie Graham and Pamela Thimmes. New York: New York University Press, 1999.

Arlandson, James Malcolm. *Women, Class, and Society in Early Christianity: Models from Luke-Acts*. Peabody, Mass.: Hendrickson, 1997.

Bachmann, Michael. *Jerusalem und der Tempel: Die geographisch-theologischen Elemente in der lukanishen Sicht des jüdischen Kultzentrums*. Stuttgart: W. Kohlhammer, 1980.

Bailey, Kenneth E. *Poet and Peasant: A Literary Cultural Approach to the Parables in Luke*. Grand Rapids: Eerdmans, 1976.

———. *Through Peasant Eyes: More Lucan Parables, Their Culture and Style*. Grand Rapids: Eerdmans, 1980.

Bakhtin, Mikhail. *Problems of Dostoevsky's Poetics*. Edited and translated by Caryl Emerson. Minneapolis: University of Minnesota Press, 1984.

Ballard, Paul H. "Reasons for Refusing the Great Supper." *Journal of Theological Studies* 23 (1972): 341–50.

Baltzer, Klaus. "The Meaning of the Temple in the Lukan Writings." *Harvard Theological Review* 58 (1965): 263–77.

Balz, Horst, and Günther Wanke. "φοβέω κτλ." Pages 189–219 in vol. 9 of *Theological Dictionary of the New Testament*. Edited by G. Kittel and G. Friedrich. Translated by G. W. Bromiley. 10 vols. Grand Rapids: Eerdmans, 1964–1976.

Barbour, R. S. "Gethsemane in the Tradition of the Passion." *New Testament Studies* 16 (1969–70): 231–50.

Bartchy, S. Scott. "Slavery (Greco-Roman)." Pages 65–73 in vol. 6 of *Anchor Bible Dictionary*. Edited by D. N. Freedman. 6 vols. New York: Doubleday, 1992.

Barton, Stephen. *Discipleship and Family Ties in Mark and Matthew*. Cambridge: Cambridge University Press, 1994.

———. *The Spirituality of the Gospels*. Peabody, Mass.: Hendrickson, 1992.

Bauckham, Richard. "Jesus and the Wild Animals (Mark 1:13): A Christological Image for an Ecological Age." Pages 3–21 in *Jesus of Nazareth: Lord and Christ: Essays on the Historical Jesus and New Testament Christology*. Edited by Joel Green and Max Turner. Grand Rapids: Eerdmans, 1994.

———. "The Rich Man and Lazarus: The Parable and the Parallels." *New Testament Studies* 37 (1991): 225–46.

Beavis, Mary Ann. "Ancient Slavery as an Interpretative Context for the New Testament Servant Parables with Special Reference to the Unjust Steward (Luke 16:1–8)." *Journal of Biblical Literature* 111 (1992): 37–54.

Beck, Brian E. *Christian Character in the Gospel of Luke*. London: Epworth, 1989.

———. "'Imitatio Christi' and the Lucan Passion Narrative." Pages 28–47 in *Suffering and Martyrdom in the New Testament: Studies Presented to G. M. Styler by the Cambridge New Testament Seminar*. Edited by William Horbury and Brian McNeil. Cambridge: Cambridge University Press, 1981.

Bernadicou, Paul J. "The Spirituality of Luke's Travel Narrative." *Review for Religious* 36 (1977): 455–66.

Betz, Hans Dieter. *The Sermon on the Mount: A Commentary on the Sermon on the Mount, including the Sermon on the Plain*. Minneapolis: Fortress, 1995.

Beyer, Hermann W. "διακονέω κτλ." Pages 81–93 in vol. 2 of *Theological Dictionary of the New Testament*. Edited by G. Kittel and G. Friedrich. Translated by G. W. Bromiley. 10 vols. Grand Rapids: Eerdmans, 1964–1976.

Blass, F., and A. Debrunner. *A Greek Grammar of the New Testament and Other Early Christian Literature*. Translated and revised by Robert W. Funk. Chicago: University of Chicago Press, 1961.

Blinzler, J. "Die literarische Eigenart des sogenannten Reiseberichts im Lukasevangelium." Pages 20–52 in *Synoptische Studien*. Edited by J. Schmid and A. Vögtle. München: Karl Zink, 1953.

Blomberg, Craig L. "Midrash, Chiasmus, and the Outline of Luke's Central Section." Pages 217–61 in *Gospel Perspectives. III. Studies in Midrash and Historiography*. Edited by R. T. France and D. Wenham. Sheffield: JSOT Press, 1983.

Bock, Darrell L. *Luke*. 2 vols. Grand Rapids: Baker Books, 1994, 1996.

Bovon, François. *Luke 1: A Commentary on the Gospel of Luke 1:1–9:50*. Minneapolis: Fortress, 2002.

Braumann, G., and C. Brown. "Child." Pages 280–85 in vol. 1 of *New International Dictionary of New Testament Theology.* Edited by C. Brown. 4 vols. Grand Rapids: Zondervan, 1975–1979.

Braun, Willi. *Feasting and Social Rhetoric in Luke 14.* Cambridge: Cambridge University Press, 1995.

Brawley, Robert L. *Text to Text Pours Forth Speech: Voices of Scripture in Luke-Acts.* Bloomington: Indiana University Press, 1995.

Brown, Raymond. *The Death of the Messiah: From Gethsemane to the Grave.* 2 vols. New York: Doubleday, 1994.

———, ed. *Mary in the New Testament.* Philadelphia: Fortress, 1978.

Brown, Schuyler. *Apostasy and Perseverance in the Theology of Luke.* Rome: Pontifical Biblical Institute, 1969.

Brun, Lyder. "Engel und Blutschweiss Lc 22,43–44." *Zeitschrift für die neutestamentliche Wissenschaft und die Kunde der älteren Kirche* 32 (1933): 265–76.

Brutscheck, Jutta. *Die Maria-Marta-Erzählung: Eine redaktionskritische Untersuchung zu Lk 10,38–42.* Frankfurt am Mein: Peter Hanstein, 1986.

Bultmann, Rudolf. *The History of the Synoptic Tradition.* Translated by John Marsh. 2d ed. New York: Harper & Row, 1968.

Cadbury, Henry J. *The Making of Luke-Acts.* London: SPCK, 1958.

Caird, G. B. *The Gospel of St. Luke.* Baltimore: Penguin, 1963.

Carter, Warren. "Getting Martha out of the Kitchen: Luke 10:38–42 Again." *Catholic Biblical Quarterly* 58 (1996): 264–80.

———. *Households and Discipleship: A Study of Matthew 19–20.* Sheffield: JSOT Press, 1994.

Casey, Michael. "Apatheia." Pages 50–51 in *The New Dictionary of Catholic Spirituality.* Edited by Michael Downey. Collegeville, Minn.: Liturgical, 1993.

Cave, C. H. "Lazarus and the Lukan Deuteronomy." *New Testament Studies* 15 (1968–69): 319–25.

Chatman, Seymour. *Story and Discourse: Narrative Structure in Fiction and Film.* Ithaca: Cornell University Press, 1978.

Cohn, Robert L. *The Shape of Sacred Space: Four Biblical Studies.* Chico, Calif.: Scholars Press, 1981.

Conzelmann, Hans. *The Theology of St. Luke.* Translated by G. Buswell. New York: Harper & Row, 1960.

Corley, Kathleen E. *Public Women, Public Meals: Social Conflict in the Synoptic Tradition.* Peabody, Mass.: Hendrickson, 1993.

Cosgrove, Charles H. "The Divine ΔEI in Luke-Acts: Investigations into the Lukan Understanding of God's Providence." *Novum Testamentum* 26 (1984): 168–90.

Craddock, Fred B. *Luke.* Interpretation: A Bible Commentary for Teaching and Preaching. Louisville: John Knox, 1990.

Creed, J. M. *The Gospel According to St. Luke: The Greek Text with Introduction, Notes, and Indices*. London: Macmillan, 1930.

Crossan, J. Dominic. *In Parables: The Challenge of the Historical Jesus*. New York: Harper & Row, 1973.

Crump, David. *Jesus the Intercessor: Prayer and Christology in Luke-Acts*. Grand Rapids: Baker, 1999.

Danker, Frederick W. *Benefactor: Epigraphic Study of a Graeco-Roman and New Testament Semantic Field*. St. Louis: Clayton, 1982.

———, ed. *A Greek-English Lexicon of the New Testament and Other Early Christian Literature*. 3d ed. Chicago: University of Chicago Press, 2000.

———. *Jesus and the New Age according to St. Luke: A Commentary on the Third Gospel*. St. Louis: Clayton, 1972.

Darr, John A. *On Character Building: The Reader and the Rhetoric of Characterization in Luke-Acts*. Louisville: Westminster John Knox, 1992.

Davies, J. H. "The Purpose of the Central Section of St. Luke's Gospel." *Studia evangelica* II (Berlin: Akademie-Verlag, 1964): 164–69.

Davies, W. D., and Dale C. Allison Jr. *A Critical and Exegetical Commentary on the Gospel According to Saint Matthew*. 3 vols. Edinburgh: T&T Clark, 1988, 1991, 1997.

Dawsey, James M. "Jesus' Pilgrimage to Jerusalem." *Perspectives in Religious Studies* 14 (1987): 217–32.

Delling, G. "συμπληρόω." Pages 308–9 in vol. 6 of *Theological Dictionary of the New Testament*. Edited by G. Kittel and G. Friedrich. Translated by G. W. Bromiley. 10 vols. Grand Rapids: Eerdmans, 1964–1976.

Delobel, Joël. "Lk 7,47 in its Context: An Old Crux Revisited." Pages 1581–90 in vol. 2 of *The Four Gospels 1992: Festschrift Franz Neirynck*. Edited by F. Van Segbroeck et al. Leuvan: University Press, 1992.

de Meeûs, X. "Composition de Lc., XIV et genre symposiaque." *Ephemerides theologicae lovanienses* 37 (1961): 847–70.

Derrett, J. Duncan M. *Law in the New Testament*. London: Darton, Longman & Todd, 1970.

———. "Law in the New Testament: The Parable of the Unjust Judge." Pages 32–47 in vol. 1 of *Studies in the New Testament*. 2 vols. Leiden: Brill, 1977, 1978.

———. "The Parable of the Unjust Steward." Pages 48–77 in *Law in the New Testament*. London: Darton, Longman & Todd, 1970.

Diderot, Denis. "Regrets on Parting with My Old Dressing Gown." Pages 309–17 in *Rameau's Nephew and Other Works*. Translated by Jacques Barzun and Ralph Bowen. Indianapolis: Bobbs-Merrill, 1964.

Dillon, Richard J. *From Eye-Witnesses to Ministers of the Word: Tradition and Composition in Luke 24*. Rome: Biblical Institute, 1978.

Donahue, John J. "The Penitent Woman and the Pharisee: Luke 7:36–50," *American Ecclesiastical Review* 142 (1960): 414–21.

Donahue, John R. *The Gospel in Parable: Metaphor, Narrative, and Theology in the Synoptic Gospels.* Philadelphia: Fortress, 1988.

———. "Tax Collectors and Sinners: An Attempt at Identification." *Catholic Biblical Quarterly* 33 (1971): 39–61.

———. "Two Decades of Research on the Rich and Poor in Luke-Acts." Pages 129–44 in *Justice and the Holy: Essays in Honor of Walter Harrelson.* Edited by Douglas A. Knight and Peter J. Paris. Atlanta: Scholars Press, 1989.

Dupont, Jacques. "L'arrière-fond biblique du récit des tentations de Jésus." *New Testament Studies* 3 (1956–57): 287–304.

Edwards, Douglas R. "Dress and Ornamentation." Pages 232–38 in vol. 2 of *Anchor Bible Dictionary.* Edited by D. N. Freedman, 6 vols. New York: Doubleday, 1992.

Egan, Harvey D. "Indifference." Pages 211–13 in A *Dictionary of Christian Spirituality.* Edited by Gordon S. Wakefield. London: SCM, 1983.

Egelkraut, H. L. *Jesus' Mission to Jerusalem: A Redaction Critical Study of the Travel Narrative in the Gospel of Luke, Lk 9:51–19:48.* Frankfurt am Main: Peter Lang, 1976.

Ehrman, Bart, and M. Plunkett. "The Angel and the Agony: The Textual Problem of Luke 22:43–44." *Catholic Biblical Quarterly* 45 (1983): 401–16.

Elliott, J. K. "Anna's Age (Luke 2:36–37)." *Novum Testamentum* 30 (1988): 100–102.

———. "Κηφᾶς: Σίμων Πέτρος: ὁ Πέτρος: An Examination of New Testament Usage." *Novum Testamentum* 14 (1972): 241–56.

Elliott, John H. "Temple versus Household in Luke-Acts: A Contrast in Social Institutions." Pages 211–40 in *The Social World of Luke-Acts: Models for Interpretation.* Edited by Jerome H. Neyrey. Peabody, Mass.: Hendrickson, 1991.

Ellis, E. Earle. *Eschatology in Luke.* Philadelphia: Fortress, 1972.

———. *The Gospel of Luke.* Rev. ed. London: Oliphants, 1974.

———. "Present and Future Eschatology in Luke." *New Testament Studies* 12 (1965–66): 27–41.

Esler, Philip F. *Community and Gospel in Luke-Acts: The Social and Political Motivations of Lucan Theology.* Cambridge: Cambridge University Press, 1987.

Evans, C. F. "The Central Section of St. Luke's Gospel." Pages 37–53 in *Studies in the Gospels: Essays in Memory of R. H. Lightfoot.* Edited by D. E. Nineham. Oxford: Basil Blackwell, 1955.

———. *Saint Luke.* Philadelphia: Trinity Press International, 1990.

Evans, Craig A. "'He Set His Face': A Note on Luke 9,51." *Biblica* 63 (1982): 545–48.

———. "'He Set His Face': Luke 9,51 Once Again." *Biblica* 68 (1987): 80–84.

———. *Luke*. Peabody, Mass.: Hendrickson, 1990.

Fee, Gordon D. "'One Thing is Needful'?, Luke 10:42." Pages 61–75 in *New Testament Textual Criticism: Its Significance for Exegesis*. Edited by Eldon J. Epp and Gordon D. Fee. Oxford: Clarendon, 1981.

Fitzmyer, Joseph A. *The Gospel According to Luke: Introduction, Translation, and Notes*. 2 vols. Garden City, N.Y.: Doubleday, 1981, 1985.

———. "The Story of the Dishonest Manager (Lk 16:1–13)." *Theological Studies* 25 (1964): 23–42.

Flender, Helmut. *St. Luke: Theologian of Redemptive History*. London: SPCK, 1967.

Fletcher, Donald R. "Condemned to Die: The Logion on Cross-Bearing: What Does It Mean?" *Interpretation* 18 (1954): 156–64.

———. "The Riddle of the Unjust Steward: Is Irony the Key?" *Journal of Biblical Literature* 82 (1963): 15–30.

Flusser, David. "Do You Prefer New Wine?" *Immanuel* 9 (1979): 26–31.

Foerster, W. "ὄρος." Pages 475–87 in vol. 5 of *Theological Dictionary of the New Testament*. Edited by G. Kittel and G. Friedrich. Translated by G. W. Bromiley. 10 vols. Grand Rapids: Eerdmans, 1964–1976.

Fowler, Roger. *A Dictionary of Modern Critical Terms*. Rev. ed. London: Routledge & Kegan Paul, 1987.

Francis, James. "Children and Childhood in the New Testament." Pages 65–85 in *The Family in Theological Perspective*. Edited by Stephen Barton. Edinburgh: T&T Clark, 1996.

Franklin, Eric. *Luke: Interpreter of Paul, Critic of Matthew*. Sheffield: JSOT Press, 1994.

Freed, Edwin D. "The Parable of the Judge and the Widow (Luke 18.1–8)." *New Testament Studies* 33 (1987): 38–60.

Friedrich, Gerhard. "Lk 9,51 und die Entrückungschristologie des Lukas." Pages 48–77 in *Orientierung an Jesus: Zur Theologie der Synoptiker für Josef Schmid*. Edited by Paul Hoffmann, et. al. Freiburg: Herder, 1973.

Fuchs, Albert. *Sprachliche Untersuchungen zu Matthäus und Lukas: Ein Beitrag zur Quellenkritik*. Rome: Biblical Institute, 1971.

Ganss, George E. "Detachment." Pages 269–70 in *The New Dictionary of Catholic Spirituality*. Edited by Michael Dooney. Collegeville, Minn.: Liturgical, 1993.

Garrett, Susan R. "Exodus from Bondage: Luke 9:31 and Acts 12:1–24." *Catholic Biblical Quarterly* 52 (1990): 656–80.

————. "'Lest the Light in You Be Darkness': Luke 11:33–36 and the Question of Commitment." *Journal of Biblical Literature* 110 (1991): 93–105.

Gasse, W. "Zum Reisebericht des Lukas." *Zeitschrift für die neutestamentliche Wissenschaft und die Kunde der älteren Kirche* 34 (1935): 293–99.

Gaventa, Beverly Roberts. *Mary: Glimpses of the Mother of Jesus*. Columbia, S. C.: University of South Carolina Press, 1995.

Geldenhuys, Norval. *Commentary on the Gospel of Luke: The English Text with Introduction, Exposition and Notes*. Grand Rapids: Eerdmans, 1951.

Giblin, Charles H. *The Destruction of Jerusalem according to Luke's Gospel: A Historical-Typological Moral*. Rome: Biblical Institute, 1985.

Gill, David. "Observations on the Lukan Travel Narrative and Some Related Passages." *Harvard Theological Review* 63 (1970): 199–221.

Gillman, John. *Possessions and the Life of Faith: A Reading of Luke-Acts*. Collegeville, Minn.: Liturgical, 1991.

Girard, L. C. *L'Évangile des voyages de Jésus, Ou la section 9:51–18:14 de saint Luc*. Paris: J. Gabalda, 1951.

Good, R. S. "Jesus, Protagonist of the Old, in Lk 5:33–39." *Novum Testamentum* 25 (1983): 19–36.

Goppelt, L. "πίνω κτλ." Pages 135–60 in vol. 6 of *Theological Dictionary of the New Testament*. Edited by G. Kittel and G. Friedrich. Translated by G. W. Bromiley. 10 vols. Grand Rapids: Eerdmans, 1964–1976.

————. "ὕδωρ." Pages 314–33 in vol. 8 of *Theological Dictionary of the New Testament*. Edited by G. Kittel and G. Friedrich. Translated by G. W. Bromiley. 10 vols. Grand Rapids: Eerdmans, 1964–1976.

Goulder, M. D. "The Chiastic Structure of the Lucan Journey." *Studia evangelica* II, 195–202. Edited by F. L. Cross. Berlin: Akademie-Verlag, 1964.

————. *Midrash and Lection in Matthew*. London: SPCK, 1974.

————. *Type and History in Acts*. London: SPCK, 1964.

Gowler, David B. "Hospitality and Characterization in Luke 11:37–54: A Socio-Narratological Approach." *Semeia* 64 (1993): 213–51.

————. *Host, Guest, Enemy and Friend: Portraits of the Pharisees in Luke and Acts*. New York: Peter Lang, 1991.

Grassi, Joseph A. "Child, Children." Pages 904–7 in vol. 1 of *Anchor Bible Dictionary*. Edited by D. N. Freedman, 6 vols. New York: Doubleday, 1992.

————. "Emmaus Revisited (Luke 24,13–35 and Acts 8,26–40)." *Catholic Biblical Quarterly* 26 (1964): 463–67.

Green, Joel B. "The Death of Jesus and the Rending of the Temple Veil (Luke 23:44–49): A Window into Luke's Understanding of Jesus and the Temple." Pages 543–57 in *Society of Biblical Literature 1991 Seminar Papers*. Edited by Eugene H. Lovering Jr. Atlanta: Scholars Press, 1991.

————. "Good News to Whom? Jesus and the 'Poor' in the Gospel of Luke." Pages 59–74 in *Jesus of Nazareth: Lord and Christ. Essays on the Historical Jesus and New Testament Christology*. Edited by Joel B. Green and Max Turner. Grand Rapids: Eerdmans, 1994.

————. *The Gospel of Luke*. Grand Rapids: Eerdmans, 1997.

————. "Jesus on the Mount of Olives (Luke 22:39–46): Tradition and Theology." *Journal for the Study of the New Testament* 26 (1986): 29–48.

————. *The Theology of the Gospel of Luke*. Cambridge: Cambridge University Press, 1995.

Grundmann, Walter. "δεῖ κτλ." Pages 21–25 of vol. 2 of *Theological Dictionary of the New Testament*. Edited by G. Kittel and G. Friedrich. Translated by G. W. Bromiley. 10 vols. Grand Rapids: Eerdmans, 1964–1976.

————. "Fragen der Komposition des lukanischen 'Reiseberichts.'" *Zeitschrift für die neutestamentliche Wissenschaft und die Kunde der älteren Kirche* 50 (1959): 252–70.

Hamel, Gildas. *Poverty and Charity in Roman Palestine, First Three Centuries* C.E. Berkeley: University of California Press, 1990.

Hamm, Dennis. "Luke 19:8 Once Again: Does Zacchaeus Defend or Resolve?" *Journal of Biblical Literature* 107 (1988): 431–37.

————. "Zacchaeus Revisited Once More: A Story of Vindication or Conversion?" *Biblica* 72 (1991): 249–52.

Han, Kyu Sam. "Theology of Prayer in the Gospel of Luke." *Journal of the Evangelical Theological Society* 43 (2000): 675–93.

Haulotte, Edgar. *Symbolique du Vêtement selon la Bible*. Paris: Aubier, 1966.

Hedrick, Charles. *Parables as Poetic Fictions: The Creative Voice of Jesus*. Peabody, Mass.: Hendrickson, 1994.

Heil, John Paul. *Jesus Walking On the Sea: Meaning and Gospel Functions of Matt 14:22–23; Mark 6:45–52 and John 6:15b–21*. Rome: Biblical Institute, 1981.

————. *The Meal Scenes in Luke-Acts: An Audience-Oriented Approach*. Atlanta: Society of Biblical Literature, 1999.

Hendrickx, Herman. *The Parables of Jesus*. San Francisco: Harper & Row, 1986.

Hengel, Martin. *The Charismatic Leader and His Followers*. Translated by C. G. Craig. Edinburgh: T&T Clark, 1981.

————. *The Cross of the Son of God*. London: SCM, 1986.

————. "φάτνη." Pages 49–55 in vol. 9 of *Theological Dictionary of the New Testament*. Edited by G. Kittel and G. Friedrich. Translated by G. W. Bromiley. 10 vols. Grand Rapids: Eerdmans, 1964–1976.

Herrenbrück, Fritz. *Jesus und die Zöllner: Historische und neutestamentlich-exegetische Untersuchungen*. Tübingen: J. C. B. Mohr (Paul Siebeck), 1990.

Herzog, William R. II. *Parables as Subversive Speech: Jesus as Pedagogue of the Op-pressed*. Louisville: Westminster John Knox, 1994.

Hiers, Richard H. "Friends by Unrighteous Mammon. The Eschatological Proletariat (Luke 16:9)." *Journal of the American Academy of Religion* 38 (1970): 30–36.

Hollander, Anne. *Seeing Through Clothes*. New York: Viking, 1978.

Holman, Hugh C. A *Handbook to Literature*. 4th ed. Indianapolis: ITT Bobbs-Merrill, 1980.

Hornsby, Teresa J. "Why Is She Crying? A Feminist Interpretation of Luke 7.36–50." Pages 91–103 in *Escaping Eden: New Feminist Perspectives on the Bible*. Edited by Harold C. Washington, Susan Lochrie Graham, and Pamela Thimmes. New York: New York University Press, 1999.

Hultgren, Arland J. *The Parables of Jesus: A Commentary*. Grand Rapids: Eerdmans, 2000.

———. "Interpreting the Gospel of Luke." *Interpretation* 30 (1976): 353–65.

Ireland, Dennis J. *Stewardship and the Kingdom of God: An Historical, Exegetical, and Contextual Study of the Parable of the Unjust Steward in Luke 16:1–13*. Leiden: Brill, 1992.

Jensen, Joseph E. "Clothing." Pages 256–66 in *Eerdmans Dictionary of the Bible*. Edited by D. N. Freedman. Grand Rapids: Eerdmans, 2000.

Jeremias, Joachim. " ᾅδης." Pages 146–49 in vol. 1 of *Theological Dictionary of the New Testament*. Edited by G. Kittel and G. Friedrich. Translated by G. W. Bromiley. 10 vols. Grand Rapids: Eerdmans, 1964–1976.

———. *The Parables of Jesus*. Rev ed. New York: Charles Scribner's Sons, 1963.

Johnson, Luke T. *Sharing Possessions: Mandate and Symbol of Faith*. Philadelphia: Fortress, 1981.

Joselit, Jenna Weissman. A *Perfect Fit: Clothes, Character, and the Promise of Amer-ica*. New York: Metropolitan/Henry Holt, 2001.

Just, Arthur A. Jr. *The Ongoing Feast: Table Fellowship and Eschatology at Emmaus*. Collegeville, Minn.: Liturgical, 1993.

Kariamadam, Paul. "The Composition and Meaning of the Lucan Travel Nar-rative (Lk. 9,51–19,46). *Bible Bhashyam* 13 (1987): 179–98.

Karris, Robert J. *Luke: Artist and Theologian: Luke's Passion Account as Literature*. New York: Paulist, 1985.

———. "Luke 24:13–35." *Interpretation* 41 (1987): 57–61.

Kee, Alistair. "The Old Coat and the New Wine: A Parable of Repentance." *Novum Testamentum* 12 (1970): 13–21.

Keener, Craig S. A *Commentary on the Gospel of Matthew*. Grand Rapids: Eerdmans, 1999.

Kenny, Anthony. "The Transfiguration and the Agony in the Garden." *Catholic Biblical Quarterly* 19 (1957): 444–52.

Kermode, Frank. *The Sense of an Ending: Studies in the Theory of Fiction with a New Epilogue*. New York: Oxford University Press, 2000.

Kilgallen, John J. "John the Baptist, the Sinful Woman, and the Pharisee." *Journal of Biblical Literature* 104 (1985): 675–79.

Kim, Kyoung-Jin. *Stewardship and Almsgiving in Luke's Theology*. Sheffield: JSOT Press, 1998.

Kingsbury, Jack Dean. *Conflict in Luke: Jesus, Authorities, Disciples*. Minneapolis: Fortress, 1991.

————. "The Pharisees in Luke-Acts." Pages 1497–1512 in vol. 2 of *The Four Gospels 1992: Festschrift Frans Neirynck*. Edited by F. Van Segbroeck, et al. Leuvan: University Press, 1992.

Kittel, G. "ἔρημος κτλ." Pages 657–60 in vol. 2 of *Theological Dictionary of the New Testament*. Edited by G. Kittel and G. Friedrich. Translated by G. W. Bromiley. 10 vols. Grand Rapids: Eerdmans, 1964–1976.

Kloppenborg, John S. "The Dishonoured Master (Luke 16,1–8a)." *Biblica* 70 (1989): 474–94.

Klostermann, Erich. *Das Lukasevangelium*. 2d ed. Tübingen: J. C. B. Mohr (Paul Siebeck), 1929.

Knowles, Michael P. " 'Everyone Who Hears These Words of Mine': Parables on Discipleship (Matt 7:24–27//Luke 6:47–49; Luke 14:28–33; Luke 17:7–10; Matt 20:1–16)." Pages 286–305 in *The Challenge of Jesus' Parables*. Edited by Richard N. Longenecker. Grand Rapids: Eerdmans, 2000.

Kodell. J. "Luke and the Children: The Beginning and End of the Great Interpolation (Luke 9:46–56; 18:9–23)." *Catholic Biblical Quarterly* 49 (1987): 415–30.

Kort, Wesley A. *Story, Text, and Scripture: Literary Interests in Biblical Narrative*. University Park: Pennsylvania State University Press, 1988.

Krämer, M. *Das Rätsel der Parabel vom ungerechten Verwalter, Lk 16,1–13*. Zurich: PAS, 1972.

Kratz, R. "θάλασσα." Pages 127–28 in vol. 2 of *Exegetical Dictionary of the New Testament*. Edited by H. Balz, G. Schneider, ET. Grand Rapids: Eerdmans, 1990–1993.

Lane, Belden C. *Landscapes of the Sacred: Geography and Narrative in American Spirituality*. New York: Paulist, 1988.

————. *The Solace of Fierce Landscapes: Exploring Desert and Mountain Spirituality*. New York: Oxford University Press, 1998.

Leach, Edmund. "Fishing for Men on the Edge of the Wilderness." Pages 579–99 in *The Literary Guide to the Bible*. Edited by Robert Alter and Frank Kermode. Cambridge: Belknap Press, 1987.

Leaney, A. R. C. *A Commentary on the Gospel according to St. Luke*. 2d ed. London: Black, 1966.

Liefeld, Walter L. "Parables on Prayer (Luke 11:5–13; 18:1–14)." Pages 240–62 in *The Challenge of Jesus' Parables*. Edited by Richard N. Longenecker. Grand Rapids: Eerdmans, 2000.

Lightfoot, R. H. *Locality and Doctrine in the Gospels*. London: Hodder & Stoughton, 1938.

Loader, William. "Jesus and the Rogue in Luke 16,1–8a: The Parable of the Unjust Steward." *Revue Biblique* 96 (1989): 518–32.

Loder, James E. *The Transforming Moment: Understanding Convictional Experiences*. New York: Harper & Row, 1981.

Loewe, William P. "Towards an Interpretation of Lk 19:1–10." *Catholic Biblical Quarterly* 36 (1974): 321–31.

Lohfink, G. *Die Sammlung Israels: Eine Untersuchung zur lukanishcen Ekklesiologie*. München: Kösel, 1975.

Lohse, E. "Missionarisches Handeln Jesu nach dem Evangelium des Lukas." *Theologische Zeitschrift* 10 (1954): 1–13.

Lövestam, Evald. *Spiritual Wakefulness in the New Testament*. Lund: GWK Gleerup, 1963.

Lull, David J. "The Servant-Benefactor as a Model of Greatness (Luke 22:24–30)." *Novum Testamentum* 28 (1986): 289–305.

Lurie, Alison. *The Language of Clothes*. New York: Random House, 1981.

McCown, C. C. "The Geography of Luke's Central Section." *Journal of Biblical Literature* 57 (1938): 51–66.

McGrath, Alister E. *Christian Spirituality: An Introduction*. Oxford: Blackwell, 1999.

Maddox, Robert. *The Purpose of Luke-Acts*. Edinburgh: T&T Clark, 1982.

Malbon, Elizabeth Struthers. *In the Company of Jesus: Character in Mark's Gospel*. Louisville: Westminster John Knox, 2000.

———. "The Jesus of Mark and the Sea of Galilee." *Journal of Biblical Literature* 103 (1984): 363–77.

———. *Narrative Space and Mythic Meaning in Mark*. San Francisco: Harper & Row, 1986.

Malina, Bruce J. *Christian Origins and Cultural Anthropology: Practical Models for Biblical Interpretation*. Atlanta: John Knox, 1986.

———. "Hospitality." Pages 408–9 in *HarperCollins Bible Dictionary*. Edited by P. J. Achtemeier et al. 2d ed. San Francisco: Society of Biblical Literature, 1996.

———. *The New Testament World: Insights from Cultural Anthropology*. 3d ed., rev. and enl. Louisville: Westminster John Knox, 2001.

Malina, Bruce J., and Richard L. Rohrbaugh. *Social-Science Commentary on the Synoptic Gospels*. Minneapolis: Fortress, 1992.

Mánek, J. "The New Exodus in the Book of Luke." *Novum Testamentum* 2 (1958): 8–23.

Manning, Robert D. *Credit Card Nation: The Consequences of America's Addiction to Credit*. New York: Basic, 2000.

Manson, T. W. *The Sayings of Jesus as Recorded in the Gospels according to St. Matthew and St. Luke Arranged with Introduction and Commentary*. London: SCM, 1949.

Marcus, Joel. *Mark 1–8: A New Translation with Introduction and Commentary*. New York: Doubleday, 2000.

Marshall, I. Howard. *The Gospel of Luke: A Commentary on the Greek Text*. Grand Rapids: Eerdmans, 1978.

———. *Luke: Historian and Theologian*. London: Paternoster, 1970.

Martin, Dale B. *Slavery as Salvation: The Metaphor of Slavery in Pauline Christianity*. New Haven: Yale University Press, 1990.

Mason, Steve. "Pharisees." Pages 1043–44 in *Eerdmans Dictionary of the Bible*. Edited by D. N. Freedman. Grand Rapids: Eerdmans, 2000.

Matera, Frank J. "Jesus' Journey to Jerusalem (Luke 9:51–19:46): A Conflict with Israel." *Journal for the Study of the New Testament* 51 (1993): 57–77.

Mattill Jr., A. J. *Luke and the Last Things: A Perspective for the Understanding of Lukan Thought*. Dillsboro, N.C.: Western North Carolina, 1979.

Mauser, Ulrich W. *Christ in the Wilderness: The Wilderness Theme in the Second Gospel and Its Basis in the Biblical Tradition*. London: SCM, 1963.

Mead, A. H. "Old and New Wine: St. Luke 5:39." *Expository Times* 99 (1988): 234–35.

Meeks, M. Douglas. *God the Economist: The Doctrine of God and Political Economy*. Minneapolis: Fortress, 1989.

Merk, Otto. "Das Reich Gottes in den lukanischen Schriften." Pages 201–20 in *Jesus und Paulus, Festschrift für Werner Georg Kümmel*. Edited by E. Earle Ellis and E. Grässer. Göttingen: Vandenheock und Ruprecht, 1975.

Metzger, Bruce M. *A Textual Commentary on the Greek New Testament*. 2d ed. New York: United Bible Societies, 1994.

Meyer, Rudolf. "κόλπος." Pages 824–26 in vol. 3 of *Theological Dictionary of the New Testament*. Edited by G. Kittel and G. Friedrich. Translated by G. W. Bromiley. 10 vols. Grand Rapids: Eerdmans, 1964–1976.

Michel, Otto. "μισέω." Pages 683–94 in vol. 4 of *Theological Dictionary of the New Testament*. Edited by G. Kittel and G. Friedrich. Translated by G. W. Bromiley. 10 vols. Grand Rapids: Eerdmans, 1964–1976.

———. "τελώνης." Pages 88–105 in vol. 8 of *Theological Dictionary of the New Testament*. Edited by G. Kittel and G. Friedrich. Translated by G. W. Bromiley. 10 vols. Grand Rapids: Eerdmans, 1964–1976.

Minear, Paul S. "Jesus' Audiences, according to Luke." *Novum Testamentum* 16 (1974): 81–109.

———. "A Note on Luke 17:7–10." *Journal of Biblical Literature* 93 (1974): 82–7.

Minor, Mitzi. *The Spirituality of Mark: Responding to God.* Louisville: Westminster John Knox, 1996.

Mitchell, Alan C. "Zacchaeus Revisited: Luke 19,8 as a Defense." *Biblica* 71 (1990): 153–76.

Miyoshi, Michi. *Der Anfang des Reiseberichts Lk 9,51–10,24: Eine redaktionsgeschichtliche Untersuchung.* Rome: Biblical Institute, 1974.

Moessner, David P. *Lord of the Banquet: The Literary and Theological Significance of the Lukan Travel Narrative.* Minneapolis: Fortress Press, 1989.

———. "Luke 9:1–50: Luke's Preview of the Journey of the Prophet like Moses of Deuteronomy." *Journal of Biblical Literature* 102 (1983): 575–605.

Moore, Stephen D. *Literary Criticism and the Gospels: The Theoretical Challenge.* New Haven: Yale University Press, 1989.

Moran, Maureen. "Review of *Feasting and Social Rhetoric in Luke* 14 by Willi Braun." *Biblical Interpretation* 7 (1999): 450–53.

Morrice, William. *Joy in the New Testament.* Exeter: Paternoster, 1984.

Moule, C. F. D. *An Idiom Book of New Testament Greek.* 2d ed. Cambridge: Cambridge University Press, 1959.

Moulton, James H., and George Milligan. *The Vocabulary of the Greek New Testament: Illustrated from the Papyri and Other Non-literary Sources.* Grand Rapids: Eerdmans, 1930.

Moxnes, Halvor. *The Economy of the Kingdom: Social Conflict and Economic Relations in Luke's Gospel.* Philadelphia: Fortress, 1988.

———. "Kingdom Takes Place: Transformation of Place and Power in the Kingdom of God in the Gospel of Luke." Pages 176–209 in *Social Scientific Models for Interpreting the Bible: Essays by the Context Group in Honor of Bruce J. Malina.* Edited by John J. Pilch. Leiden: Brill, 2000.

———. "Meals and the New Community in Luke." *Svensk exegetisk Årsbok* 51 (1986): 158–67.

Muddiman, John. "Fast, Fasting." Pages 773–76 in vol. 2 of *Anchor Bible Dictionary.* Edited by D. N. Freedman, 6 vols. New York: Doubleday, 1992.

Muecke, D. C. *The Compass of Irony.* London: Methuen & Co., 1970.

Muir, Stephen C. Review of Willi Braun, *Feasting and Social Rhetoric in Luke* 14. *Novum Testamentum* 38 (1996): 408–9.

Myers, J. M. "Dress and Ornaments." Pages 869–71 in vol. 1 of *The Interpreter's Dictionary of the Bible.* Edited by G. A. Buttrick. 4 vols. Nashville: Abingdon, 1962.

Nash, James A. "On the Subversive Virtue: Frugality." Pages 416–36 in *Ethics of Consumption: The Good Life, Justice, and Global Stewardship.* Edited by

David A. Crocker and Toby Linden. New York: Rowman & Littlefield, 1998.

Nash, Kathleen S. "Widow." Pages 1377–78 in *Eerdmans Dictionary of the Bible*. Edited by D. N. Freedman. Grand Rapids: Eerdmans, 2000.

Navone, John. *Themes of St. Luke*. Rome: Gregorian University, 1970.

———. "The Way of the Lord." *Scripture* 20 (1968): 24–30.

Neale, David A. *None but the Sinners: Religious Categories in the Gospel of Luke*. Sheffield: JSOT Press, 1991.

Nelson, Peter K. "The Flow of Thought in Luke 22:24–27." *Journal for the Study of the New Testament* 43 (1991): 113–23.

———. *Leadership and Discipleship*: A Study of Luke 22:24–30. Atlanta: Scholars Press, 1994.

Neyrey, Jerome H. "Ceremonies in Luke-Acts: The Case of Meals and Table Fellowship." Pages 361–87 in *The Social World of Luke-Acts: Models for Interpretation*. Edited by Jerome H. Neyrey. Peabody, Mass.: Hendrickson, 1991.

———. *The Passion according to Luke*: A Redaction Study of Luke's Soteriology. New York: Paulist, 1985.

———. "The Symbolic Universe of Luke-Acts: 'They Turn the World Upside Down.'" Pages 271–304 in *The Social World of Luke-Acts: Models for Interpretation*. Edited by Jerome H. Neyrey. Peabody, Mass.: Hendrickson, 1991.

Nolland, John. *Luke*. 3 vols. Dallas: Word, 1989, 1993.

Nuttall, Geoffrey F. *The Moment of Recognition: Luke as Story-Teller*. London: University of London Athlone Press, 1978.

O'Brien, P. T. "Prayer in Luke-Acts." *Tyndale Bulletin* 24 (1973): 111–27.

O'Collins, Gerald. "Crucifixion." Pages 1207–10 in vol. 1 of *Anchor Bible Dictionary*. Edited by D. N. Freedman, 6 vols. New York: Doubleday, 1992.

Oepke, A. "παῖς." Pages 639–52 in vol. 5 of *Theological Dictionary of the New Testament*. Edited by G. Kittel and G. Friedrich. Translated by G. W. Bromiley. 10 vols. Grand Rapids: Eerdmans, 1964–1976.

Ogg, George. "The Central Section of the Gospel according to St Luke." *New Testament Studies* 18 (1971): 39–53.

Osiek, Carolyn, and David L. Balch. *Families in the New Testament World: Households and House Churches*. Louisville: Westminster John Knox, 1997.

Osten-Sacken, Peter von der. "Zur Christologie des lukanischen Reiseberichts." *Evangelische Theologie* 33 (1973): 476–96.

O'Toole, Robert F. "The Kingdom of God in Luke-Acts." Pages 147–62 in *The Kingdom of God in 20th-Century Interpretation*. Edited by Wendell Willis. Peabody, Mass.: Hendrickson, 1987.

———. Review of Willi Braun, *Feasting and Social Rhetoric in Luke 14*. *Catholic Biblical Quarterly* 59 (1997): 149–50.

———. *The Unity of Luke's Theology: An Analysis of Luke-Acts*. Wilmington, Delaware: Michael Glazier, 1984.

Ott, Wilhelm. *Gebet und Heil: Die Bedeutung der Gebetsparänese in der lukanischen Theologie*. München: Kösel, 1965.

Palmer, Humphrey. "Just Married, Cannot Come." *Novum Testamentum* 18 (1976): 241–57.

Parrott, Douglas M. "The Dishonest Steward (Luke 16.1–8a) and Luke's Special Parable Collection." *New Testament Studies* 37 (1991): 499–515.

Parson, Mikeal. *The Departure of Jesus in Luke-Acts: The Ascension Narratives in Context*. Sheffield: JSOT Press, 1987.

Peterson, Eugene H. *Subversive Spirituality*. Grand Rapids: Eerdmans, 1997.

———. *Take and Read, Spiritual Reading: An Annotated List*. Grand Rapids: Eerdmans, 1996.

Petzer, Kobus. "Style and Text in the Lucan Narrative of the Institution of the Lord's Supper (Luke 22.19b–20)." *New Testament Studies* 37 (1991): 113–29.

Pilgrim, Walter E. *Good News to the Poor: Wealth and Poverty in Luke-Acts*. Minneapolis: Augsburg, 1981.

Plummer, Alfred. *A Critical and Exegetical Commentary on the Gospel According to S. Luke*. Edinburgh: T&T Clark, 1922.

Plutarch. *Moralia*, vol. 7. Loeb Classical Library. Translated by Philip De Lacy and B. Einarson. Cambridge: Harvard University Press, 1959.

Plymale, Steven F. *The Prayer Texts of Luke-Acts*. New York: Peter Lang, 1991.

Pope, M. H. "Number, Numbering, Numbers." Pages 561–67 in vol. 3 of *The Interpreter's Dictionary of the Bible*. Edited by G. A. Buttrick. 4 vols. Nashville, 1962.

Powell, Mark Allan. "Narrative Criticism." Pages 239–55 in *Hearing the New Testament: Strategies for Interpretation*. Edited by Joel B. Green. Grand Rapids: Eerdmans, 1995.

———. "The Religious Leaders in Luke-Acts: A Literary-Critical Study." *Journal of Biblical Literature* 109 (1990): 93–110.

———. *What Are They Saying About Luke?* New York: Paulist, 1989.

———. *What is Narrative Criticism?* Minneapolis: Fortress, 1990.

Price, Robert M. *The Widow Traditions in Luke-Acts: A Feminist-Critical Scrutiny*. Atlanta: Scholars Press, 1997.

Radl, W. "ἔρημος." Pages 51–52 in vol. 2 of *Exegetical Dictionary of the New Testament*. Edited by H. Balz, G. Schneider, ET. Grand Rapids: Eerdmans, 1990–1993.

Ravens, D. A. S. "Zacchaeus: The Final Part of a Lucan Triptych?" *Journal for the Study of the New Testament* 41 (1991): 19–32.

Rawson, Beryl. "Adult-Child Relationships in Roman Society." Pages 7–30 in *Marriage, Divorce, and Children in Ancient Rome*. Edited by Beryl Rawson. Oxford: Oxford University Press, 1991.

———. *The Family in Ancient Rome: New Perspectives*. Ithaca: Cornell University Press, 1986.

Reicke, Bo. "Instruction and Discussion in the Travel Narrative." *Studia evangelica* I. Berlin: Akademie-Verlag, 1959, 206–16.

Reid, Barbara E. *Choosing the Better Part? Women in the Gospel of Luke*. Collegeville, Minn.: Liturgical, 1996.

———. "Prayer and the Face of the Transfigured Jesus." Pages 39–53 in *The Lord's Prayer and Other Prayer Texts from the Greco-Roman Era*. Edited by James H. Charlesworth. Valley Forge, Pa.: Trinity, 1994.

———. *The Transfiguration: A Source- and Redaction-Critical Study of Luke 9:28–36*. Paris: J. Gabalda, 1993.

Rengstorf, Karl H. "ἁμαρτωλός κτλ." Pages 317–35 of vol. 1 of *Theological Dictionary of the New Testament*. Edited by G. Kittel and G. Friedrich. Translated by G. W. Bromiley. 10 vols. Grand Rapids: Eerdmans, 1964–1976.

———. "δοῦλος κτλ." Pages 261–80 in vol. 2 of *Theological Dictionary of the New Testament*. Edited by G. Kittel and G. Friedrich. Translated by G. W. Bromiley. 10 vols. Grand Rapids: Eerdmans, 1964–1976.

———. "ποταμός κτλ." Pages 595–623 in vol. 6 of *Theological Dictionary of the New Testament*. Edited by G. Kittel and G. Friedrich. Translated by G. W. Bromiley. 10 vols. Grand Rapids: Eerdmans, 1964–1976.

Resseguie, James L. "Automatization and Defamiliarization in Luke 7:36–50." *Literature and Theology* 5 (1991): 137–50.

———. "Defamiliarization and the Gospels." *Biblical Theology Bulletin* 20 (1990): 147–53.

———. "Defamiliarization in the Gospels." *Mosaic: A Journal for the Interdisciplinary Study of Literature* 21 (1988): 25–35.

———. "Interpretation of Luke's Central Section (Luke 9:51–19:44) Since 1856." *Studia Biblica et Theologica* 5 (1975): 3–36.

———. "New Testament as Literature." Pages 815–17 of *Eerdmans Dictionary of the Bible*. Edited by D. N. Freedman. Grand Rapids: Eerdmans, 2000.

———. "Point of View in the Central Section of Luke (9:51–19:44)." *Journal of the Evangelical Theological Society* 25 (1982): 41–47.

———. "Reader-Response Criticism and the Synoptic Gospels." *Journal of the American Academy of Religion* 52 (1984): 307–24.

———. *Revelation Unsealed: A Narrative Critical Approach to John's Apocalypse*. Leiden: Brill, 1998.

———. *The Strange Gospel: Narrative Design and Point of View in John*. Leiden: Brill, 2001.

Rhoads, David, Joanna Dewey and Donald Michie. *Mark as Story: An Introduction to the Narrative of a Gospel.* 2d ed. Minneapolis: Fortress, 1999.

Ringe, Sharon H. *Luke.* Philadelphia: Westminster John Knox, 1995.

———. "Luke 9:28–36: the Beginning of an Exodus." *Semeia* 28 (1983): 83–99.

Ritzer, George. *Enchanting a Disenchanted World: Revolutionizing the Means of Consumption.* Thousands Oaks, Calif.: Pine Forge, 1999.

———. *The McDonaldization of Society.* Thousand Oaks, Calif.: Pine Forge, 2000.

Robinson, B. P. "The Place of the Emmaus Story in Luke-Acts." *New Testament Studies* 30 (1984): 481–97.

Rohrbaugh, Richard L. "The Pre-Industrial City in Luke-Acts: Urban Social Relations." Pages 125–49 in *The Social World of Luke-Acts: Models for Interpretation.* Edited by Jerome H. Neyrey. Peabody, Mass.: Hendrickson, 1991.

Roth, S. John. *The Blind, the Lame, and the Poor: Character Types in Luke-Acts.* Sheffield: JSOT Press, 1997.

Sanders, E. P. *Jewish Law from Jesus to the Mishnah: Five Studies.* Philadelphia: Trinity, 1990.

Sanders, James A. "The Ethic of Election in Luke's Great Banquet Parable." Pages 245–71 in *Essays in Old Testament Ethics.* Edited by J. L. Crenshaw, and J. T. Willis. New York: KTAV, 1974.

Schmid, Josef. *Das Evangelium nach Lukas.* 4th ed. Regensburg: Pustet, 1960.

Schmidt, Karl Ludwig. *Der Rahmen der Geschichte Jesu: Literarkritische Untersuchungen zur ältsten Jesusüberlieferung.* Berlin: Trowitzsch und Sohn, 1919.

Schmidt, Thomas E. *Hostility to Wealth in the Synoptic Gospels.* Sheffield: JSOT Press, 1987.

Schneider, Gerhard. "Engel und Blutschweiss (Lk 22, 43–44): 'Redaktionsgeschichte' im Dienste der Textkritik." *Biblische Zeitschrift* 20 (1976): 112–16.

Schneider, Johannes. "Zur Analyse des lukanischen Reiseberichtes." Pages 207–29 in *Synoptische Studien.* Edited by J. Schmid and A. Vögtle. München: Karl Zink, 1953.

Schor, Juliet B. *Do Americans Shop Too Much?* Boston: Beacon, 2000.

———. *The Overspent American: Upscaling, Downshifting, and the New Consumer.* New York: Basic, 1998.

Schottroff, Luise. *Lydia's Impatient Sisters: A Feminist Social History of Early Christianity.* Translated by Barbara and Martin Rumscheidt. Louisville: Westminster John Knox, 1995.

Schrenk, G. "ἐδικέω κτλ." Pages 442–46 in vol. 2 of *Theological Dictionary of the New Testament.* Edited by G. Kittel and G. Friedrich. Translated by G. W. Bromiley. 10 vols. Grand Rapids: Eerdmans, 1964–1976.

Schubert, Paul. "The Structure and Significance of Luke 24." Pages 165–86 in *Neutestamentliche Studien für Rudolf Bultmann*. 2d ed. Edited by W. Eltester. Berlin: Alfred Töpelmann, 1957.

Schulz, Siegfried. Q: *Die Spruchquelle der Evangelisten*. Zürich: Theologischer Verlag, 1972.

Schürmann, H. *Das Lukasevangelium*. Freiburg: Herder, 1969.

Schüssler Fiorenza, Elizabeth. "A Feminist Critical Interpretation for Liberation: Martha and Mary: Luke 10:38–42." *Religion and Intellectual Life*: A *Journal for Associates for Religion and Intellectual Life* 3 (1986): 21–36.

Schweizer, Eduard. *The Good News according to Luke*. Atlanta: John Knox, 1984.

Scott, Bernard Brandon. *Hear Then the Parable: A Commentary on the Parables of Jesus*. Minneapolis: Fortress, 1989.

Seccombe, David P. *Possessions and the Poor in Luke-Acts*. Linz: Fuchs, 1983.

Seesemann, H. "ὀσφύς." Pages 496–97 in vol. 5 of *Theological Dictionary of the New Testament*. Edited by G. Kittel and G. Friedrich. Translated by G. W. Bromiley. 10 vols. Grand Rapids: Eerdmans, 1964–1976.

Seim, Turid Karlsen. *The Double Message: Patterns of Gender in Luke-Acts*. Nashville: Abingdon, 1994.

Sellew, Philip. "Interior Monologue as a Narrative Device in the Parables of Luke." *Journal of Biblical Literature* 111 (1992): 239–53.

Sellin, Gerhard. "Komposition, Quellen und Funktion des lukanischen Reiseberichtes (9.51–19.28)." *Novum Testamentum* 20 (1976): 100–35.

Sheeley, Stephen M. *Narrative Asides in Luke-Acts*. Sheffield: JSOT Press, 1992.

Smalley, Steven S. "Spirit, Kingdom and Prayer in Luke-Acts." *Novum Testamentum* 15 (1973): 59–71.

Smith, Dennis E. "Table Fellowship as a Literary Motif in the Gospel of Luke." *Journal of Biblical Literature* 106 (1987): 613–38.

———. "Table Fellowship." Pages 302–4 in vol. 6 of *Anchor Bible Dictionary*. Edited by D. N. Freedman, 6 vols. New York: Doubleday, 1992.

Smith-Christopher, Daniel L. "Fasting." Page 456 in *Eerdmans Dictionary of the Bible*. Edited by D. N. Freedman. Grand Rapids: Eerdmans, 2000.

Squires, John T. *The Plan of God in Luke-Acts*. Cambridge: Cambridge University Press, 1993.

Stählin, G. "χήρα," Pages 440–65 in vol. 9 of *Theological Dictionary of the New Testament*. Edited by G. Kittel and G. Friedrich. Translated by G. W. Bromiley. 10 vols. Grand Rapids: Eerdmans, 1964–1976.

Starcky, J. "Obfirmavit faciem suam ut iret Jerusalem: Sens et portée de Luc ix, 51. *Recherches de science religieuse* 39 (1951): 197–202.

Steele, E. Springs. "Luke 11:37–54—A Modified Hellenistic Symposium?" *Journal of Biblical Literature* 103 (1984): 379–94.

Stein, Robert H. *An Introduction to the Parables of Jesus.* Philadelphia: Westminster, 1981.

———. "Luke 14:26 and the Question of Authenticity." *Forum* 5 (1989): 187–92.

Strack, H. and P. Billerbeck, *Kommentar zum Neuen Testament aus Talmud und Midrasch.* 6 vols. München: Beck, 1922–61.

Strauss, Mark L. *The Davidic Messiah in Luke-Acts: The Promise and its Fulfillment in Lucan Christology.* Sheffield: JSOT Press, 1995.

Streeter, B. H. *The Four Gospels: A Study of Origins.* London: Macmillan, 1924.

Sweet, J. P. M. *Revelation.* Philadelphia: Westminster, 1979.

Sweetland, Dennis M. *Our Journey with Jesus: Discipleship according to Luke-Acts.* Collegeville, Minn.: Liturgical, 1990.

Sylva, Dennis D. "The Temple Curtain and Jesus' Death in the Gospel of Luke." *Journal of Biblical Literature* 105 (1986): 239–50.

Talbert, Charles H. *Literary Patterns, Theological Themes, and the Genre of Luke-Acts.* Missoula, Mont.: Scholars Press, 1974.

———. *Reading Luke: A Literary and Theological Commentary on the Third Gospel.* New York: Crossroad, 1982.

———. "The Way of the Lukan Jesus: Dimensions of Lukan Spirituality." *Perspectives in Religious Studies* 9 (1982): 237–49.

Talmon, Shemaryahu. "The 'Desert Motif' in the Bible and in Qumran Literature." Pages 31–63 in *Biblical Motifs: Origins and Transformations.* Edited by Alexander Altmann. Cambridge: Harvard University Press, 1966.

Tannehill, Robert C. "The Lukan Discourse on Invitations (Luke 14, 7–24)." Pages 1603–16 in vol. 2 of *The Four Gospels 1992, Festschrift Frans Neirynck.* Edited by F. Van Segbroeck, et al. Leuven: University Press, 1992.

———. *Luke.* Nashville: Abingdon, 1996.

———. *The Narrative Unity of Luke-Acts: A Literary Interpretation.* 2 vols. Philadelphia: Fortress, 1986, 1990.

———. Review of Willi Braun, *Feasting and Social Rhetoric in Luke 14. Biblica* 77 (1996): 564–67.

———. "The Story of Zacchaeus as Rhetoric: Luke 19:1–10." *Semeia* 64 (1994): 201–11.

———. *The Sword of His Mouth: Forceful and Imaginative Language in Synoptic Sayings.* Philadelphia: Fortress, 1975.

"τετράπλους." Page 353 in vol. 3 of *Exegetical Dictionary of the New Testament.* Edited by H. Balz and G. Schneider, ET. Grand Rapids: Eerdmans, 1990–1993.

Thébert, Yvon. "The Slave." Pages 138–74 in *The Romans.* Edited by Andrea Giardina. Chicago: University of Chicago, 1993.

Thompson, Henry O. "Jordan River." Pages 953–58 in vol. 3 of *Anchor Bible Dictionary*. Edited by D. N. Freedman, 6 vols. New York: Doubleday, 1992.

Tiede, David L. "The Kings of the Gentiles and the Leader Who Serves: Luke 22:24–30." *Word and World* 12 (1992): 23–8.

Topel, L. John. "On the Injustice of the Unjust Steward: Lk 16:1–13." *Catholic Biblical Quarterly* 37 (1975): 216–27.

Trites, Allison A. "The Prayer Motif in Luke-Acts." Pages 168–86 in *Perspectives on Luke-Acts*. Edited by Charles Talbert. Edinburgh: T&T Clark, 1978.

Trompf, G. W. "La Section Médiane de L'Évangile de Luc: L'Organisation des Documents." *Revue d'histoire et de philosophie religieuses* 53 (1973): 141–54.

Twitchell, James B. *Lead Us into Temptation: The Triumph of American Materialism*. New York: Columbia University Press, 1999.

Tyson, Joseph B., ed. *Luke-Acts and the Jewish People: Eight Critical Perspectives*. Minneapolis: Augsburg, 1988.

Veblen, Thorstein. *The Theory of the Leisure Class*. 1899. Amherst, N.Y.: Prometheus, 1998.

Via, Dan O., Jr. *The Parables: Their Literary and Existential Dimension*. Philadelphia: Fortress, 1967.

Waetjen, Herman. "Theological Criteria and Historical Reconstruction: Martha and Mary, Luke 10:38–42." In *Center for Hermeneutical Studies in Hellenistic and Modern Culture* 53 (1986): 1–63.

Weinert, Francis D. "The Meaning of the Temple in Luke-Acts." *Biblical Theology Bulletin* 11 (1981): 85–89.

Weiser, Alfons. *Die Knechtsgleichnisse der synoptischen Evangelien*. Munich: Kösel, 1971.

Wenham, J. W. "Synoptic Independence and the Origin of Luke's Travel Narrative." *New Testament Studies* 27 (1981): 507–15.

Wheeler, Sondra Ely. *Wealth as Peril and Obligation: The New Testament on Possessions*. Grand Rapids: Eerdmans, 1995.

White, Richard C. "A Good Word for Zacchaeus? Exegetical Comment on Luke 19:1–10." *Lexington Theological Quarterly* 14 (1979): 89–96.

———. "Vindication for Zacchaeus?" *Expository Times* 91 (1979–80): 21.

Wickes, D. R. *The Sources of Luke's Perean Section*. Chicago: University of Chicago, 1912.

Wiedemann, Thomas. *Adults and Children in the Roman Empire*. New Haven: Yale University Press, 1989.

Wilckens, U. "στολή." Pages 687–91 in vol. 7 of *Theological Dictionary of the New Testament*. Edited by G. Kittel and G. Friedrich. Translated by G. W. Bromiley. 10 vols. Grand Rapids: Eerdmans, 1964–1976.

Williams, Francis E. "Is Almsgiving the Point of the 'Unjust Steward'?" *Journal of Biblical Literature* 83 (1964): 293–97.

Wimmer, Joseph F. *Fasting in the New Testament: A Study in Biblical Theology.* New York: Paulist, 1982.

Windisch, H. "ζύμη κτλ." Pages 902–6 in vol. 2 of *Theological Dictionary of the New Testament.* Edited by G. Kittel and G. Friedrich. Translated by G. W. Bromiley. 10 vols. Grand Rapids: Eerdmans, 1964–1976.

Witherington III, Ben. *Women in the Ministry of Jesus: A Study of Jesus' Attitudes to Women and their Roles as Reflected in His Earthly Life.* Cambridge: Cambridge University Press, 1984.

Wolter, Michael. "'Reich Gottes' bei Lukas." *New Testament Studies* 41 (1995): 541–63.

Wright, Addison G. "The Widow's Mites: Praise or Lament?—A Matter of Context." *Catholic Biblical Quarterly* 44 (1982): 256–65.

Yarbro Collins, Adela. "Numerical Symbolism in Jewish and Early Christian Apocalyptic Literature." ANRW 21.2:1221–87. Part 2, *Principat,* 21.2. Edited by H. Temporini and W. Hasse.

York, John O. *The Last Shall Be First: The Rhetoric of Reversal in Luke.* Sheffield: JSOT Press, 1991.

Zerwick, Maximilian. *Biblical Greek: Illustrated by Examples.* Rome: Scripta Pontificii Instituti Biblici, 1963.

Ziesler, J. A. "Luke and the Pharisees." *New Testament Studies* 25 (1978–79): 146–57.

# Modern Author Index

Abrams, M. H., 122n.9, 144n.99
Allison, Dale C., Jr., 135n.75
Applegate, Judith, 146n.9
Arlandson, James Malcolm, 146n.11

Bachmann, Michael, 155n.68
Bailey, Kenneth E., 132n.44,
   135n.80, 144nn.88,91, 159n.62
Bakhtin, Mikhail, 154n.32
Balch, David L., 137n.105,
   138nn.6,9, 144n.92, 146n.1,
   147n.27
Ballard, Paul H., 149n.54
Baltzer, Klaus, 155n.68
Barbour, R. S., 127n.80
Bartchy, S. Scott, 46, 138n.2
Barton, Stephen C., 121nn.2,3,
   135n.79, 145n.114, 146n.2
Bauckham, Richard, 105, 123n.10,
   157n.30
Beavis, Mary Ann, 138n.7, 140n.34
Beck, Brian E., 25, 128n.85, 133n.58,
   137n.104
Bernadicou, Paul J., 121n.2, 142n.58
Betz, Hans Dieter, 97, 154n.64,
   155n.66
Beyer, Hermann W., 139n.15
Blinzler, J., 130n.38
Blomberg, Craig L., 132nn.44,45

Bock, Darrell L., 123n.14, 129n.14,
   135n.77, 145n.118
Bovon, François, 125n.49
Braumann, G., 141n.51
Braun, Willi, 79, 102, 137n.105,
   148n.43, 149nn.46,58, 150n.65,
   156nn.9,10,11
Brawley, Robert L., 124n.21, 154n.32
Brown, C., 141n.51
Brown, Raymond, 127nn.77,78,
   128n.86, 145nn.114,115,116,
   155nn.71,72
Brun, Lyder, 127n.78
Brutscheck, Jutta, 152n.97
Bultmann, Rudolf, 135n.82

Cadbury, Henry J., 125n.39, 130n.29,
   152n.100
Caird, G. B., 131n.38
Carlston, C. E., 136n.87
Carter, Warren, 138n.2, 139n.17,
   141nn.49,51, 151n.92
Casey, Michael, 139n.19
Cave, C. H., 132n.45
Chatman, Seymour, 122n.11
Cohn, Robert L., 126n.56
Conzelmann, Hans, 35–36, 37,
   130n.37, 131n.38, 133n.51,
   135n.69

Corley, Kathleen E., 146n.10
Cosgrove, Charles H., 130n.33,
   134n.70, 158n.50
Craddock, Fred B., 141n.48
Creed, J. M., 131n.38
Crossan, J. Dominic, 139n.26,
   140n.34
Crump, David, 21, 25, 122n.7,
   126n.61, 127nn.74,78,80,82,
   128n.83, 130n.34

Danker, Frederick W., 131n.38, 138n.5
Darr, John A., 147n.17, 148n.30
Davies, J. H., 134n.66
Davies, W. D., 135n.75
Dawsey, James M., 133n.59
de Meeûs, X., 148n.43
Degenhardt, Hans, 158n.42
Delling, G., 134n.68
Delobel, Joël, 147n.25
Derrett, J. Duncan M., 143n.82,
   149n.54, 160n.81
Dewey, Joanna, 123n.2, 129n.4
Diderot, Denis, 155n.5
Dillon, Richard J., 129nn.14,21
Diogenes Laertius, 102
Donahue, John J., 147n.25
Donahue, John R., 144n.90, 146n.4,
   158n.42
Dupont, Jacques, 124n.16

Edwards, Douglas R., 152n.2
Egan, Harvey D., 139n.19
Egelkraut, H. L., 131n.38
Ehrman, Bart D., 127n.78
Elliott, J. K., 125n.36, 142n.70
Elliott, John H., 74, 148n.32
Ellis, E. Earle, 129n.2, 131n.38,
   140n.28
Esler, Philip F., 145n.114, 146n.1,
   150n.68
Evans, C. A., 134nn.66,68, 141n.54,
   142n.59, 149n.54, 153nn.9,28,30,
   154n.60, 159n.59, 160n.68

Evans, C. F., 35, 93, 126nn.53,59,
   130n.38, 132n.44

Fee, Gordon D., 151n.95
Fitzmyer, Joseph A., 53, 91, 126n.52,
   127nn.72,75, 130nn.31,34,
   135n.72, 140n.30, 141nn.43,50,
   142nn.60,64, 143n.86, 145n.114,
   147n.25, 151nn.83,88,
   153nn.5,14,30, 159n.54,
   160nn.69,70,81
Flender, Helmut, 134n.67
Fletcher, Donald R., 136n.103,
   161nn.89,98
Flusser, David, 151n.84
Foerster, W., 126n.56
Fowler, Roger, 122n.9
Francis, James, 141n.51
Franklin, Eric, 137n.105
Freed, Edwin D., 143nn.75,79,81,86
Friedrich, Gerhard, 134n.67
Fuchs, Albert, 133n.61

Ganss, George E., 139n.19
Garrett, Susan R., 148n.37
Gasse, W., 130n.38
Gaventa, Beverly Roberts, 145n.115
Geldenhuys, Norval, 131n.38
Giblin, C. H., 134n.66
Gill, David, 36, 131n.38, 133n.60
Gillman, John, 158nn.42,44, 159n.54
Girard, L. C., 131n.39
Good, R. S., 151n.84
Goppelt, L., 147n.15
Goulder, M. D., 132nn.44,45
Gowler, David B., 137n.105, 147n.16,
   148nn.31,34,42, 150nn.65,66
Grassi, Joseph A., 141n.51
Green, Joel, 54, 121n.5,
   123nn.4,7,13, 124n.16,
   125nn.38,45, 126nn.51,61,
   128n.87, 129n.16, 131n.38,
   133n.58, 136n.91, 137n.109,
   138n.10, 139n.13, 140n.37,

142nn.57,64, 144n.91, 145n.117,
146n.8, 147nn.21,22,24,
148nn.31,41, 149n.61,
150nn.64,65,72,76,79, 151n.84,
152nn.98,107, 153nn.6,17,
154nn.42,59,63,
155nn.65,70,72,75, 156nn.14,16,
159nn.54,56, 160nn.67,69,76,81
Grundmann, Walter, 36, 130n.38,
133n.54, 134n.70

Hamel, Gildas, 96, 152n.2,
153nn.19,25,30,
155n.37,42,47,54,58
Hamm, Dennis, 158n.46, 159n.54
Han, Kyu Sam, 122n.7
Haulotte, Edgar, 152n.2
Hedrick, Charles, 143n.75, 157n.20
Heil, John Paul, 124n.30, 125n.32,
146n.1, 149n.61, 150n.72,
152n.101
Hemingway, Ernest, 7
Hendrickx, Herman, 157n.25,
161n.99
Hengel, Martin, 135nn.81,82,83,
136nn.99,101, 153n.13
Herrenbrück, Fritz, 146n.4
Herzog, William R., III, 52, 141n.42,
143n.79, 144n.91, 157nn.33,39,
158nn.40,41, 160n.68
Hiers, Richard H., 160n.78,
161nn.89,97
Hollander, Anne, 154n.39
Holman, C. Hugh, 122nn.9,10
Hornsby, Teresa J., 146n.9
Hultgren, Arland J., 131n.38, 138n.7,
144n.89

Ireland, Dennis J., 159n.66

Jensen, Joseph E., 152n.2
Jeremias, Joachim, 135n.84, 140n.37
Johnson, Luke T., 158n.42, 161n.99
Joselit, Jenna Weissman, 154n.39

Just, Arthur A., Jr., 129n.14, 130n.34,
146n.1

Kariamadam, Paul, 131n.38, 132n.44
Karris, Robert J., 146n.1, 152n.2
Kee, Alistair, 151n.87
Keener, Craig S., 135n.83
Kenny, Anthony, 127n.77
Kermode, Frank, 63,
145nn.106,107,108
Kilgallen, John J., 147n.25
Kim, Kyoung-Jin, 161n.94
Kingsbury, Jack Dean, 131n.38,
137n.105
Kittel, G., 123n.8
Kloppenborg, John S., 160nn.78,81
Klostermann, Erich, 130n.38
Knowles, Michael P., 140nn.36,39
Kodell, J., 151n.51
Kort, Wesley A., 133n.62
Krämer, M., 159n.66

Lane, Belden C., 122n.1, 123n.12,
139n.19, 153nn.15,16
Leach, Edmund, 123n.8
Leaney, R. C., 134n.67
Liefeld, Walter L., 122n.7
Lightfoot, R. H., 131n.39
Loader, William, 159n.66
Loder, James E., 130n.35
Loewe, William P., 159n.53
Lohfink, G., 136n.87
Lohse, E., 131n.39
Lövestam, Evald, 139nn.21,27
Lull, David J., 139n.11
Lurie, Alison, 154n.39

McCown, C. C., 131–132n.39
McGrath, Alister, 2, 45, 121nn.1,2,
126nn.54,57
Maddox, Robert, 129n.2
Malbon, Elizabeth Struthers, 123n.8,
125nn.32,33, 126n.56,
142nn.65,68

Malina, Bruce J., 82, 147n.15, 148n.33, 150nn.77,78,81, 153n.12, 156n.16

Mánek, J., 126n.71

Manning, Robert D., 155n.2

Manson, T. W., 144n.101, 151n.83, 160n.70

Marcus, Joel, 124n.30, 125n.43, 137n.105

Marshall, I. Howard, 125nn.42,49, 129n.14, 136nn.92,100, 140n.37, 144n.96, 145n.118, 151n.95, 157n.29, 158n.46, 161n.97

Martin, Dale B., 140n.28

Mason, Steve, 137n.105

Matera, Frank J., 131n.38

Mattill, A. J., Jr., 49, 139n.26

Mauser, Ulrich W., 123nn.8,9

Mead, A. H., 151n.84

Meeks, M. Douglas, 124n.25, 156nn.6,17

Meeûs, X. de, 148n.43

Merk, Otto, 128n.2

Metzger, Bruce M., 151n.95

Meyer, Rudolf, 157n.39

Michel, Otto, 145n.103, 146n.4

Michie, Donald, 123n.2, 129n.4

Milligan, George, 141n.46

Minear, Paul S., 123n.3, 135n.87, 140n.36

Minor, Mitzi, 121n.2

Mitchell, Alan C., 158n.46, 159n.54

Miyoshi, Michi, 135nn.73,82

Moessner, David P., 35, 127n.73, 131n.38, 132nn.40,46,47, 133n.50

Moore, Stephen D., 122n.9

Moran, Maureen, 149n.61

Morrice, William, 146n.2

Moule, C. F. D., 133n.61, 145n.116, 147n.25

Moulton, James H., 141n.45

Moxnes, Halvor, 42, 112, 121n.6, 128n.2, 138nn.8,113,114, 139n.16, 144n.93, 146nn.1,3,
148nn.34,38,40, 149n.50, 150n.80, 154n.63, 155n.65, 159n.63, 160n.82, 161nn.88,95

Muddiman, John, 150n.77

Muecke, D. C., 129n.22

Muir, Steven, 149n.61

Myers, J. M., 152n.2

Nash, James A., 158n.43

Nash, Kathleen S., 142n.62

Navone, John, 122n.7, 146n.1, 149n.51

Neale, David A., 125n.39, 146nn.8,10, 159n.54

Nelson, Peter K., 138nn.4,7,9,10, 139n.11, 146n.1

Neyrey, Jerome H., 128n.86, 146n.1, 152n.2, 154n.63, 155n.65

Nolland, John, 52, 96, 125nn.35,42, 128n.89, 129n.15, 135n.71, 138n.10, 141n.45, 142n.66, 143n.82, 145n.118, 147n.25, 150nn.67,71, 151n.84, 154n.57, 155n.72, 157nn.24,35

Nuttall, Geoffrey F., 31, 32, 129nn.13,24

O'Brien, P. T., 122n.7

O'Collins, Gerald, 136n.101

Oepke, A., 141n.51

Ogg, George, 130n.38

Osiek, Carolyn, 137n.105, 138nn.6,9, 144n.92, 146n.1, 147n.27

Osten-Sacken, Peter von der, 36, 131n.38, 133n.55

O'Toole, Robert F., 128n.2, 146n.2, 149n.62

Ott, Wilhelm, 122n.7

Palmer, Humphrey, 149n.54

Parrott, Douglas M., 159n.66

Parson, Mikeal, 134n.67

Peterson, Eugene, 121n.2

Petzer, Kobus, 150n.74

Pilgrim, Walter E., 158n.42, 159n.67
Plummer, Alfred, 122nn.7,8, 124n.22, 125n.50, 129n.14, 134n.66, 139n.24, 147n.18, 151n.83
Plunkett, Mark A., 127n.78
Plutarch, 102, 156n.10
Plymale, Steven F., 122n.7
Pope, M. H., 124n.29
Powell, Mark Allan, 122n.9, 123n.14, 136n.104, 137nn.105,113, 158n.42
Price, Robert M., 151n.89

Radl, W., 123n.8
Ravens, D. A. S., 159n.54
Rawson, Beryl, 141n.51, 151n.52
Reicke, Bo, 36
Reid, Barbara E., 122n.7, 147n.19, 152n.2
Rengstorf, K. H., 123n.2, 138n.3, 146n.7
Resseguie, James L., 122n.9, 123nn.6,11, 124nn.15,29, 126nn.62,63, 131n.38, 133n.57, 134n.67, 146n.9, 148n.43, 152n.2
Rhoads, David, 123n.2, 129n.4
Ringe, Sharon H., 124n.30, 126n.71, 131n.38, 142n.64, 143n.82, 150n.69
Ritzer, George, 155n.1
Robinson, B. P., 128n.1, 130n.34
Rohrbaugh, Richard L., 82, 148n.33, 149n.56, 150nn.65,77,78, 153n.12
Roth, S. John, 56–57, 142nn.64,66, 143n.75, 149n.50

Sanders, E. P., 148n.28
Sanders, J. A., 149n.54
Schmid, Josef, 134n.67
Schmidt, Karl Ludwig, 34, 130n.36
Schmidt, Thomas F., 40, 136nn.91,93, 144n.101, 145n.102, 156n.12
Schneider, Gerhard, 127n.78

Schneider, Johannes, 36, 130n.38, 132n.43
Schor, Juliet B., 155nn.1,3
Schottroff, Luise, 143n.77
Schrenk, G., 143n.85
Schubert, Paul, 130n.33, 133n.61, 134n.70
Schulz, Siegfried, 135nn.73,82
Schürmann, H., 127n.72
Schüssler Fiorenza, Elizabeth, 151n.89
Schweizer, Eduard, 127n.78, 128n.88
Scott, Bernard Brandon, 52, 141n.44, 143n.83, 154n.45, 157nn.19,34
Seccombe, David P., 148n.40, 158n.42, 160nn.69,78
Seesemann, H., 139n.21
Seim, Turid Karlsen, 142n.67, 144n.88, 145nn.111,113,114,119, 147n.15, 151n.90
Sellew, Philip, 157n.20
Sellin, Gerhard, 133n.61
Sheeley, Steven, 124n.23
Smalley, Stephen S., 122n.7
Smith, Dennis E., 145n.1, 148n.43
Smith-Christopher, Daniel L., 150n.77
Squires, John T., 134n.70
Stählin, G., 142n.63, 143nn.76,82
Starcky, J., 134n.66
Steele, E. Springs, 147n.26
Stein, Robert H., 144n.101, 150n.63
Storbaeus, 156n.9
Strauss, Mark L., 35, 127nn.72,73, 132n.48
Streeter, B. H., 132n.39
Sweet, J. P. M., 126n.62
Sweetland, Dennis M., 144n.98
Sylva, Dennis D., 155nn.72,73

Talbert, Charles H., 121n.2, 132n.44, 135n.84, 151n.84
Talmon, Shemaryahu, 123n.8

Tannehill, Robert C., 125n.44,
126n.59, 129n.17, 135nn.76,83,
136n.104, 144nn.95,97,
145nn.109,112,114,116, 149n.61,
150n.82, 154n.50, 158n.45,
159nn.54,64
Thébert, Yvon, 138n.2
Thompson, Henry O., 123n.2
Tiede, David L., 139n.18
Tolstoy, Leo, 10
Topel, L. John, 161n.89
Trites, Allison A., 122n.7
Trompf, G. W., 131n.38
Twitchell, James B., 156n.5
Tyson, Joseph B., 137n.105

Veblen, Thorstein, 156n.6
Via, Dan O., Jr., 141n.47

Weinert, Francis D., 155n.68

Weiser, Alfons, 140nn.28,32,38
Wenham, J. W., 132n.45
Wheeler, Sondra Ely, 157n.28
White, Richard C., 159n.54
Wickes, D. R., 131n.39
Wiedemann, Thomas, 141n.51
Williams, Francis E., 161n.97
Wimmer, Joseph F., 150n.77
Windisch, H., 137n.107
Witherington, Ben, III, 143n.75,
147n.25
Wolter, Michael, 128n.2
Wright, Addison G., 56, 142nn.64,65

Yarbro Collins, Adela, 124n.29
York, John O., 150n.67

Zerwick, Maximillian, 124n.26,
147n.25
Ziesler, J. A., 137n.105

# Subject Index

abundance, 16, 18
accumulation, 100, 103, 112, 114, 118
afterlife, 105–6
almsgiving, 75, 119, 161n.89
altruism, 4, 26, 75, 117
ambition, 78
Anna, 57–58, 82, 142nn.70,71
anxiety, 84–85, 95–97, 99, 117, 141n.47
architectural landscape, 122n.12
atmosphere, 133n.62
attentiveness, 48–49, 118
awakening, 19–20

balanced reciprocity, 86, 97, 112, 117, 121n.6
banquet, 78–80, 86, 106
baptism, 11, 26, 115
benefaction, 47–48
birds, 96
blessing, blessedness, 66–67
bosom of Abraham, 107
boundaries, 70, 71, 83, 85–86
bread, 16, 33–34, 124n.25
brokenness, 17–18, 29, 34, 38–41, 43, 60–63, 68, 116

calming, of storm, 6, 18–19
"cathedrals of consumption," 101

celebration, 83
children, 44, 45, 53–55, 67, 68, 117, 141nn.51,55
Christian life, 36, 128n.1
Cleopas, 30, 32
cloaks, 92–93
clothing, 1–2, 87, 89–94, 106, 117–18, 152nn.1,2
cloud, 23
consumerism, consumption, 3, 82, 100, 101, 105, 113–14, 117, 118, 156n.5; see also hyperconsumerism
control, 116
cross, 41, 43, 133n.58
crowds, 40

darkness, 98
David, 82
"days and day," 64–65
Dead Poet's Society (film), 10
death, 13, 29
defamiliarization, 126n.63
demoniac, 90, 91, 99
demonic, 125n.45
dependence, upon God, 97
desert, 6, 9, 12–16, 26, 115
designer clothing, 94, 101
detachment, 48–49, 118
Deuteronomy, 35, 132n.44

devil, 13–15
dialogue, 7–8
"Diderot effect," 102, 155–56n.5
discipleship, 2, 36, 38–41, 46, 51, 61, 116, 133n.58, 144n.98
dishonest steward, 159n.67
dishonesty, 110–11, 160n.69
dispossession, 108, 114
distractions, 117
divorce, 67
downward mobility, 68
dropsy, 102–3, 113, 156n.11

eating, 85
economic justice, 75, 119
economic landscapes, 2, 6, 100
egalitarian leadership, 48
Emmaus road, 3, 29, 30–34, 116, 128n.1
emptiness, 15, 17
eternal life, 13
etiquette, 70, 78
evil, 75
exodus, 3–4, 23, 29, 37, 39, 126n.71
expectation, 33
extortion, 158n.46

faith, 18, 20, 117
family, 1, 45, 60–66, 67–68, 116
fasting, 58, 82–84, 86–87, 119
feast, 78, 86
fellowship, 69
flowers, 96
fool, 105
forgiveness, 147n.25
formulaic spirituality, 72–73, 83, 137n.105
frugality, 158n.43

garments, 1–2
generalized reciprocity, 4, 11, 26, 75, 97, 110, 112, 117, 121n.6, 148n.42
generosity, 47, 78, 97, 117, 149n.50
girding, 49, 50, 89

God: awakening of, 19; controls sea, 20; extravagance, 16; grace, 12, 15, 16, 26; power, 17; as traveling companion, 43, 116; will, 10, 25, 50, 119
greed, 102

Hades, 107
handwashing, 74, 148n.28
hard road, 37–38, 43
hate, 62, 144n.101
hearing, 21–22
heaven, 11, 20
Herod, 93
*Hills Like White Elephants* (Hemingway), 7–8
homelessness, 39
honor, 76–77
hospitality, 69, 70, 71, 146n.15
households, 1, 45, 67
hunger, 58
hyperconsumerism, 3, 101–2, 105–8, 113
hypocrisy, 42

images, 2
indifference, 48–49, 118
individualism, 27
indolence, 89, 117, 118
inner landscape, 7, 9
insiders, 79–80
integrity, 49, 50, 115
inward journey, 6
inward substance, 75–76
inward transformation, 43
irony, 32, 50, 161n.98

Jesus: ascension, 91; baptism, 11; calms trouble, 19–20; clothing, 91–94, 99; death, 36, 136n.99; fishing, 17; prayer, 4–5, 16, 21, 24–26, 119, 127n.82; as prophet, 35; suffering, 35–36; table manners, 81; temptation, 13–15,

115–16, 124n.16; transfiguration, 22

Jordan, 6, 9, 10–11, 26, 115

journey, 3–4, 6, 27, 30, 115, 133n.58

journey to Jerusalem, 3, 29, 34–43, 130–31n.38

joy, 69, 146n.2

Judith, 142nn.70,71

kingdom of God, 23, 34, 39, 69, 86, 108, 110, 115, 128n.2

knowing God's will, 4

lake, 9, 17–20, 116

landscapes, 1

Last Supper, 80–82

leadership, 46–48, 67

liberation, 46

light, 98

listening, 21, 23

literary criticism, 5

lording over, 47, 48

love, 62, 144n.101

mammon, 113, 159n.67, 161n.98

manna, 16

margins, marginalized, 54–55, 79, 108–9, 117

marriage, 64, 65–66, 67

Martha, 84–85, 117–18, 151n.89

Mary (mother of Jesus), 66–67, 145n.116

Mary Magdalene, 32

material resources, 4

meals, 1, 6–7, 69, 70

messianic banquet, 78–80

metaphors, 45

Mount of Olives, 5, 24–25, 119

Mount of Transfiguration, 1, 21–22, 99

mountain, 5, 6, 9, 10, 20–23, 27, 119

narrative criticism, 5, 122n.9

natural family, 66–67

negative reciprocity, 4, 11, 26, 75, 122n.6

new clothes, 90–91

new exodus, 23, 34, 39

new Israel, 16, 23, 34

new spiritual family, 66–67

new wine, 83–84

obedience, 51, 67, 140n.27

oppression, 2

ordinary, 63–65

orphan, 58

outsiders, 79–80

outward change, 44

outward form, 42, 75–76

outward journey, 6

Passover, 80–81

Perfect Storm, The (film), 9

persistence, 56, 60

Peter, 17–18, 116

Pharisees, 41–43, 51, 71, 73–76, 82, 147–48n.27

physical landscapes, 1, 6, 26

pictures, 45

plenty, 101, 114

political landscape, 122n.12

possessions, 109–10, 113, 116, 118

pounds, 51–53

poverty, 4, 17, 142n.69; see also rich and poor

powerlessness, 144n.90

prayer, 4–5, 21, 23, 24–26, 119

prodigal son, 89, 90–91, 99

purity, 74–75, 76, 86

rapacity, 75, 148n.39

readiness, 89

reciprocity, 77–78, 97, 112, 121n.6

redemption, 33

responsibility, 53

resurrection, 29

reward, 77

rich and poor, 2, 57, 158n.42

rich farmer, 113
Rich Man and Lazarus, 4, 94–95,
    105–8
rich ruler, 2, 3, 109–10, 114, 118
ruling, 47

Satan, 115
satisfaction, 58
scribes, 89, 99
sea, 9
security, 41, 43
seeing/hearing pattern, 21–22
self, 80, 104, 116–17, 119
self-denial, 41
self-deprecation, 76
self-giving, 57, 67, 81
self-humiliation, 82
self-indulgence, 41–43, 45, 76–77,
    104
self-sacrifice, 81
self-sufficiency, 16, 43, 55, 67, 116,
    118
servanthood, 138n.7
setting, 6; *see also* landscape
shame, 76–77, 143n.82
Simon the Pharisee, 71–73, 146n.15,
    147nn.17,20
sinners, 18, 70, 108–9, 117, 146n.10,
    151n.86
"slaves of God," 46
slaves, slavery, 1, 7, 44, 45, 46–53,
    67, 117, 118
sleep, 25
social conventions, 74
social justice, 75
social landscape, 1, 6, 45
soliloquy, 157n.20
sower, 85
spiritual awakenings, 17–18, 26, 31,
    116
spiritual dullness and fatigue, 49,
    71, 72, 105, 129n.20
spiritual fitness, 119
spiritual formation, 35–37, 39, 116

spiritual journey, 133n.58
spiritual landscape, 9
spiritual map, 74–75
spirituality, 2–5, 36, 121n.2
stories, 2
storm, 6, 19, 116
stranger, 58, 130n.27
strength, 26, 27, 55–56
suffering and death, 37
sweat, 24, 25, 128n.86

table fellowship, 6, 69, 117,
    151n.86
talents, 52, 53
tax collectors, 4, 42, 70, 82, 108, 117,
    151n.86, 158n.44
temple veil, 98–99
temptation, 26
terror, 12
testing, 12, 15
threshold experience, 9, 11, 26, 115
tithing mint and rue and herbs,
    75–76
transfiguration, 92
twelve (number), 16, 124n.29

uncontrollable space, 9, 12, 17, 26,
    115
unjust judge, 58–59, 143nn.75,79
unjust steward, 110–12, 160n.81
unprofitable slave, 50–51
upward mobility, 67

vigilance, 118
visual revelation, 22
vulnerability, 54–55, 117, 144n.90

wakefulness, 49, 118, 139n.26
way, the, 12, 129n.3
weakness, 54–55
wealth, 103, 105, 108, 110–12,
    160n.69; *see also* rich and poor
wedding banquet, 49, 76, 118
white garments, 92, 153n.22

wickedness, 75, 148n.39
widows, 1, 44, 45, 55–60, 67–68, 117
wild animals, 123n.9
wilderness, 12, 123n.9, 124n.16
word of God, 20–21, 27, 43, 67
worldly cares, 97

*Year of Living Dangerously, The* (film), 10–11
yeast, 42

Zacchaeus, 2, 4, 108–9, 114, 118, 158nn.44,46